Complete Poems

Blaise Cendrars

Complete Poems

Translated by Ron Padgett

Introduction by Jay Bochner

University of California Press

Berkeley   Los Angeles   Oxford

The publisher gratefully acknowledges the contribution pro-
vided by the Literature in Translation endowment, which is
supported by a generous grant from Joan Palevsky.

Versions of some of these translations appeared in *Paris Re-
view, The Ant's Forefoot, Juillard, Best & Co., Works, Sulfur,
Shiny International, Gas, Poetry 75, The World,* and *The Po-
etry Project Newsletter,* and in *Kodak* (New York: Adventures
in Poetry, 1976).

Published 1992 by the
University of California Press
Berkeley and Los Angeles, California

University of California Press
Oxford, England

Library of Congress Cataloging-in-Publication Data

Cendrars, Blaise, 1887—1961.
    [Poems. English]
    Complete poems / Blaise Cendrars ; translated from the
French by Ron Padgett ; introduction by Jay Bochner.
        p.   cm.
    Translation of: Poésies complètes.
    Includes index.
    ISBN 0-520-06579-4
    1. Cendrars, Blaise, 1887–1961—Translations into
English.
    I. Padgett, Ron.   II. Title.
PQ2605.E55A27   1992
841'.912—dc20   91-25903
                                                    CIP

Printed in the United States of America
1 2 3 4 5 6 7 8 9

Contents

Translator's Preface

This translation follows the text of the 1947 edition of Cendrars's *Poésies complètes*, which, according to his heir and biographer, Miriam Cendrars, is the one he felt to be the most faithful to his idea of his complete poetry. I have followed Cendrars's own copy of that edition, with his handwritten corrections, that is now in the Swiss National Library. Cendrars excluded *Séquences*, the early poems he later called "a sin of youth," and I have followed suit. I have also omitted a few short poems and fragments that have turned up since his death. Also, I have taken the liberty of eliminating the French of two of Cendrars's notes ("A Little Note on Literary History" from *Nineteen Elastic Poems* and "Document" from *Kodak*), though I do include English translations of them in the endnotes of the present volume. Also, I have restored the original title of *Kodak*, which the French division of that company forced him to change (to *Documentaries*). The fact is that from edition to edition Cendrars tinkered with the stanza breaks and punctuation of some of his poems, and later on in life he didn't notice—or mind—minor inconsistencies. In this sense, there never has been a perfect, definitive collection of his complete poems in French.

It took me a while to discover Cendrars. In college I translated one of his short poems from an anthology, but I didn't have much of a sense of his work until, in Paris in 1965, I was asked to translate a selection for *The Paris Review*. His *Poésies complètes* came as a revelation. The freshness, inventiveness, and wide range of the work were dazzling, and what appealed to me about the man was his good-humored orneriness, his outlaw sensibility, and his informality, all of which seemed so American.

A few years later I tackled *The Trans-Siberian*, his most widely translated and perhaps most popular poem. I was familiar with several English versions of it, but in Cendrars's French I kept hearing a slightly different poem. My version had a lot of exuberance: I was nearing thirty, and, in my own work, writing about *my* adolescence, as he had at twenty-six, and in the translation I let myself go. I've pulled it back a bit now, but I hope some of that youthful energy still drives the translation.

From *The Trans-Siberian* to *Kodak* is quite a stylistic leap, in fact a good example of Cendrars's versatility. All the poems in *Kodak* are "found" poems. It is interesting to see so much of Blaise Cendrars coming through in someone else's words (Gustave Le Rouge's *Mysterious Doctor Cornelius* was the primary source for *Kodak*). It made me happy to find beauty and wit emanating from what had originally been the language of the pulp novel, and what was exciting about translating these poems was the challenge of modulating the English accordingly. It was especially important not to try to "improve" the original text. Besides, it didn't need improvement.

Cendrars described *Kodak* as "verbal snapshots," but they were snapshots of fictitious scenes. In *Travel Notes* and *South American Women*, he made verbal pictures of his own life. What appealed to me about these poems was their lack of what we ordinarily think of as imagination, their immediacy, freshness, and simplicity, and the feeling that you are traveling alongside this great guy Blaise Cendrars. Going to Brazil was exotic in the 1920s, and these poems have exotic things in them, but they are not exotic. As in *Kodak*, what is interesting is the way Cendrars makes poetry out of language that is not particularly poetic. He uses very few metaphors, for example. The style is diaristic, offhand, notational, sometimes minimalist. It is particularly interesting to think of him writing these poems at a time when they would have been considered increasingly unfashionable by the prevailing avant-garde literary movement (the surrealists). But then, Cendrars was so avant-garde he was off the graph.

Noticing that I had translated quite a lot of his poetic work made me think of doing it all. For years I had been circling around his long poem *Easter in New York*. For me it was a hard poem to like and an even harder one to translate. Its rhymed alexandrines tend to function as self-contained units, trapping the translator inside each couplet; then, from time to time, the couplets mysteriously abandon rhyme and meter. The poem's themes—religious anxiety, poverty, crushing loneliness, the individual dwarfed by modern urban life—do not make for lively reading. But something kept bringing me back to the poem, until, one summer in the country, surrounded by quiet, trees, and the feeling that all is well in the world, I had a breakthrough: the poem felt "right" and the English rhymes suddenly started coming to me in clusters. I sat out in the sun and translated the whole poem in my head, writing down only the rhymes. When the flow lessened, I would sit back and let my mind drift, allowing French and English words and phrases to bang around the axis formed by the original's end-rhymes. Some passages did not come easily, and I hope that an occasional awkwardness will be camouflaged by some equally awkward moments in the original that are clearly intentional— they reinforce the poem's sincerity (if one can accept the idea that artfulness can be sincere). In any case, sincerity is crucial here, for the poem works only if the reader believes the poet.

For a long time I had been telling myself that I had to finish my spinach (*Easter in New York*) before I could have dessert (*Panama, or the Adventures of My Seven Uncles*). If in *Easter* and *The Trans-Siberian* Cendrars had been able to write about his travels, in *Panama* he was able to stay home and go even further, through the adventures of his "uncles." This mobile and expansive poem is filled with colors, adventures, mysteries, shifts in diction, imaginary autobiography, humor, anecdotes, and history, all of which seem to be happening simultaneously. It's fun to "ride" on this poem that almost veers out of control, like an amusement park ride that both thrills and scares you.

After I was invited to put together the present volume, I translated the remaining poems: *The War in the Luxembourg* (the last part of which Max Jacob described as some of the most beautiful poetry he had ever read), the funnily modernistic *Unnatural Sonnets* (which I was tempted to call *Twisted Sonnets*), the *Black African Poems* (which are reminiscent of the African tales Cendrars assembled in his *Anthologie nègre*), the *Various Poems* (which includes the often-quoted "Homage to Guillaume Apollinaire"), and, finally, the legendary poem that Cendrars started during the First World War and never finished, *To the Heart of the World*. In doing these final translations and looking back over the whole work, I began to see that despite the wide stylistic and thematic range, these poems do indeed fit together: they all reflect some aspect of Blaise Cendrars— his insatiable curiosity, classlessness, idiosyncratic scholarship, unselfconscious bohemianism, obsession with writing, and boldness; his love of painting, music, cinema, and dance; his penchant for the fabulous; and, at the base of it all, his metaphysical way of looking at the world.

A few words about translating. It is customary for translators to apologize for not doing justice to the original. I too respect the poetry I've translated, but I do not see my translations (or anyone's) as being inevitably inferior to the originals. Perhaps my being a poet (not a professional translator) allows me to feel I have a license. My reverence for the original tails off about halfway across the Atlantic. Then the words in English start to glow, and I get involved in making poetry, American poetry, and if that means straying from the original a bit, I do it. In the case of Cendrars's poems, it's another way of being faithful to the original.

Of course I try to avoid misrepresentation and errors. I've shown this translation to friends and colleagues for their advice and spent many hours at various libraries, particularly the New York Public Library at Forty-Second Street and Fifth Avenue, where Cendrars devoted many a day to reading and keeping out of the cold in early 1912. I've also tried to keep up with the burgeoning Cendrars scholarship. Ultimately, though, for me the main trick in translating Cendrars is to catch the tone and follow it through the shifting patterns of his poetry. To do this, it would have been wonderful to have had his help.

A couple of years ago I had the following dream. Cendrars had arrived on campus a few days before a colloquium in his honor. "All my film biographers are here," he said, gesturing to the documentary filmmakers we walked past, all of whom were black. We went up and down stairs. "You make everything sound like a misty porn film," he said, referring to my translations of his poetry. The implication was that I was smoothing out the rough spots. He began to recite, in his own English version, one of his poems. I checked it against my version. The third line consisted of the word *casket*, which I had translated as *case*. He raised an eyebrow as he hit that word. I penciled in the correction on my manuscript, realizing that this was the ultimate way to check my work. "I could come to Paris for a while and work with you," I suggested. "I could stay for a couple of months. I'd just take time off from everything and work on this." His face sparkled with skepticism and mirth.

Fortunately, many other people have helped me. Editors and fellow poets who have published some of the versions in this book are Larry Bensky, Maxine Groffsky, Tom Clark, Jack Hopper, David Rosenberg, Clayton Eshleman, Anne Waldman, Larry Fagin, Trevor Winkfield, Joseph McLaughlin, Bill Berkson, Michael Friedman, Jerome Sala, Kevin Opstedahl, and Patricia Storace. Friends who gave me valuable advice include James Schuyler, Kenward Elsmlie, Tom Veitch, David Ball, Nicole Ball, Christine Tysh, Jean Boulte, Vivian Bittencourt, Frank Kemp, and William Lawlor. The staffs of the New York Public Library, the Swiss National Library, the Bronx Zoo, and the Bibliothèque Littéraire Jacques Doucet were diligent and expert. Thanks also to Fr. Matthew Kelty of the Abbey of Gethsemani; Gunnar Harding, Cendrars's Swedish translator; and James Whittemore and Donald Kimmick of the Seaman's Church Institute of New York and New Jersey. I am grateful to all the members of the Blaise Cendrars International Society, on whose collective knowledge I have drawn, but especially to Jean-Pierre Goldenstein, Marius Michaud, Rino Cortiana, Georgiana Colvile, Yzabelle Martineau, Jim Christy, Jay Bochner, Monique Chefdor, and Miriam Cendrars. These last three merit extra-special gratitude: Jay for correcting the translation and adding to the notes and for his introduction to this volume; Monique for her knowledge and understanding of Cendrars, for her own translations of Cendrars, and for generously checking my translation; and Miriam for her warm welcome and constant support, as well as her invaluable advice and painstaking reading of this translation. Without the help of these three, this book would not have been possible.

I also wish to express my gratitude for help from François Samuelson, former director of the Bureau du Livre Français in New York, and from the late Gregory Kolovakos, director of the New York State Council on the Arts Literature Program, which provided a grant toward the completion of this project. Thanks also go to Jerome Rothenberg, Marjorie Perloff, Elaine Cohen, Michael Davidson, and Paul Auster; to my friend and agent Robert Cornfield; and, at the University of California Press, to Scott Mahler, Shirley Warren, Rebecca Frazier, Jenia Walter, and Stanley Holwitz. I am very grateful to David Bullen for the beautiful design of this book. My wife Patricia has made many contributions to this translation, in ways she probably doesn't realize, not the least of which is being a good sounding board. Finally, I want to acknowledge previous translators of Cendrars's poetry, especially John Dos Passos, George Reavey, Monique Chefdor, Ron Hornung, and Anselm Hollo. Thank you, all.

Introduction

Blaise Cendrars was born in Paris, on the rue Saint-Jacques, or so he would have it in his last poem, *To the Heart of the World*. A poem has a license to lie, if we can call it lying, and Cendrars, in all his work from 1912 to 1961, continuously exercised that same right to construct a myth for himself. The problem that has always arisen is that readers, and possibly Cendrars himself, have taken the poetic myth as the mere transcription from life of his own real voyage. It thus becomes difficult to establish a "true" biography separate from a poeticized one; we have a body of ascertainable, and sometimes extraordinary, fact upon which to hang a motley of fantastical clothes, some fancy "stretchers" as Huck Finn called the inventions of his own author. Stretchers give breadth, myth, and, let us not forget, humor. Cendrars had all three in abundance, if readers will only follow, or swallow, for the fun of the chase and, in the end, the spiritual value of the adventure. So, Blaise Cendrars was born in a poem in Paris, in the building on the Left Bank where the *Romance of the Rose* was written; that was the medieval and urban parentage he wanted.

Before the myth, a boy named Frédéric Louis Sauser is born on 1 September 1887 in La Chaux-de-Fonds, Switzerland, the third child of Georges Frédéric Sauser, merchant, and Marie-Louise Dorner. La Chaux-de-Fonds, near Neuchâtel, has been the center of the Swiss watch industry since the beginning of the eighteenth century. It is a small city, with streets set out at neat right angles and a population of upstanding burghers in the best Swiss tradition, except that it was also the home base for the great anarchist Kropotkin, who arrived about ten years before Freddy's birth. Though Cendrars may have had various connections to different stripes of anarchists in the last years before World War I, in both New York and Paris, his family background in La Chaux-de-Fonds and other Swiss cities is securely bourgeois. In any event, he is moved from this town in his infancy, possibly for a stay in Egypt. Certainly by the age of eight he and his family have moved to Naples.

Cendrars's life is full of voyages even before he learns to travel under his own steam. After Alexandria and Naples, with perhaps England and Paris in between, and after a failed attempt to be a good schoolboy at the local commercial school in Neuchâtel, he launches the grand adventure: a break with his parents, flight crisscrossing Germany, and the eventual landing in Saint Petersburg. Or, more realistically, his father despairs of his boy's truancy and entrusts him to the care of one H. A. Leuba, member of the small La Chaux-de-Fonds colony dealing in timepieces in the imperial Russian city. Freddy works for Leuba from 1904 to 1907, during which time he establishes a lifelong pattern of alternating travel with long sessions in libraries. He most probably travels at least to the famous Nijni-Novgorod fair and on the Trans-Siberian railroad, the subject of his second long poem. There seems little doubt that he witnesses various manifestations of the budding revolution: the devastated Russian troops returning on the Trans-Siberian from defeat at the hands of the Japanese at Port Arthur, Bloody Sunday in January 1905, and the general strike of that year. The Port Arthur debacle provides the background for his *Trans-Siberian* poem, while the 1926 novel *Moravagine* is full of the abortive insurrections in Saint Petersburg. Later texts tell of further travels in this period, to China, Armenia, and the mouth of the Lena; but some of these may be the travels of a reader, perhaps of Kropotkin's own explorations in eastern Russia, for example.

In 1907 Freddy returns to Switzerland, apparently ready to be "serious." He is at university in Basel, perhaps in Leipzig, then in Bern where he signs up for philosophy courses. But he seems to have broken with his father. In February of 1908 his mother dies. He studies music, and makes friends with a group of Polish students, among whom is one Féla Poznanska. In the summer of 1909 he may raise bees on a French farm; in April of 1910 he is an extra in *Carmen* in Brussels, and by October of that year he is in Paris, with Féla, on the rue Saint-Jacques. To make ends meet they translate letters and documents, and hope for longer manuscripts. He is now accumulating his own. He meets a few artists, including the young Marc Chagall, and gets to know a very seedy side of the city. But this first assault upon the bastion of art is a failure, for lack of funds; in March of 1911 Féla leaves to join relatives in New York, and the following month Freddy returns to Saint Petersburg. He gives language lessons and virtually lives at the library. He tries for a post as Parisian correspondent for a Russian bank in order to return to Paris, but to no avail. Finally, Féla mails him a boat ticket for New York, where he arrives on 11 December 1911, on board the *Birma* out of Libau, which is to say with a boatload of immigrants from eastern Europe in steerage.

Freddy and Féla live for a while with her relatives in the Bronx, and later in an old wooden house on West Ninety-sixth Street, the last one left there at that time. They meet Caruso and see him sing Puccini, but generally Freddy finds far too little cultural activity to feed his huge hunger. If he discovers Stieglitz's Little Galleries at 291 Fifth Avenue, it is to find that the real new work is being done back in Paris. He submits to menial jobs he manages to hold for a few days at a time, such as pianist in a Bowery movie-house, but he can sustain no interest in making a living, only in reading, doing his own inventories of modern French and German art, and writing at the brand-new Forty-second Street library. It is a time of oppressive poverty, described later by Cendrars as the worst period in his life (yet his is a life of chronic poverty, in which windfalls disappear in a day). Féla teaches, at first, at the Ferrer School, an anarchist center founded by Emma Goldman and others, and Freddy no doubt meets some of the artists and writers who are getting their start there. But John Sloan and George Bellows are not doing work that can attract a budding European modernist (and Man Ray probably does not attend the Ferrer studio until after it moves in the fall of 1912). The school's director is a young Will Durant (Ariel is a fifteen-year-old student) and all the talk is of European writers, Maeterlinck for example. Freddy is desperate for a way past this sort of neosymbolism, and there is little doubt that the city itself, rather than the culture it wishes to ape, is the strongest new influence on him, as distasteful as that may seem. The first city of modernity introduces, then, the poet's first important poem, *Easter in New York*. It is also the site of a rebirth; Freddy takes on the name of Blaise Cendrars, this burning phoenix apparently rising out of a few smoldering lines of Nietzsche: "And everything of mine turns to mere cinders / What I love and what I do." After a stay of about six months he leaves again for Paris, via Switzerland, armed with a poem and a name, but without Féla.

From now through August of 1914, for a period of about two years, Cendrars participates in what must be the most promising avant-garde period in history. He works on projects with Guillaume Apollinaire and has poems published in his magazine *Les Soirées de Paris*. He publishes *Easter in New York* himself, as a special number of *Les Hommes Nouveaux*, a semianarchist review he starts with Emil Szittya, as well as the magnificent two-meter-high *Prose of the Trans-Siberian*, printed vis-à-vis Sonia Delaunay's abstract painting. Among Cendrars's best friends are Fernand Léger and Chagall; he supplies titles for the latter's paintings. Robert and Sonia Delaunay often treat him to dinner; the three, along with Arthur Cravan, the pre-Dadaist who billed himself as the nephew of Oscar Wilde (and he was, though no one believed it) and the world's greatest poet-boxer (he fought Jack Johnson, ignominiously, in 1916 in Spain) would then go to Bal Bullier dances in "modern" attire dipped in painters' colors. There are poems for Roger de La Fresnaye, Alexander Archipenko, Léger and Chagall, and friendships with other painters at the studios for poor artists called La Ruche: Chaim Soutine, Jacques Lipchitz, Joseph Csaky, Moise Kisling, and Cendrars's best wandering and drinking companion after the war, Modigliani, who has left us some five or six portraits of the poet. Many of these painters do art work for Cendrars's books and are in turn the writer's subjects. He participates in exhibits and readings from Saint Petersburg to Berlin, polemics with poetasters, projects for little magazines, concerts such as the première of Stravinsky's *Sacre du Printemps*, in May 1913, where one result of the ruckus is that Cendrars spends the night with an orchestra seat for a collar. It is an exhilarating period of adventurous creation. It is also a period of great poverty for all these now-famous people, something we should try not to overromanticize. Cendrars is among the poorest, and unable to manage even the few francs that come his way; he splurges and sponges, sometimes eats and sometimes prefers to print his own poems. In that month of May Féla rejoins Blaise in Paris. *Panama* and *Elastic Poems* (at that point only seventeen) are written, but then war will postpone any possibility of immediate publication. Féla and Blaise have their first son, Odilon, born in April of 1914. One would have expected the world to be opening up rather than closing down, but everyone can see war coming. Blaise and his friend the Italian poet and editor Ricciotto Canudo draft an appeal, published in the newspapers on 29 July 1914, calling for all foreigners to enlist on the side of the French. A few days later he is on his way into the Foreign Legion, "First Foreign Regiment of Paris." Before he leaves for the front in September he and Féla marry, largely because of the rising xenophobia she is already being subjected to in her little suburban town. Now her baby has a real "poilu," a soldier for a father, one who is quickly marched off to Frise, then Herbécourt. In May of 1915 he survives the attacks in Artois, where 100,000 are lost in the month. Carency cemetery, the Bois de la Vache, Vimy Ridge, Notre-Dame-de-Lorette, Givenchy; a list of glorious disasters in the hopes of a few feet of no-man's-land and a few inches in the Parisian dailies. The four foreign regiments sustain such enormous losses that the remnants are transferred to "la Marocaine," the original and most famous Foreign Legion. At Souchez the Marocaine division suffers half of all the losses for the whole of the Tenth Army. Sainte-Marie-les-Mines, then Roye, where there is some relief, and then a two-week leave for Paris in July. Roye again, then the assault of the Navarin Farm in Champagne where, on 28 September 1915, Cendrars loses his right arm.

So he has to learn to write all over again, passing the pen over to his left hand. He is astonished to discover that the same day he loses his arm his greatest literary hero, Remy de Gourmont, dies. Despite the pain and sense of loss his amputation causes him throughout his life, he is private and discreet about it in his work. For example, a full volume entitled *La Main coupée* (literally, the severed hand) does not discuss his own arm, though he is himself on stage at war throughout. The left hand becomes, in the signature to letters, his familiar "la main amie," the friendly hand.

Paris in 1915 is deserted culturally, but one by one artists and writers drift back (many are in self-imposed exile, dodging the draft like Duchamp and Picabia in New York). Cendrars finishes earlier poems and writes stunningly surrealistic prose pieces such as *Profound Today*, to be published as small pamphlets. He reinvolves himself, in poetry readings and concerts at the Salle Huyghens with Apollinaire, Max Jacob, and Pierre Reverdy, or Erik Satie, Darius Milhaud, Arthur Honegger, and Francis Poulenc. But, after a year or so in the avant-garde, Cendrars prefers to leave Paris to its cliques. In 1917 he is living in the countryside with Féla and his two sons, near Méréville. He writes surreal texts like *The End of the World Filmed by the Angel of Notre-Dame* in a barn among the watercress fields, where he works for the wives of farmer-soldiers at the front. He also frequents the families of gypsies he met in the Legion. A chapter a month of the visionary *L'Eubage* gets him 100 francs apiece from the couturier Jacques Doucet, who is already collecting avant-garde manuscripts. Nineteen-seventeen is also the year he begins to see less and less of Féla; in Paris he meets Raymone, a young aspiring actress who becomes the moral center of his life. He also goes to Cannes and works in film, a career he dreams of sporadically for a number of years. His first work is with Abel Gance's *J'accuse*. He recruits mutilated veterans to play the final scene in which he rises with them from the battlefield to show the civilians what they have wrought. Then he is assistant director on Gance's *La Roue*, hiring Honegger for the music and probably having a decisive influence on the radical fast cutting the film is best remembered for. In 1920 he starts to make his own film in Rome, but his star has a serious accident, and financial manipulators bankrupt the studio he is working in.

Meanwhile Cendrars becomes the artistic director of La Sirène editions, where, with the help of Jean Cocteau, he publishes the moderns alongside their progenitors, such as Lautréamont and de Gourmont. He is receiving his first recognition in English, with *I Have Killed* in *The Plowshare*, the literary magazine of the artists' colony at Woodstock, New York, and various translations in *Broom*, the most luxurious of the American expatriate little magazines. He has the reputation of being the main purveyor of African culture in Paris and writes the scenario for Milhaud's *The Creation of the World*, with sets and costumes by Léger. Another scenario, with music by Satie and sets by Francis Picabia, is left in manuscript; Picabia replaces it with his famous *Relâche*. The incident is emblematic of Cendrars's pre-Dada role and how he played it; typically, instead of defending his participation, he leaves again, this time for South America.

Originally invited by the Brazilian *modernistas* as their model for a modern poet, Cendrars lectures on language in São Paulo and explores the plains and jungles, participating if not actually leading in the discovery of the country by its indigenous poets in search of roots. He will travel to South America five times between 1924 and 1930. Meanwhile, and ironically, he has himself abandoned writing poetry. The complete poetry, as represented in this volume, was written in twelve years of revolutionary activity, from 1912 to 1924. Cendrars now turns to novels, the first of which, *Sutter's Gold* (1925), is written with the same directness of style we find in his "documentary" poems, such as *Kodak*. In *Sutter's Gold* Cendrars rediscovers the forgotten figure of General Sutter, the

Swiss adventurer who founded an agricultural empire in northern California only to see it collapse when gold is discovered on his own land. This most accessible of Cendrars's prose works will eventually be translated into fifteen languages. The following year *Moravagine* appears, Cendrars's most famous novel. It recounts the hallucinatory voyages of a madman and his doctor-observer through the early upheavals of the century, from Russian revolution to World War I. It is as if Moravagine himself, though but a single ingenious and gleefully vicious consciousness, is the instigator of all chaos, whether in Berlin or the Amazon jungle. Finally, to continue the composition by threes initiated with the epic poems of 1912–1914, a third novel, *Dan Yack* (1929), appears in two very distinct volumes: the first follows Dan Yack's adventures and survival in Antarctica, the second shows him recording his memories in a small, snowbound hut in the French Alps. A double novel of the cold, yet the warmest and most openly personal of the early novels, with the clearest portrayal of a view of life made up of alternating and complementary action and contemplation.

Cendrars begins the thirties covering the trail of Jean Galmot for *Vu* magazine, the result being *Rhum* (1930), his first reportage. The thirties are, for him, mainly news work, or novelistic writing on documentary subjects: editorial or translation jobs on Al Capone and O. Henry, unfinished novels on Jim Fiske and John Paul Jones; a 1935 volume on the underworld throughout France; a 1936 volume on Hollywood, which must be one of the first models for those ironic tours of famous places where one continually fails to meet the important people. Always attracted to the marginal, he covers the first crossing of the *Normandie* for *Paris-Soir* but reports only on the hold and its workers (Colette and others write about first class). The Hollywood book is the product of his trip for the film première of *Sutter's Gold*, in which James Cruze (of *Covered Wagon* fame) has directed Edward Arnold and Binnie Barnes. The project has been in the works since 1930, when Eisenstein negotiated with Cendrars in Paris, but the American studio never let the Russian make a film. The final version, in which we no longer see the hand of one of its early scriptwriters, William Faulkner, is without interest, as Cendrars well knows.

From about 1924 to the Second World War, and when he is more or less stationary in France, Cendrars lives mostly in a small town outside of Paris called Le Tremblay-sur-Maudre, where Picabia and the art dealer Vollard are his neighbors. Another neighbor is Jacques-Henry Lévesque, who publishes *Orbes*, a last Dada-spirit journal that features Cendrars, Picabia, and Duchamp above all others. Lévesque will be the first to publish an anthology of Cendrars's work (1944) and first to write a book on him (1947). Cendrars might also be in Biarritz staying with his Peruvian friend and benefactress Eugenia Errazuriz; John Dos Passos finds him nearby in Montpazier and returns to the States with his translations of Cendrars's poetry, *Panama* (1931), an elegant and rare volume with the American's watercolors. Cendrars also has a Paris address, the Alma-Hôtel, and makes short forays into town. In December of 1934, for example, he ferrets out Henry Miller and is the first important writer to congratulate him, in person and then in print, for *Tropic of Cancer.*

Near the end of the thirties Cendrars returns to fiction, or at least to a renewed amalgam of fiction and documentary, in three volumes of short pieces that can for convenience be classified under the generic title of the first, *Histoires vraies* (*True Stories*). These tales, presented as witnessed truths, are the early models for his post–World War II fictions (again, radical writing to be interrupted by a war). In 1939 he is a war correspondent for a consortium of French newspapers and travels to Britain, reports from a British submarine, and is attached to British headquarters in France. As war breaks out he is in Belgium, then Lille, Arras, Amiens, and Paris. A great photograph dated 12 May 1940 shows him in a boxcar, reclining on his good arm atop the evacuated gold reserves of the Bank of France, 280 million francs' worth. He is in flight by car through the Loire valley, thence to Marseilles where he is arrested for his English "uniform." His reportage, *Chez l'Armée anglaise* (*With the English Army*), is interdicted by the Germans in Paris, and he settles down to a secretive and apparently inactive life for the duration in Aix-en-Provence.

From July 1940 through August 1943 Cendrars writes nothing. He is reading a great deal in the works of the church fathers in the town's famous Méjanes Library. There are plenty of hints he may be assisting Resistance groups, since the militia men come after him several times and wreck his car. He helps the filmmaker Max Ophuls and his family out of the country (the young son later makes *The Sorrow and the Pity*). But, in the first years of this war, he seems paralyzed as a writer, unless perhaps he is busy doing things we do not know about. Then, suddenly after three years of silence, and with no sign whatever of tentativeness, he launches into the four volumes of memoirs that make up the great achievement of his maturity.

Of the four, only the second, *La Main coupée* (1946; *Lice*) can be considered reasonably straightforward narrative. The three others, *L'Homme foudroyé* (1945; *The Astonished Man*), *Bourlinguer* (1948; *Planus*), and *Le Lotissement du ciel* (1949; presently being translated) wrench time and place out of their old orders, to mix and reassemble them into a vast, exteriorized panorama of the self in the twentieth century. This autobiographical saga, as it has been called for lack of a more precise term, is alternately truculent and full of humor about Cendrars's obsessions and those of innumerable other formidable characters he has met (and created). In the finale, *Le Lotissement du ciel*, he plunges backward into his past to free his spirit, and our own, to "levitate" with the saints who were inspired enough to fly in the skies.

The last decades of Cendrars's life are less rushed. After marrying Raymone in 1949 in the Swiss village of his paternal family (Féla died during the war, in England), he settles for good in Paris. There are reprints of older works to oversee: *Dan Yack* finally in one volume in 1951; a third edition of *Moravagine* in 1956 with its invaluable "Pro Domo" epilogue on how the book was written; the complete poetry in 1957 (after a first 1947 volume entitled *Poésies complètes*), under the fine title *Du Monde entier au coeur du monde*. There are radio plays, introductions, interviews, notably a thirteen-part series for radio later published in 1952 as *Blaise Cendrars vous parle* (*Blaise Cendrars Speaks*); this volume constitutes the author's last version of his life as myth, or as suspect truth. Cendrars works on a number of fiction projects: one on the *Carissima* (Mary Magdalena), which would have paralleled *Le Lotissement* in many ways, and, the only project to see the day, *Emmène-moi au bout du monde! . . .* (1956; *To the End of the World*). This scabrous account of the exploits of an old actress, Thérèse, and her legionnaire lover, Jean de France, is a detective story without a solution and a roman à clef that impinges uncomfortably on the lives of certain Parisian notables. *Emmène-moi* is a vigorous and youthful tumble after the high-flying double levitation of Saint Teresa and Saint John in the *Lotissement*.

In 1956 and 1958 Cendrars suffers strokes that leave him partially paralyzed. At the end of 1958 André Malraux comes to Cendrars's apartment on the rue Jean-Dolent to give the much-diminished author the award of commander of the Légion d'Honneur. Over the next year he produces only a few scribbled pages of new work. In January of 1961 he is awarded the Grand Prix Littéraire de Paris. Perhaps these prizes at the end of his life are a consolation, or perhaps they are a disappointment, a reminder of past neglect. He dies on 21 January 1961, at the age of seventy-three, having lived to see three of the eight volumes of his complete works appear in a fine hardcover edition from Denoël; this is, I am sure, a better way to end, a sign that his readers can begin to take his work seriously.

THE POETRY

Cendrars's early poetry is written under the influence of Remy de Gourmont's *Latin mystique*, a book that provided medieval models for a young poet attempting to escape the then current mode of neosymbolism. However, de Gourmont was also a supporter of precisely that same sort of heavily symbolic interior groping which was the model of the time, as in the work of Maeterlinck for example, who received the Nobel Prize for literature about the time Cendrars stepped off the boat in New York. Cendrars's earliest poems, *Séquences* (1912), are the product of this double influence, via the single conduit of de Gourmont, with their Latin liturgical title and running epigraphs, and their self-conscious, exacerbated sexuality. These twenty-five short poems, which Cendrars chose never to republish, detail the frustrated relationships of hands, mouths, breasts, and bellies as the speaker probes for what he calls in one of the poems an "interior nudity."

But this sort of narcissistic eroticism, with its forced imagery, soon must have appeared to Cendrars to be a dead end, while the plainer diction speaking of simpler, more outward subjects of de Gourmont's Latin fathers was a natural medium for rendering the modern world just opening up for a poet in 1912, especially in New York. In *Easter in New York*, the religious theme is brought to the fore in its contrast with the victimization of immigrant populations piling up in lower Manhattan, and of course it is already foregrounded in the title, which tells us the crucial day of the poem, and in the epigraph from the Latin in which the wood of the cross is implored to relent its pull on Christ's body. Meanwhile, Cendrars walks a dangerous tightrope, for a modernist, with the close identification of the speaker-poet and the Christ. Part of the success of the poem is in the fact that the poet, ultimately, is *not* Christ, but instead is always measuring his own failure to sympathize sufficiently against the infinite compassion of a Jesus who, repeatedly, will not function for a modern world. The desperate or exhausted repetition of the poem's last line is testimony to the failure and the painful consciousness of the distance between savior and poet: "I stop thinking about you. I stop thinking about you."

Easter in New York was new, in 1912, in its return, or at least in its beginning of a return, to the use of a common, spoken language for poetic lyricism. There are only a few sporadic—maybe even accidental—examples of such diction in *Séquences*, but *Easter in New York* employs it throughout. There are in fact barely any occasions given over to metaphor. Most of the poetic flights in the poem are about a symbolic, religious code that is lacking in this world, a world this new poem is resolved to contend with; as if to say metaphor itself is ailing for lack of belief or relevance and is not to be trusted.

Remnants of the medieval impulse survive in *The Trans-Siberian*, in the "Prose" of the title in French (after the low Latin *prosa*, as Cendrars explained it; a sort of speaking forth, which he considered less pretentious and confining), and in such lines as "I foresaw the coming of the big red Christ of the Russian Revolution," where a new ideology usurps an older figure. But the brash and violent originality of this long poem successfully obscures its antecedents. The format alone was spectacular; a fold-out sheet six and a half feet tall, with the poem on the right in multiple typefaces and different colored inks, and on the left a full length *pochoir* (a sort of silk screen), an abstraction by a then unknown Sonia Delaunay. A projected 150 copies were advertised as equaling, at two meters a copy, the height of the Eiffel Tower, which is invoked in the last line of the poem and at the very bottom of the painting. But presumably nowhere near that many were actually completed, and a copy is rare enough to have been sold in 1991 for $100,000. It is first a poem for the eyes, though it can hardly be read in the glance that would take it all in at once (its first public reading was by a friend who, candle in hand, had to start on a chair and end on her knees); *The Trans-Siberian* is not only one of the first truly modern poems, but a modern multimedia object as well.

The influence of Whitman, along with that of Rimbaud, is apparent in the break with all rules of regular line length, beat, or rhyme. The poem's lyricism resides in how the line is allowed to breathe, sometimes in a syllable, sometimes in twenty-four or more. In complete control of the typography and using the full width of a seven-inch page, Cendrars preferred to set almost all of his extended "breaths" on one long line. Many blocks of print are justified only at the right-hand margin, and numerous sections are highlighted by font size and position on the page. He uses repetition and refrain, but makes almost no other concessions to traditional poetic form. After the incantatory rhyming of the first three lines, two nice exceptions are the ironic twenty-line section, sometimes rhyming, sometimes assonant, on the prostitute as a bodiless flower, and the following couplet that flashes a rhyme for a poet's name while declaring that these new poets have lost the ability to rhyme:

> "Pardonnez-moi de ne plus connaître l'ancien jeu des vers"
> Comme dit Guillaume Apollinaire
>
> ("Pardon my forgetting how to play the ancient game of Verse"
> As Guillaume Apollinaire says.)

The poem is full of admitted failures, both at braving the perils that engulf everyone around the narrator and at expressing adequately in poetry the furious state of the world: "I don't know how to take it all the way," runs one refrain, and that applies equally to the job of living and the job of writing. *The Trans-Siberian* is certainly a heroic poem, even an epic one despite its compression into 420 lines, but the hero is carried along, submits, resists, sympathizes, and flees, so he is hardly the master of his adventure. The poem alternately fragments and reassembles the self, the prostitute Jeanne, the war, and the desolate landscape into a moving cubist and expressionist vision of a painful new world; this is a poem which, physically, cleaves to its twentieth-century contents.

In *Panama*, the third and last long poem of these early years, 1912–1914, fragmentation is still greater, as there is no longer the train and its long, straight trip to focus the action. *Panama* doesn't so much tell the adventures or stories of seven uncles—plus one narrating "nephew"—as it embodies their yearning back to a family home in Europe from all corners of the earth. Again Cendrars's format is novel, both fun and to the point. The soft cover of the original edition is folded vertically to constitute both front and back of the volume. It copies an old Union Pacific train schedule and invites casual pocketing. Within the text of more than five hundred lines, Cendrars reproduced, as stanza breaks, the schematic train routes from the American schedule, in seemingly endless variations on the Chicago to Los Angeles or San Francisco routes, as if the many voyages of the poem itself were the multiplied variations of the same wanderlust and inevitable homesickness. Also reproduced in the poem is a first stab at found poetry: Denver, Colorado's full-page advertisement for itself, sandwiched between the lines, "You go under the Eiffel Tower—looping the loop—to come down on the other side of the world" and "Then you go on." In *Panama*, we meet, we leave, then we blend, in our minds, the places we visit so quickly that the idea of a voyage recedes leaving in its place the sense of all places coexisting simultaneously.

The language of *Panama* is as far as possible from the high rhetorical style inherited by the poets of the early 1900s. Arguably Cendrars's lines are not (and are not trying to be) "beautiful." Instead, objects, names, advertisements, book titles, and conversations replace higher sentiments or ideas about such things. It is a poetry of presentation, with emotion held in reserve behind the rapid-fire juxtaposition of the wide world's quotidian. Poetry is declared to flow not from high-blown musings but from financial fiascos like France's attempt to build the Panama Canal: "Stock Market quotations are our daily prayers." In such manner the poem asserts its place in the world, yet sails easily clear of lecturing on poetics or the lessons of history. The scattered histories of the seven uncles bring the wide, hard world to bear on the private anguish of a yearning, uprooted child. Eventually the uncles come to weigh very heavily upon the narrator, who is alternately a young boy shunted from school to school and country to country and a young adult pursuing his fate in the wake of lost family. This Cendrars-like person comes, at the end of the poem, to a temporary rest in Paris (again and always Paris with Cendrars), poised for a moment, before his compulsion to renew himself in wandering imposes itself once more, even to travel beyond the possible:

Suns moons stars
Apocalyptic worlds
You all still have a good role to play

. . . .

I'd like to be a fifth wheel.

Most of the *Nineteen Elastic Poems* were written at the same time as *Panama* and published in small international avant-garde magazines: for example, number 4 as late as February 1914 in the Berlin *Der Sturm*, and numbers 13, 16, and 17 in the July-August 1914 issue of *Les Soirées de Paris*. Like *Panama*, the poems had to await the end of the war for their appearance as a volume, at which point, in 1919, Cendrars added two more (19 poems to match 1919); this was one of their elasticities.

The physical presentation of the poems was not avant-garde (though there was a portrait of the author by Modigliani), and thus, aside from the lack of rigor threatened in the title, Cendrars seemed to be announcing a return to more conventional modes. Of course, in the context of the proliferating productions of an avant-garde that everyone knew he had himself pioneered, this deceptive appearance was another striking move against the grain. The radical practices of *Nineteen Elastic Poems* had immediate effect in the avant-garde, in their modest magazine appearances and even in manuscript, since two were first published without Cendrars's knowledge: one in *De Stijl*, in the Netherlands, another in *Le Cabaret Voltaire*, the one-issue founding magazine of Dada in Zurich. Essentially, Cendrars had driven his modernization of diction and subject matter to one of its logical outcomes, to write "occasional" poems of Parisian life in colloquial language. This does not mean the poems are simple, or easy to understand; often the contrary is the case. Much of the context for a conversation in a café, and the processes which ought to link comments and images, are missing, dismissed in favor of an immediate if confusing sense of our presence on the scene. Some of the poems are so entirely embedded in precise events as to have become obscure within a few years, or even months.*

* We are deeply indebted to Jean-Pierre Goldenstein for his meticulous searches after the almost lost references and sources. The notes Ron Padgett has appended to his translations reflect this research.

The sense of an authentic, personal voice in conversation is over-whelming in *Nineteen Elastic Poems:* fresh, enthused, private or confid-ing, bemused or poignant, always, it seems, undisguised:

> ˙ It's useless not wanting to talk about yourself
> You have to cry out sometimes

Certainly it is oddly intimate to hear "I" admit so naturally to being the poet himself at his writing desk:

> Christ
> It's been more than a year now since I stopped thinking about you
> Since I wrote my . . . poem *Easter*

These poems, like the previous ones, are filled with references to the books of others, but the sense is hardly "intertextual" or erudite when the poem reads, "There is also one pretty page," and proceeds to quote from it.

"Une jolie page" is a good tag for Cendrars's most radical elasticizing of the concept of poetry; number 10, "News Flash," is probably the first found poem, copied (with some changes) from a Parisian daily. At one stroke Cendrars anticipates Duchamp's ready-mades and goes well be-yond collage in the undermining of romantic ideas of originality. *Nine-teen Elastic Poems* is a first primer of found, cubist, assemblage, and collage techniques, all put to relevant use and variation. Another poem, "Mee Too Buggi," is also found, with the exception of its opening line and the fact that it doesn't explicitly admit to its "other," Tonga origin. In that poem the swiped material is odd to Western eyes because its point of view is so foreign to Western culture; the poem is an extraordinary act on Cendrars's part of decolonializing perception.

But what struck readers of *Nineteen Elastic Poems* first was the modern subject matter, presented with engaging enthusiasm even though the poet did not seem duped by progress. Trains, radios, machines, advertising, headlines, pop culture, had already appeared in other work, but never with this concentration. Modernity occupies the foreground entirely in these short, nonnarrative lyrics, matching subject to novel treatment per-fectly. I don't think this is contradicted even by the Tonga poem "Mee Too Buggi," in which modernist form demonstrates its sources in so-called primitivism. The poems were new inside and out, like the poet reborn to the newness of a world rushing ahead with no regard for culture as a civilizer.

Only two further volumes of poetry would appear, both in 1924: *Kodak (Documentaire)*, with a portrait by Picabia, and *The Formosa*, which is part one of *Feuilles de route (Travel Notes)*, with a drawing by the Brazilian artist Tarsila. Though other parts of *Travel Notes* appeared in reviews through the latter half of the twenties, 1924 remains the latest dating of any of them, so we may mark that year as the end of Cendrars's life as a poet, after which time he wrote only prose. Perhaps *Kodak* and *Travel Notes* represented a culmination and a finale in his mind; certainly he had put poetry in a very special corner, far away from expressionist lyricism, from literary movements and trends, removed from any grandiose claims to eternal and beautiful art which might reflect back upon the eternal fame of the creating artist.

Still, *Kodak* has its great, if unpretentious, beauties. It has its affinities to travelogue, even more obvious in *Travel Notes*, but of a sort far from either exalted exoticism or Michelin's tour of historical monuments. The poems are made almost entirely of description, quite eventless, like snapshots in a family album. We flip the pages but make few profound links. Each poem is largely mute, showing without saying much, while just below these surfaces of heat, rain, and mud, of cool bungalows, unfamiliar birds, trees, flowers and fish, lies an odd sort of secret quotidian; a strange one, someone else's, as if only the American (or Japanese) knew what it was we were being shown, and only Cendrars knew how to write it down without overinterpreting it. And at the same time, as I have said, it does not seem to add up, especially with the elephant hunt near the end in which it seems the huge beast in the jungle is always getting away, right next to you! The finale of eight stunning and weird menus constitutes an unexpectedly sublime ending to the album, a magical decantation of all the disparate localities that have supplied the travelogue's poems. Yet, should not menus come beforehand? As with any menu, you cannot possibly eat it all, from "Truffled green turtle liver" through "Canadian bear ham" and "Cream of silkworm cocoon" to "Hedgehog ravensara." The menus are also an index, a parting taste to save as a reminder of the variety and strangeness of experience, and a parting invitation to reopen the album when the right hunger strikes.

I have said these few words about *Kodak* to prompt the reader to respond directly to what is on the page before revealing the extraordinary game Cendrars has played behind the scenes. The only trip Cendrars took for these snapshots is through a book by someone else, a writer of popular novels he knew named Gustave Le Rouge. The plagiarism was "discovered" by Francis Lacassin in 1966, but twenty years earlier Cendrars had already given it away in *L'Homme foudroyé*, writing that he had been cruel enough to show an (unnamed) volume of poems to Le Rouge which he had scissor-and-pasted out of the latter's adventure novels. Presumably his point had been to prove to Le Rouge that he was himself something of a poet, if an "anti-poetic" one, capable of shedding light on the "real" in his fictions. But, though most all of *Kodak* is lifted from Le Rouge's *Le Mystérieux Docteur Cornélius*, it is only Cendrars who is shedding real light. He has cut away all the narrative claptrap, extracted "facts" that Le Rouge saw only as background and atmosphere, and substituted felt landscapes for dross and silly or moralistic stories. Beyond that, the "finding" of this poetry never ridicules its source or its dissimulated author. It seems to have been a way for Cendrars himself to disappear as an author and to become another.

Travel Notes, on the other hand, is definitely Cendrars's own trip, the journal of his first voyage to South America. Though its language may seem similar to that of *Kodak*, in various ways the volume is in complete contrast to its companion of that year; *Travel Notes* is entirely ingenuous in presentation, bringing the poet back into play personally in his own voice and in his own logbook. The objectivity of *Kodak* is here replaced by personal and unpretentious response, for example the poet's anticipated delight at seeing, at a specific latitude and longitude and time one afternoon, the ocean turn from slate to ultramarine. In another poem the poet lists the contents of his trunk, summarizing a whole way of life (and incidentally telling the scholar exactly what manuscripts he was working on at the time). The writing, at least in appearance, is no more formal than that of a postcard, or an "ocean letter," as he calls it at various times, except for the fact that he is perfectly conscious of what he is doing as a writer, to personal correspondence on the one hand and to poetry on the other. He wants to displace both, making his friendly messages home into an act of poetry-making and his poetry-making into a way of living, instead of the sign of a separation from it:

The ocean letter is not a new poetic genre
It's a practical message with a descending rate and a lot cheaper than a
    radiogram . . .
But when . . . you send ocean letters
It's poetry

So not only is there no pretentiousness in these poems but they also constitute an attack upon pretentiousness, upon rhetorical embellishment and artistic "superiority." And throughout, Cendrars demonstrates a sense of humor about the job, an enjoyment of living, and a whole range of irony and sarcasm about the arrogant insularity of Western attitudes. As he wrote so often, poetry is in the street.

That statement might sum up the stylistic progression of Cendrars's twelve years as a publishing poet; a series of increasingly radical descents from the tower into the street until, to confirm the myth about him that he may have controlled only more or less, his poetry disappeared into his life. By the end, a life had been successfully transformed into poetry, by almost no artificial operations at all, only a certain tone in the delivery.

All along the path of this rapid progression are transformations of poetic expression that are, each by each, wonderfully fresh and invigorating lessons for poetry in the twentieth century. Always a lesson in stripping down rhetoric and poetic habit, in getting to the point, in speaking to the reader. Profusion of experience, brotherhood beneath exoticism, easy familiarity with a daily living pervaded by modernity, these are the aspects of a way of life that foster Cendrars's brand of poetry. And, with all that directness, he still gives us the essentially poetic, the powerful sense that what cannot be said or what is always left to be said is intensely felt.

Jay Bochner, Université de Montréal

Easter in New York

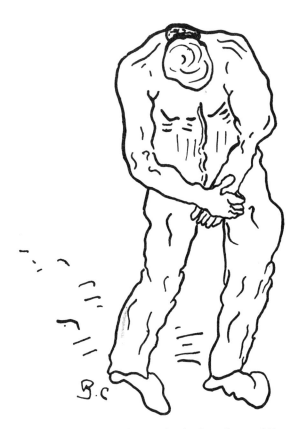

Cendrars's frontispiece drawing for the first edition of *Easter in New York*.

Easter in New York

To Agnès

Lord, today is your feast day.
I read about your Passion in an old play,

And your good words and your anguish and your groans
That weep in the book, in quiet monotones.

An old-time monk tells me about your death.
He was writing your story in golden script

In a missal balanced on his knees.
Inspired by You, he worked reverently.

Sheltered by the altar, sitting dressed in white,
He worked slowly all week, deep into the night.

Time stopped at the threshold of his retreat.
He forgot himself, bent over your portrait.

At Vespers, when the bells chimed above,
The good friar knew not if it was his Love

Or your Father's, Lord, or yours
That pounded loudly on the monastery doors.

I am like that good monk tonight, I am upset.
In the room next door, a being sad and silent

Waits behind the door, waits that I come asking!
It's You, it's God, it's me—it's the Everlasting.

I didn't know You then—and not today.
When I was little I didn't know how to pray.

Tonight, though, I think of You with awe.
My soul is a grieving widow at the foot of your Cross;

My soul is a widow in black—it's your Mother
Without tears or hope, as Carrière painted her.

I know all the Christs hanging in museums;
But tonight You walk, Lord, next to me.

I stride quickly toward the lower part of town,
Hunched over, heart shrunk, spirits down.

Your wide-open side is like a big sun
And your hands throb with sparks all around.

The apartment windows are all filled with blood
And the women behind them are like flowers of blood,

Orchids, strange, bad, withered blooms,
Chalices inverted underneath your wounds.

They never drank of your blood collected there.
They have red on their lips, and lacy underwear.

White, like candles, are the Passion
Flowers, the sweetest in the Good Virgin's garden.

It was the same time as now, around the ninth hour,
When your Head, Lord, dropped onto your Heart.

I'm sitting at the ocean's edge
And I remember a German hymn

That told, with very quiet words, very simple and pure,
The beauty of your Face in torture.

In a church, in Siena, in a burial vault,
I saw the same face, beneath a curtain, on the wall.

And in a hermitage, in Burrié-Vladislasz,
It's plated with gold in a reliquary behind glass.

Clouded cabochons were used for eyes
And the farmers knelt down to kiss Your eyes.

Veronica's handkerchief bears the print
And that's why Saint Veronica is Your saint.

It's the best relic carried in procession,
It cures every illness and transgression.

It does thousands and thousands of other miracles,
But I've never seen any of those spectacles.

Maybe I lack the faith, Lord, and the goodness
To see this form of your Beauty's radiance.

Still, Lord, I took a dangerous voyage
To see a beryl intaglio of your image.

Lord, make my face, buried in my hands,
Leave there its agonizing mask.

Lord, don't let my two hands, pressed there
Against my lips, lick the foam of wild despair.

I'm sad and sick. Perhaps because of You,
Perhaps because of someone else. Perhaps because of You.

Lord, the poor masses for whom you made the Sacrifice
Are here, penned in, heaped up, like cattle, in poorhouses.

Huge dark ships come in around the clock
And dump them off, pell-mell, onto the dock.

There are Italians, Greeks, Bulgarians,
Spaniards, Persians, Russians, and Mongolians.

They're circus animals that leap meridians.
They're thrown a piece of rotten meat, like swine.

Even such a lousy pittance makes them happy.
On suffering people, Lord, have pity.

Lord, in the ghetto swarm the hordes of Jews.
They come from Poland and are all refugees.

I know they held your Trial, Lord;
But believe me, they aren't completely bad.

They sit in shops, under copper lamps,
Sell old clothes, books, arms, and stamps.

Rembrandt loved to paint them in their cast-off clothes.
Me, tonight I pawned a microscope.

Alas, Lord, after Easter you won't be here anymore!
Have pity on the Jews in their hovels, Lord.

Lord, the humble women who were with you at Golgotha
Are hidden, in filthy backrooms, on obscene sofas,

They're polluted by the wretchedness of men.
Dogs have gnawed their bones, and in gin

They hide their hardened, scaly vice.
Lord, when one of these women speaks to me I wince.

I wish I were You, so I could love these prostitutes.
Lord, have pity on the prostitutes.

Lord, I'm in the neighborhood of vagrants,
Good thieves, bums, and fences.

I think of the two thieves who shared your torture,
I know you deign to smile on their misfortune.

Lord, one wants a rope with a noose on the end,
But they aren't free, ropes, they cost a couple of cents.

This old robber talked like a philosopher.
I gave him some opium so he'd get to heaven faster.

I think also of the street singers,
The blind violinist, the one-armed organ-grinder,

The straw-hat, paper-rose singer; surely
These are the ones who sing throughout eternity.

Lord, give them a little something, more than gaslight glimmer,
Lord, give them a little money right down here.

Lord, the curtain parted when you died,
And what was seen behind, no one has said.

In the night the street is like a gash,
Filled with gold and blood, fire and trash.

The ones you drove out of the temple with your lash
Flog passersby with a fistful of evil acts.

The Star that disappeared then from the tabernacle
Burns on the walls in the raw light of public spectacles.

Lord, the illuminated Bank is like a safe,
Where the Blood of your death coagulates.

The streets empty out and then grow dark.
I stagger down the sidewalk like a drunk.

I'm scared by the shadows the big buildings cast down.
I'm scared. Someone follows me. I don't dare look around.

Closer and closer comes this limping step.
I'm scared. I'm dizzy. I deliberately stop.

A scary creep gave me a sharp look,
Then went on by, vicious, like a shark.

Lord, since you were King things haven't changed much.
Evil has made your Cross into a crutch.

I go down some rickety steps to a café
And here I am, sitting, with a glass of tea.

Their backs seem to smile, these Chinese,
Who bow, shiny as magot figurines.

Painted all in red, the shop is small
With curious prints in bamboo frames along the wall.

Hokusai painted the hundred views of a mountain.
What would your face look like, painted by a Chinese artist? . . .

This idea, Lord, at first made me less glum.
I saw you foreshortened in your martyrdom.

But the painter would have painted your torment
With a cruelty beyond the western temperament.

With your skin sliced off by twisted blades,
Your nerves ripped out by tongs and rakes,

They'd have put your neck in an iron choker,
Burned through your eyes with a red-hot poker.

Great black dragons with smoking tongues
Would have blown red flames into your lungs.

With your tongue ripped out, and fingernails,
You'd have been impaled on a sharp stake.

Thus you'd have suffered the vilest torture
Because there is no crueler posture.

And then they would have thrown you to the swine,
Who'd have eaten out your belly and intestines.

I'm alone now, the others have all left,
I'm stretched out on a bench against the wall.

I would have found a church and gone inside;
But there are no bells in this city, Lord.

I think of the silent bells—where are the ancient bells?
Where are the anthems and sweet canticles?

Where are the long services and where the litanies?
Where is the music and where the liturgies?

Where are your nuns, Lord, where your proud prelates?
Where the white dawn, amice of all your Saints?

The joy of Paradise is drowned in the dust,
The mystic fires have stopped glowing in stained glass.

Dawn is slow, and in this little sty
Shadows are crucified against the walls and die.

You look in the mirror: red flickering on black,
It's like a night-Golgotha reflected back.

The smoke, below the light, is like a dingy sheet
That winds its way around you, head to foot.

Above, the dim lamp, like your Head,
Hangs down, sad, cadaverous, dead.

Strange reflections quiver on the panes . . . I'm scared
And I'm sad, Lord, sad to be so sad.

"*Dic nobis, Maria, quid vidisti in via?*"
"The humble morning light, shivering."

"*Dic nobis, Maria, quid vidisti in via?*"
"A wild whiteness, like hands quivering."

"*Dic nobis, Maria, quid vidisti in via?*"
"The augury of spring, in my breast, throbbing."

Lord, cold as a shroud the dawn slipped away
And left the skyscrapers naked in the day.

Already a giant noise resounds across the day.
Already the trains are lurching and roaring away.

The subways run and thunder underground.
The bridges shake with the railway's sound.

The city trembles. Cries and smoke and flames,
Steam whistles give out screechy screams.

A crowd enfevered by the toil that pays
Jostles and disappears down long passageways.

The dim sun, in the roofs' plumed confusion—it
Is your Face soiled with spit.

Lord, I come back tired, alone, and utterly dejected . . .
My room is as empty as a tomb . . .

Lord, I'm all alone and I have a fever . . .
My bed is as cold as a coffin . . .

Lord, I close my eyes and my teeth chatter . . .
I'm too alone. I'm cold. I call your name . . .

A thousand tops spin before my eyes . . .
No, a thousand women . . . No, a thousand cellos . . .

I think, Lord, about how miserable I've been . . .
I think, Lord, about all the days that are gone . . .

I stop thinking about You. I stop thinking about You.

New York, April 1912

The Prose of the
Trans-Siberian
and of Little
Jeanne of France

Young man, probably Cendrars, and a train.

•

The Prose of the Trans-Siberian and of Little Jeanne of France
Dedicated to the musicians

Back then I was still young
I was barely sixteen but my childhood memories were gone
I was 48,000 miles away from where I was born
I was in Moscow, city of a thousand and three bell towers and seven
    train stations
And the thousand and three towers and seven stations weren't enough
    for me
Because I was such a hot and crazy teenager
That my heart was burning like the Temple of Ephesus or like Red
    Square in Moscow
At sunset
And my eyes were shining down those old roads
And I was already such a bad poet
That I didn't know how to take it all the way.

The Kremlin was like an immense Tartar cake
Iced with gold
With big blanched-almond cathedrals
And the honey gold of the bells . . .
An old monk was reading me the legend of Novgorod
I was thirsty
And I was deciphering cuneiform characters
Then all at once the pigeons of the Holy Ghost flew up over the square
And my hands flew up too, sounding like an albatross taking off
And, well, that's the last I remember of the last day
Of the very last trip
And of the sea.

Still, I was a really bad poet.
I didn't know how to take it all the way.
I was hungry

And all those days and all those women in all those cafés and all those
    glasses
I wanted to drink them down and break them
And all those windows and all those streets
And all those houses and all those lives
And all those carriage wheels raising swirls from the broken pavement
I would have liked to have rammed them into a roaring furnace
And I would have liked to have ground up all their bones
And ripped out all those tongues
And liquefied all those big bodies naked and strange under clothes that
    drive me mad . . .
I foresaw the coming of the big red Christ of the Russian Revolution . . .
And the sun was an ugly sore
Splitting apart like a red-hot coal.

Back then I was still quite young
I was barely sixteen but I'd already forgotten about where I was born
I was in Moscow wanting to wolf down flames
And there weren't enough of those towers and stations sparkling in
    my eyes
In Siberia the artillery rumbled—it was war
Hunger cold plague cholera
And the muddy waters of the Amur carrying along millions of corpses
In every station I watched the last trains leave
That's all: they weren't selling any more tickets
And the soldiers would far rather have stayed . . .
An old monk was singing me the legend of Novgorod.

Me, the bad poet who wanted to go nowhere, I could go anywhere
And of course the businessmen still had enough money
To go out and seek their fortunes.
Their train left every Friday morning.
It sounded like a lot of people were dying.
One guy took along a hundred cases of alarm clocks and cuckoo clocks
    from the Black Forest
Another took hatboxes, stovepipes, and an assortment of Sheffield
    corkscrews

Another, coffins from Malmo filled with canned goods and sardines
    in oil
And there were a lot of women
Women with vacant thighs for hire
Who could also serve
Coffins
They were all licensed
It sounded like a lot of people were dying out there
The women traveled at a reduced fare
And they all had bank accounts.

Now, one Friday morning it was my turn to go
It was in December
And I left too, with a traveling jewel merchant on his way to Harbin
We had two compartments on the express and 34 boxes of jewelry from
    Pforzheim
German junk "Made in Germany"
He had bought me some new clothes and I had lost a button getting on
    the train
—I remember, I remember, I've often thought about it since—
I slept on the jewels and felt great playing with the nickel-plated
    Browning he had given me
I was very happy and careless

It was like Cops and Robbers
We had stolen the treasure of Golconda
And we were taking it on the Trans-Siberian to hide it on the other side
    of the world
I had to guard it from the thieves in the Urals who had attacked the
    circus caravan in Jules Verne
From the Khunkhuz, the Boxers of China
And the angry little Mongols of the Great Lama
Ali Baba and the Forty Thieves
And the followers of the terrible Old Man of the Mountain
And worst of all, the most modern
The cat burglars
And the specialists of the international express.

And still, and still
I was as sad as a little boy
The rhythms of the train
What American psychiatrists call "railroad nerves"
The noise of doors voices axles screeching along frozen rails
The golden thread of my future
My Browning the piano the swearing of the card players in the next
    compartment
The terrific presence of Jeanne
The man in blue glasses nervously pacing up and down the corridor
    and glancing in at me
Swishing of women
And the whistle blowing
And the eternal sound of the wheels wildly rolling along ruts in the sky
The windows frosted over
No nature!
And out there the Siberian plains the low sky the big shadows of the
    Taciturns rising and falling
I'm asleep in a tartan
Plaid
Like my life
With my life keeping me no warmer than this Scotch
Shawl
And all of Europe seen through the wind-cutter of an express at top
    speed
No richer than my life
My poor life
This shawl
Frayed on strongboxes full of gold
I roll along with
Dream
And smoke
And the only flame in the universe
Is a poor thought . . .

Tears rise from the bottom of my heart
If I think, O Love, of my mistress;
She is but a child, whom I found, so pale
And pure, in the back of a bordel.

She is but a fair child who laughs,
Is sad, doesn't smile, and never cries;
But the poet's flower, the silver lily, trembles
When she lets you see it in the depths of her eyes.

She is sweet, says nothing you can hear,
With a long, slow trembling when you draw near;
But when I come to her, from here, from there,
She takes a step and shuts her eyes—and takes a step.

For she is my love and other women
Are but big bodies of flame sheathed in gold,
My poor friend is so alone
She is stark naked, has no body—she's too poor.

She is but an innocent flower, all thin and delicate,
The poet's flower, a pathetic silver lily,
So cold, so alone, and so wilted now
That tears rise if I think of her heart.

And this night is like a hundred thousand others when a train slips
    through the night
—Comets fall—
And a man and a woman, no matter how young, enjoy making love.

The sky is like the torn tent of a rundown circus in a little fishing village
In Flanders
The sun like a smoking lamp
And way up on the trapeze a woman does a crescent moon
The clarinet the trumpet a shrill flute a beat-up drum
And here is my cradle

My cradle
It was always near the piano when my mother, like Madame Bovary,
    played Beethoven's sonatas
I spent my childhood in the hanging gardens of Babylon
Playing hooky, following the trains as they pulled out of the stations
Now I've made the trains follow me
Basel–Timbuktu
I've played the horses at tracks like Auteuil and Longchamps
Paris–New York
Now the trains run alongside me
Madrid–Stockholm
Lost it all at the gay pari-mutuel
Patagonia is what's left, Patagonia, which befits my immense sadness,
    Patagonia and a trip to the South Seas
I'm on the road
I've always been on the road
I'm on the road with little Jeanne of France
The train does a somersault and lands on all fours
The train lands on its wheels
The train always lands on all its wheels

"Blaise, say, are we really a long way from Montmartre?"

A long way, Jeanne, you've been rolling along for seven days
You're a long way from Montmartre, from the Butte that brought you
    up, from the Sacré-Coeur you snuggled up to
Paris has disappeared with its enormous blaze
Everything gone except cinders flying back
The rain falling
The peat bogs swelling
Siberia turning
Heavy sheets of snow piling up
And the bell of madness that jingles like a final desire in the bluish air
The train throbs at the heart of the leaden horizon
And your desolation snickers . . .

"Say, Blaise, are we really a long way from Montmartre?"

Troubles
Forget your troubles
All the cracked and leaning stations along the way
The telegraph lines they hang from
The grimacing poles that reach out to strangle them
The world stretches out elongates and snaps back like an accordion in
    the hands of a raging sadist
Wild locomotives fly through rips in the sky
And in the holes
The dizzying wheels the mouths the voices
And the dogs of misery that bark at our heels
The demons are unleashed
Scrap iron
Everything clanks
Slightly off
The clickety-clack of the wheels
Lurches
Jerks
We are a storm in the skull of a deaf man . . .

"Say, Blaise, are we really a long way from Montmartre?"

Of course we are, stop bothering me, you know we are, a long way
An overheated madness bellows in the locomotive
Plague and cholera rise like burning embers around us
We disappear right into a tunnel of war
Hunger, that whore, clutches the clouds scattered across the sky and
    craps on the battlefield piles of stinking corpses
Do what it does, do your job . . .

"Say, Blaise, are we really a long way from Montmartre?"

Yes, we are, we are
All the scapegoats have swollen up and collapsed in this desert
Listen to the cowbells of this mangy troop
Tomsk Chelyabinsk Kansk Ob' Tayshet Verkne-Udinsk Kurgan Samara
    Penza-Tulun

Death in Manchuria
Is where we get off is our last stop
This trip is terrible
Yesterday morning
Ivan Ulitch's hair turned white
And Kolia Nikolai Ivanovitch has been biting his fingers for two
   weeks . . .
Do what Death and Famine do, do your job
It costs one hundred sous—in Trans-Siberian that's one hundred rubles
Fire up the seats and blush under the table
The devil is at the keyboard
His knotty fingers thrill all the women
Instinct
OK gals
Do your job
Until we get to Harbin . . .

"Say, Blaise, are we really a long way from Montmartre?"

No, hey . . . Stop bothering me . . . Leave me alone
Your pelvis sticks out
Your belly's sour and you have the clap
The only thing Paris laid in your lap
And there's a little soul . . . because you're unhappy
I feel sorry for you come here to my heart
The wheels are windmills in the land of Cockaigne
And the windmills are crutches a beggar whirls over his head
We are the amputees of space
We move on our four wounds
Our wings have been clipped
The wings of our seven sins
And the trains are all the devil's toys
Chicken coop
The modern world
Speed is of no use
The modern world

The distances are too far away
And at the end of a trip it's horrible to be a man with a woman . . .

"Blaise, say, are we really a long way from Montmartre?"

I feel so sorry for you come here I'm going to tell you a story
Come get in my bed
Put your head on my shoulder
I'm going to tell you a story . . .

Oh come on!

It's always spring in the Fijis
You lay around
The lovers swoon in the high grass and hot syphilis drifts among the
     banana trees
Come to the lost islands of the Pacific!
Names like Phoenix, the Marquesas
Borneo and Java
And Celebes shaped like a cat

We can't go to Japan
Come to Mexico!
Tulip trees flourish on the high plateaus
Clinging vines hang down like hair from the sun
It's as if the brushes and palette of a painter
Had used colors stunning as gongs—
Rousseau was there
It dazzled him forever
It's a great bird country
The bird of paradise the lyre bird
The toucan the mockingbird
And the hummingbird nests in the heart of the black lily
Come!
We'll love each other in the majestic ruins of an Aztec temple
You'll be my idol

Splashed with color childish slightly ugly and really weird
Oh come!

If you want we'll take a plane and fly over the land of the thousand lakes
The nights there are outrageously long
The sound of the engine will scare our prehistoric ancestors
I'll land
And build a hangar out of mammoth fossils
The primitive fire will rekindle our poor love
Samovar
And we'll settle down like ordinary folks near the pole
Oh come!

Jeanne Jeannette my pet my pot my poot
My me mama poopoo Peru
Peepee cuckoo
Ding ding my dong
Sweet pea sweet flea sweet bumblebee
Chickadee beddy-bye
Little dove my love
Little cookie-nookie
Asleep.

She's asleep
And she hasn't taken in a thing the whole way
All those faces glimpsed in the stations
All the clocks
Paris time Berlin time Saint Petersburg time all those stations' times
And at Ufa the bloody face of the cannoneer
And the absurdly luminous dial at Grodno
And the train moving forward endlessly
Every morning you set your watch ahead
The train moves forward and the sun loses time
It's no use! I hear the bells
The big bell at Notre-Dame
The sharp bell at the Louvre that rang on Saint Bartholomew's Day
The rusty carillons of Bruges-the-Dead

The electric bells of the New York Public Library
The campaniles of Venice
And the bells of Moscow ringing, the clock at Red Gate that kept time
    for me when I was working in an office
And my memories
The train thunders into the roundhouse
The train rolls along
A gramophone blurts out a tinny Bohemian march
And the world, like the hands of the clock in the Jewish section of
    Prague, turns wildly backwards.

Cast caution to the winds
Now the storm is raging
And the trains storm over tangled tracks
Infernal toys
There are trains that never meet
Others just get lost
The stationmasters play chess
Backgammon
Shoot pool
Carom shots
Parabolas
The railway system is a new geometry
Syracuse
Archimedes
And the soldiers who butchered him
And the galleys
And the warships
And the astounding engines he invented
And all that killing
Ancient history
Modern history
Vortex
Shipwreck
Even that of the *Titanic* I read about in the paper

So many associations images I can't get into my poem
Because I'm still such a really bad poet
Because the universe rushes over me
And I didn't bother to insure myself against train wreck
Because I don't know how to take it all the way
And I'm scared.

I'm scared
I don't know how to take it all the way.
Like my friend Chagall I could do a series of irrational paintings
But I didn't take notes
"Forgive my ignorance
Pardon my forgetting how to play the ancient game of Verse"
As Guillaume Apollinaire says
If you want to know anything about the war read Kuropotkin's *Memoirs*
Or the Japanese newspapers with their ghastly illustrations
But why compile a bibliography
I give up
Bounce back into my leaping memory . . .

At Irkutsk the trip suddenly slows down
Really drags
We were the first train to wind around Lake Baikal
The locomotive was decked out with flags and lanterns
And we had left the station to the sad sound of "God Save the Czar."
If I were a painter I would splash lots of red and yellow over the end of
    this trip
Because I think we were all slightly crazy
And that an overwhelming delirium brought blood to the exhausted
    faces of my traveling companions
As we came closer to Mongolia
Which roared like a forest fire.
The train had slowed down
And in the perpetual screeching of wheels I heard
The insane sobbing and screaming
Of an eternal liturgy

I saw
I saw the silent trains the black trains returning from the Far East and
    going by like phantoms
And my eyes, like tail lights, are still trailing along behind those trains
At Talga 100,000 wounded were dying with no help coming
I went to the hospitals in Krasnoyarsk
And at Khilok we met a long convoy of soldiers gone insane
I saw in quarantine gaping sores and wounds with blood gushing out
And the amputated limbs danced around or flew up in the raw air
Fire was in their faces and in their hearts
Idiot fingers drumming on all the windowpanes
And under the pressure of fear an expression would burst like an abcess
In all the stations they had set fire to all the cars
And I saw
I saw trains with 60 locomotives streaking away chased by hot horizons
    and desperate crows
Disappearing
In the direction of Port Arthur.

At Chita we had a few days' rest
A five-day stop while they cleared the tracks
We stayed with Mr. Iankelevitch who wanted me to marry his only
    daughter
Then it was time to go.
Now I was the one playing the piano and I had a toothache
And when I want I can see it all again those quiet rooms the store and
    the eyes of the daughter who slept with me every night
Mussorgsky
And the lieder of Hugo Wolf
And the sands of the Gobi Desert
And at Khailar a caravan of white camels
I'd swear I was drunk for over 300 miles
But I was playing the piano—it's all I saw
You should close your eyes on a trip
And sleep
I was dying to sleep

With my eyes closed I can smell what country I'm in
And I can hear what kind of train is going by
European trains are in 4/4 while the Asian ones are 5/4 or 7/4
Others go humming along are like lullabies
And there are some whose wheels' monotone reminds me of the heavy
    prose of Maeterlinck
I deciphered all the garbled texts of the wheels and united the scattered
    elements of a violent beauty
Which I possess
And which drives me

Tsitsihar and Harbin
That's as far as I go
The last station
I stepped off the train at Harbin a minute after they had set fire to the
    Red Cross office.

O Paris
Great warm hearth with the intersecting embers of your streets and your
    old houses leaning over them for warmth
Like grandmothers
And here are posters in red in green all colors like my past in a word
    yellow
Yellow the proud color of the novels of France
In big cities I like to rub elbows with the buses as they go by
Those of the Saint-Germain—Montmartre line that carry me to the
    assault of the Butte
The motors bellow like golden bulls
The cows of dusk graze on Sacré-Coeur
O Paris
Main station where desires arrive at the crossroads of restlessness
Now only the paint store has a little light on its door
The International Pullman and Great European Express Company has
    sent me its brochure
It's the most beautiful church in the world
I have friends who surround me like guardrails
They're afraid that when I leave I'll never come back

All the women I've ever known appear around me on the horizon
Holding out their arms and looking like sad lighthouses in the rain
Bella, Agnès, Catherine, and the mother of my son in Italy
And she who is the mother of my love in America
Sometimes the cry of a whistle tears me apart
Over in Manchuria a belly is still heaving, as if giving birth
I wish
I wish I'd never started traveling
Tonight a great love is driving me out of my mind
And I can't help thinking about little Jeanne of France.
It's through a sad night that I've written this poem in her honor
Jeanne
The little prostitute
I'm sad so sad
I'm going to the Lapin Agile to remember my lost youth again
Have a few drinks
And come back home alone

Paris

City of the incomparable Tower the great Gibbet and the Wheel

Paris, 1913

Panama, or the Adventures of My Seven Uncles

Proof for Raoul Dufy's cover design for *Panama*, with handwritten note by Cendrars at lower left.

Panama, or the Adventures of My Seven Uncles

To Edmond Bertrand
bartender at the Matachine

Books
There are books that talk about the Panama Canal
I don't know what the card catalogs say
And I don't pay any attention to the financial pages
Although the Stock Market quotations are our daily prayers

The Panama Canal is intimately linked to my childhood . . .
I used to play under the table
And dissect flies
My mother used to tell me about the adventures of her seven brothers
My seven uncles
And when she got letters
Dazzlement!
Those letters with beautiful exotic stamps inscribed with lines from
    Rimbaud
She didn't tell me any stories on those days
And I stayed sad under my table

It was also around that time that I read the story of the Lisbon
    earthquake
But I really believe
That the Panama crash had a much wider effect
Because it turned my childhood upside down.

I had a nice picture book
And for the first time I saw
The whale
The big cloud
The walrus
The sun

The great walrus
The bear the lion the chimpanzee the rattlesnake and the fly
The fly
The terrible fly
"Mommy, the flies! The flies! And the tree trunks!"
"Go to sleep now, child."
Ahasuerus is idiotic

I had a nice picture book
A big greyhound named Dourak
An English maid
As a banker
My father lost three-fourths of his fortune
Like a number of upright people who lost their money in that crash,
My father
Less stupid
Lost other people's money.
Bang bang.
My mother wept.
And that night I was sent to sleep with the English maid

Then after an enormous number of days . . .
We'd had to move
And the few rooms of our little apartment were crammed with furniture
We no longer had our villa on the coast
I was alone for entire days
Among the stacks of furniture
I could even break the dishes
Split open the armchairs
Demolish the piano . . .
Then after an enormous number of days
A letter came from one of my uncles

It was the Panama crash that made me a poet!
It's great
My whole generation is like that
Young people

Who experienced weird ricochets
You don't play with the furniture anymore
You don't play with old stuff anymore
You break every dish you can get your hands on
You sail away
You hunt whales
You kill walruses
You're always afraid of the tse-tse fly
Because we don't like to sleep

The bear the lion the chimpanzee the rattlesnake had taught me how to
    read . . .
Oh that first letter I deciphered alone, letter more teeming than all of
    creation
My uncle said:
I'm working as a butcher in Galveston
The slaughterhouses are 15 miles from town
I'm the one who takes the bleeding animals back along the sea, in the
    evening
And when I go by, the octopuses stand up
Sunset . . .
And there was still something else
Sadness
And homesickness.

Uncle, you disappeared in the cyclone of 1895
Since then I've seen the rebuilt town and strolled along the seashore
    where you took the bleeding animals
There was a Salvation Army band playing in a lattice bandstand
I was offered a cup of tea
They never found your body
And when I turned twenty I inherited the 400 dollars you'd saved
I also have the cookie box that served as your reliquary
It's made of tin
All your poor religion
A button from a uniform
A Kabyle pipe

Some cocoa beans
A dozen watercolors by you
And the photos of prize animals, the giant bulls you're holding by the
    halter
You're in shirtsleeves with a white apron

I like animals too
Under the table
Alone
I'm already playing with the chairs
Wardrobes doors
Windows
Modern-style furniture
Preconceived animals
That sit enthroned in houses
Like reconstructed antediluvian beasts in museums
The first wooden stool is an aurochs!
I break the windowpanes
And I threw all that out
The city, a pasture for my dog
The pictures
The books
The maid
The visits
Ha ha!

How am I supposed to study for my tests?
You sent me to all the boarding schools in Europe
High schools
Prep schools
University
How am I supposed to study for my tests
When a letter slides under the door
I saw
This beautiful pedagogy!
In the movies, I saw the trip it took
It took sixty-eight days to get to me

Loaded with spelling errors
My second uncle:
I married the woman who makes the best bread in the district
I live three days away from my nearest neighbor
I'm prospecting for gold in Alaska now
I've never found more than 500 francs' worth in my shovel
Life doesn't get paid what it's worth, either
Three of my fingers have been frozen
It's cold here . . .
And there was still something else
Sadness
And homesickness.

O uncle, my mother told me everything
You stole some horses to run away with your brothers
You became a cabin boy on a tramp steamer
You broke your leg jumping from a moving train
And after the hospital, you were in jail for sticking up a stagecoach
And you used to write poetry inspired by Musset
San Francisco
That's where you read the story of General Sutter who conquered
    California
And who, a multimillionaire, lost all his money when gold was
    discovered on his land
For a long time you hunted in the Sacramento valley where I worked
    clearing land
But what happened
I understand your pride
Eating the best bread in the district and the rivalry among neighbors 12
    women in a thousand square kilometers
They found you
A rifle bullet through the head
Your wife wasn't there
Now she's married to a jam magnate

I'm thirsty
Good God

Jesus Christ
Christ!
I feel like reading the *Neuchâtel Tattler* or the *Pamplona Courier*
In the middle of the Atlantic you're no more comfortable than in an
    editorial office
I go round in the cage of meridians like a squirrel in his
Look there's a Russian with a friendly face
Where to go
He doesn't know where to put down his baggage either
In Leopoldville or in Sejera near Nazareth, at Mr. Junod's or my old
    friend Perl's
In the Congo in Bessarabia in Samoa
I know all the timetables
All the trains and the connections
Time of arrival time of departure
All the steamers all the fares all the taxes
It's all the same to me
I have some addresses
Sponging my way
I come back from America on board the *Volturno* for 35 francs from
    New York to Rotterdam

It's the baptism of the line
The engines keep throwing endless left-rights
Boys
Splash
Buckets of water
An American his fingers stained with ink keeps time
Wireless telegraph
People are dancing with their knees among orange peels and empty
    cans
A delegation is seeing the captain
The Russian revolutionary erotic experiences
Gaoupa
The dirtiest Hungarian word
I'm escorting a Neapolitan marchioness 8 months pregnant
I'm the one taking the emigrants from Kishinev to Hamburg

It was in 1901 that I saw the first automobile,
Broken down,
At a street corner
That little train the Solothurnians call "the steam iron"
I'll call my consul
Send me over a 3rd-class ticket immediately
The Uranium Steamship Co.
I want my money's worth
The ship is dockside
A mess
The cargo doors wide open
I leave it the way you leave a filthy whore

En route
I didn't bring enough toilet paper
And I bring out
Like the god Tangaloa who fished the world up out of the water
The last letter of my third uncle:
Papeete, September 1, 1887
My dear, dear sister
I've become a Buddhist, a member of a political sect
I'm here to buy dynamite
You can buy it here at grocery stores the way you buy chicory in France
In little packets
Then I'll go back to Bombay and blow up the English
Things are getting hot
I'll never see you again . . .
And there was still something else
Sadness
And homesickness.

Knocking around
I've done time in Marseille and they took me back to school by force
All voices cry out together
The animals and the rocks
It's the mute who speaks most beautifully
I've been a libertine and have taken every liberty with the world

You who used to have faith why didn't you arrive on time
At your age
Uncle
You used to be a cute kid and you really knew how to play the cornet
That's what (as they say) did you in
You loved music so much that you preferred the whining of bombs to
    evening-dress symphonies
You worked with happy Italians building a railroad near Baghavapur
A live wire
You were a natural leader
With your good humor and beautiful singing voice
You were the favorite of the women around the camp
Like Moses you flattened your crew boss
You fled
For 12 years there was no word of you
And like Luther a thunderbolt made you believe in God
In your solitude
You learned Bengali and Urlu to learn how to make bombs
You were in contact with secret committees in London
It was at Whitechapel that I picked up your trail again
You're a convict
Your life circumcised
So much so that
I feel like killing someone with a sap or a waffle iron just to get the
    chance to see you
Because I never have seen you
You must have a long scar across your forehead

As for my fourth uncle, he was the valet of General Robertson who
    fought in the Boer War
His letters came rarely and said things such as
His Excellency has deigned to increase my salary by £50
Or
His Excellency brings 48 pairs of shoes to war
Or
I do His Excellency's nails each morning . . .
But I know

There was still something else
Sadness
And homesickness.

Uncle Jean, you're the only one of my seven uncles I ever saw
You had come back because you were ill
You had a big trunk made of hippopotamus hide that was always
    buckled up
You shut yourself up in your room to recuperate
When I saw you for the first time, you were asleep
Your face showed terrible suffering
A long beard
You slept for two weeks
And as I was leaning over you
You woke up
You were crazy
You wanted to kill grandmother
They locked you up in the asylum
And that's where I saw you for the second time
Strapped
In the straitjacket
They wouldn't let you off the ship
You made pathetic motions with your hands
As if you were going to row
Transvaal
You were in quarantine and the Horse Guards had trained a cannon on
    your ship
Pretoria
A Chinaman almost strangled you
Tugela
Lord Robertson died
On the way back to London
His Excellency's wardrobe fell into the water, like a dagger in your heart
You died in Switzerland in the Saint-Aubain insane asylum
Your last wits
Your last rites
And that's where I saw you for the third time

It was snowing
Walking behind your hearse I was arguing with the ushers about their
    tip
You loved only two things in this world
A cockatoo
And the pink fingernails of His Excellency

There's no hope
And we have to work
Shut-in lives are the densest
Steganic tissues
Remy de Gourmont lives at number 71 rue des Saints-Pères
Cartridge thread or twine
"One man can encounter another man, but a mountain can never
    encounter another mountain"
Says the Hebrew proverb
Precipices meet
I was in Naples
1896
When I received the *Little Illustrated Journal*
Captain Dreyfus being stripped in front of the army
My fifth uncle:
I'm head cook at the Club Hotel in Chicago
I have 400 kitchen boys under me
But I don't like Yankee cooking
Please note my new address
Tunis etc.
Regards from Aunt Adèle
Please note my new address
Biarritz etc.

O uncle, you're the only one who never felt homesick
Nice London Budapest Bermuda Saint Petersburg Tokyo Memphis
All the great hotels fought to get you
You are the master
You invented a number of sweet dishes that bear your name
Your art

You give yourself you sell yourself you are eaten
No one ever knows where you are
You don't like to stay put
It seems you own a *History of Cuisine down the Ages and throughout
 the World*
In 12 vols. octavo
With portraits of the most famous cooks of all time
You knew about everything that was going on
You were always everywhere anything was happening
Maybe you're in Paris.
Your menus
Are the new poetry

I left all that behind
I'm waiting
The guillotine is the masterpiece of plastic art
Its click
Perpetual motion
The blood of bandits
The songs of the light shake the towers
The colors crash over the city
Poster bigger than you and me
Open mouth that cries out
And in which we are burning
The three hot-blooded young people
Hananiah Mishael Azariah
Adam's Express Co.
Behind the Opera
We must play leapfrog
Froggy went a-courtin'
Springboard woman
The pretty toy in the advertisement
Let's go!
"Siméon, Siméon"
Paris good-bye

Denver, the Residence City and Commercial Center

DENVER is the capital of Colorado and the commercial metropolis of the Rocky Mountain Region. The city is in its fifty-fifth year and has a population of approximately 225.000 as indicated by the U. S. Census of 1910. Many people who have not visited Colorado, believe Denver is situated in the mountains. This city is located 12 miles east of the foothills of the Rocky Mountains, near the north central part of the state, at the junction of the Platte River and Cherry Creek. The land is rolling, giving the city perfect drainage. Altitude one mile above sea level. Area 60 square miles.

Ideal Climate, Superior Educational Advantages Unequalled Park System

DENVER has the lowest death rate of the cities of the United States.

DENVER has 61 grade schools, 4 high schools, 1 manual training school, 1 trade and 1 technical school.

DENVER has 209 churches of every denomination.

DENVER has 29 parks; total area 1,238 acres.

DENVER has 11 playgrounds — 8 in parks, 3 in individual tracts.

DENVER has 56 miles of drives in its parks.

Commercial and Manufacturing City

Annual Bank C l e a r i n g s, $ 487,848,305.95.

Per capita clearings, $ 180.00.

Annual manufacturing output, $ 57,711,000 (1912).
Eighteen trunk lines entering Denver, tapping the richest agricultural sections of the United States.

DENVER has 810 factories, in which 16,251 wage earners were employed during 1911. The output of factories in DENVER in 1911 was valued at $ 52,000,000. The payroll for the year was $ 12,066,000 — OVER A MILLION DOLLARS A MONTH !

DENVER, COLORADO, BERLIN, GERMANY and MANCHESTER, ENGLAND, are cited by Economists as examples of inland cities which have become great because they are located at a sort of natural cross-roads.

For detailed information, apply to the *Denver Chamber of Commerce.*   *Prospectus free.*

It's a riot
There are hours that chime
Quai-d'Orsay-Saint-Nazaire!
You go under the Eiffel Tower—looping the loop—to come down on
    the other side of the world

Then you go on

The catapults of the sun lay siege to the irascible tropics
Rich Peruvian owner of a guano business in Angamos
Acaraguan Bananan is launched
In the shade
The hospitable mulattos
I spent more than a winter on those islands of the blessed
The secretary bird is dazzling
Beautiful buxom women
You have iced drinks out on the terrace
A torpedo boat burns like a cigar
A game of polo in the pineapple grove
And the mangroves fan the studious young girls
My gun
A shot
An observatory on the side of a volcano
Big snakes in the dried-up riverbed
Cactus hedge
A donkey trumpets, tail in the air
The cross-eyed little Indian girl wants to sell herself in Buenos Aires
The German musician borrowed my silver-handled riding crop and a
    pair of suede gloves
That fat Dutchman is a geographer
People play cards waiting for the train
It's the Malaysian woman's birthday
I received a package with my name on it, 200,000 pesetas, and a letter
    from my sixth uncle: .
Wait for me at the trading post until next spring
Have a good time take your drinks straight up and don't spare the
    women

The best electuary
Dear nephew . . .
And there was still something else
Sadness
And homesickness.

O uncle, I waited a year for you and you didn't come
You'd left with a group of astronomers who were going to study the sky
    over the western coast of Patagonia
You were acting as interpreter and guide
Your advice
Your experience
No one could sight the horizon with a sextant better than you
The instruments balanced
Electromagnetic
In the fjords of Tierra del Fuego
At the edge of the world
In the glow of electric fish you gathered protozoic moss adrift between
    two oceans
You collected meteorites made of iron peroxide
One Sunday morning:
You saw a mitered bishop emerge from the waters
He had a tail like a fish and he sprinkled you when he made the sign of
    the cross
You fled into the mountains screaming like a wounded lemur
That same night
A hurricane destroyed the camp
Your companions had to give up all hope of finding you alive
Carefully they packed up their scientific instruments
And, three months later,
The poor intellectuals,
They came upon a campfire one night where gauchos were talking
    about you
I had come to meet you
Tupa
The beauties of nature
The stallions screw each other

200 black bulls bellow
Argentine tango

So?
So there aren't any more beautiful stories?
Lives of the Saints
Das Nachtbeuchlein von Schuman
Cymbalum mundi
La Tariffa delle Putane di Venegia
Navigation by Johann Struys, Amsterdam, 1528
Shalom Aleichem
The Crocodile of Saint-Martin
Strindberg demonstrated that the earth is not round
Already Gavarni had abolished geometry
Pampas
Disk
The Iroquois women of the wind
Hot sauces
The propeller of gems
Maggi
Byrrh
Daily Chronicle
The wave is a quarry where the sculpting storm cuts away chunks of
    dressed stone
Quadrigas of foam that take the bit in their teeth
Eternally
Since the creation of the world
I whistle
A shudder of wreckage

My seventh uncle
No one ever knew what happened to him
They say I look like you

I dedicate this poem to you
Mr. Bertrand
You gave me strong drink to immunize me against the fevers of the
    canal
You subscribed to the Press Argus to get all the clippings about me
Last Frenchman in Panama (there aren't even 20)
I dedicate this poem to you
Bartender at the Matachine
Thousands of Chinese died where the blazing Bar now stands
Your own distillery
You got rich burying the victims of cholera
Send me the photograph of the forest of cork oaks that grow on the 400
    locomotives abandoned by the French undertaking
The living dead
The palm tree grafted in the loading bucket of a crane overgrown with
    orchids
The cannons of Aspinwall gnawed by toucans
The tortoise nets
The pumas that nest in the caved-in gas tank
The locks punctured by swordfish
The pump pipes clogged with a colony of iguanas
The trains stopped by invasions of caterpillars
And the Louis XV coat of arms on the gigantic anchor whose presence
    in the forest you were never able to explain to me
Every year you replace the doors in your bar, encrusted with the
    signatures
Of everyone who comes through
Those 32 doors what a testimony
The living tongues of that damned canal you cherish so

This morning is the first day on earth
Isthmus
Where you see simultaneously all the heavenly bodies in the sky and all
    the forms of vegetation
Unparalleled equatorial mountains
Unique zone

The Amidon Paterson steamer is still there
The colored initials of the Atlantic & Pacific Tea Co.
The Los Angeles Limited that leaves at 10:02 to arrive on the third day
    and is the only train in the world with a beauty parlor
The Trunk the signals and the toy cars
To teach you how to spell the ABC of life beneath the ruler of departing
    whistles
Toyo Kisen Kaisha
I have some bread and cheese
A clean collar
Poetry dates from today

The Milky Way around my neck
The two hemispheres on my eyes
At top speed
There are no more breakdowns
If I had time to save a little money I'd fly in the airplane races
I've reserved a seat on the first train through the tunnel beneath the
    English Channel
I'm the first flyer to cross the Atlantic in a monocoque
900 million

Earth Earth Seas Oceans Skies
I'm homesick
I follow every face and I'm scared of mailboxes
The cities are wombs
I don't follow the roads anymore
Lines
Cables
Canals
Nor suspension bridges!

Suns moons stars
Apocalyptic worlds
You all still have a good role to play
A seltzer bottle sneezes
The literary tittle-tattle keeps moving

Very low
At the Rotonde
As if at the very bottom of a glass

I'm waiting

I'd like to be a fifth wheel
Storm
Noon at two P.M.
Nothing and everywhere

—PARIS AND ITS SUBURBS. *Saint-Cloud, Sèvres, Montmorency,*
   Courbevoie, Bougival, Rueil, Montrouge, Saint-Denis, Vincennes,
   Etampes, Melun, Saint-Martin, Méréville, Barbizon, Forges-en-
   Bière.

June 1913–June 1914

Nineteen Elastic Poems

One of Modigliani's two frontispiece portraits of Cendrars for
the first edition of *Nineteen Elastic Poems*.

1. Newspaper

Christ
It's been more than a year now since I stopped thinking about You
Since I wrote my next-to-last poem "Easter"
My life has changed a lot since
But I'm still the same
I've even wanted to become a painter
Here are the pictures I've done and which hang on the walls tonight
For me they open strange views onto myself which make me think
    of You.

Christ
Life
That's what I've ransacked

My paintings hurt me
I'm too passionate
Everything is oranged up.

I spent a sad day thinking about my friends
And reading the paper
Christ
Life crucified in the wide-open paper I hold at arm's length
Wing-spread
Rockets
Turmoil
Cries.
You'd think an airplane is dropping.
It's me.

Passion
Fire
Serials
Newspaper
It's useless not wanting to talk about yourself
You have to cry out sometimes

I'm the other one
Too sensitive

August 1913

2. Tower

1910
Castellammare
I was dining on an orange in the shade of an orange tree
When, suddenly . . .
It wasn't the eruption of Vesuvius
It wasn't the cloud of grasshoppers, one of the ten plagues of Egypt
Nor Pompeii
It wasn't the resuscitated cries of giant mastodons
It wasn't the heralded Trumpet
Nor Pierre Brisset's frog
When, suddenly,
Fires
Jolts
Surging
Spark of simultaneous horizons
My sex

O Eiffel Tower!
I didn't give you golden slippers
I didn't make you dance on crystal tiles
I didn't vow you to the Python like a Carthaginian virgin
I didn't clothe you in the peplos of Greece
I never made you wander about in a circle of menhirs
I didn't name you Rood of David or Wood of the Cross
Lignum Crucis
O Eiffel Tower
Giant fireworks of the Universal Exposition!
Over the Ganges
At Benares
Among the onanistic spinning tops of Hindu temples
And the colored cries of the multitudes of the East

You lean, graceful Palm Tree!
It was you who in the legendary era of the Hebrews
Confounded men's tongues
O Babel!
And a few thousand years later, it was you who fell again in tongues of
    fire onto the Apostles gathered in your church
On the open sea you're a mast
And at the North Pole
You shine with all the magnificence of the aurora borealis with your
    radio waves
The lianas grow through and around the eucalyptus
And you are floating, old trunk, on the Mississippi
When
Your mouth opens
And a cayman grabs a black man's thigh
In Europe you're like a gallows
(I'd like to be the tower, to hang from the Eiffel Tower!)
And when the sun goes down behind you
Bonnot's head rolls beneath the guillotine
In the heart of Africa it's you running
Giraffe
Ostrich
Boa
Equator
Monsoons
In Australia you've always been taboo
You're the gaff hook Captain Cook used to steer his boat of adventurers
O celestial plummet!
For the Simultaneous Delaunay, to whom I dedicate this poem,
You're the brush he dips in light

Gong tom-tom Zanzibar jungle animal X rays express scalpel symphony
You are everything
Tower
Ancient god
Modern animal

Solar spectrum
Subject of my poem
Tower
World tour tower
Moving tower

August 1913

3. Contrasts

The windows of my poetry are wide open onto the boulevards and in its
    shop windows
Shine
The jewels of light
Listen to the violins of the limousines and the xylophones of the
    linotypes
The stenciler washes up in the washcloth of the sky
Everything is splashes of color
And the women's hats going by are comets in the burning evening

Unity
There is no more unity
All the clocks now say midnight after being set back ten minutes
There is no more time.
There is no more money.
At the Chamber
They're wasting the marvelous elements of raw materials

At the bar
The workers in blue overalls drink red wine
Every Saturday, the numbers game
You play
You bet
From time to time a gangster goes by in a car
Or a child plays with the Arch of Triumph . . .
I advise M. Cochon to house his homeless in the Eiffel Tower.

Today
Under new management
The Holy Ghost is sold in small amounts in the smallest shops
I read with pure delight the calico rolls
Calla lily rows

It's only the pumice stones of the Sorbonne that have never flowered
On the other hand the Samaritaine sign plows the Seine
And toward Saint-Séverin
I hear
The relentless bells of the trolleys

It's raining light bulbs
Montrouge Gare de l'Est Métro Nord-Sud Seine omnibus people
One big halo
Depth
Rue de Buci they yell *L'Intransigeant* and *Paris-Sports*
The aerodrome of the sky is now, all fiery, a picture by Cimabue
And in front
The men are
Tall
Dark
Sad
And smoking, factory stacks

October 1913

4.

I. PORTRAIT

He's asleep
He wakes up
Suddenly, he paints
He takes a church and paints with a church
He takes a cow and paints with a cow
With a sardine
With heads, hands, knives
He paints with a bull's pizzle
He paints with all the dirty passions of a little Jewish town
With all the exacerbated sexuality of the Russian provinces
For France
Without sensuality
He paints with his thighs
He has eyes in his ass
And it's suddenly your portrait
It's you reader
It's me
It's him
It's his fiancée
It's the corner grocer
The milkmaid
The midwife
There are tubs of blood
They wash the newborn in
Skies of madness
Mouths of modernity
The Tower as corkscrew
Hands
The Christ
The Christ is him

He spent his childhood on the Cross
He commits suicide every day
Suddenly, he is not painting
He was awake
Now he's asleep
He's strangled by his own tie
Chagall is astonished to still be alive

II. STUDIO

The Beehive
Stairways, doors, stairways
And his door opens like a newspaper
Covered with visiting cards
Then it closes.
Disorder, total disorder
Photographs of Léger, photographs of Tobeen, which you don't see
And on the back
On the back
Frantic works
Sketches, drawings, frantic works
And paintings . . .
Empty bottles
"We guarantee the absolute purity of our tomato sauce"
Says a label
The window is an almanac
When the gigantic cranes of lightning empty the booming barges of the
    sky and dump buckets of thunder
Out fall

Pell-mell

Cossacks Christ a shattered sun
Roofs
Sleepwalkers goats
A lycanthrope
Pétrus Borel

Madness winter
A genius split like a peach
Lautréamont
Chagall
Poor kid next to my wife
Morose delectation
The shoes are down at heel
An old jar full of chocolate
A lamp that's split in two
And my drunkenness when I go see him
Empty bottles
Bottles
Zina
(We've talked about her a lot)
Chagall
Chagall
In the graduations of light

October 1913

5. My Dance

Plato does not grant city rights to the poet
Wandering Jew
Metaphysical Don Juan
Friends, close ones
You don't have customs anymore and no new habits yet
We must be free of the tyranny of magazines
Literature
Poor life
Misplaced pride
Mask
Woman, the dance Nietzsche wanted to teach us to dance
Woman
But irony?

Continual coming and going
Procuring in the street
All men, all countries
And so you are no longer a burden
It's like you're not there anymore . . .

I am a gentleman who in fabulous express trains crosses the same old
    Europe and gazes disheartened from the doorway
The landscape doesn't interest me anymore
But the dance of the landscape
The dance of the landscape
Dance-landscape
Paritatitata
I all-turn

February 1914

6. She Has a Body on Her Dress

A woman's body is as bumpy as my skull
Glorious
If you're embodied with a little spirit
Fashion designers have a stupid job
As stupid as phrenology
My eyes are kilos that weigh the sensuality of women

Everything that recedes, stands out comes forward into the depth
The stars deepen the sky
The colors undress
"She has a body on her dress"
Beneath her arms heathers hands lunules and pistils when the waters
    flow into her back with its blue-green shoulder blades
Her belly a moving disk
The double-bottomed hull of her breasts goes under the bridge of
    rainbows
Belly
Disk
Sun
The perpendicular cries of the colors fall on her thighs
The Sword of Saint Michael

There are hands that reach out
In its train the animal all the eyes all the fanfares all the regulars at the
    Bal Bullier
And on her hip
The poet's signature

February 1914

7. Hammock

Onoto-face
Complicated dial at the Gare Saint-Lazare
Apollinaire
Moves forward, falls behind, sometimes stops.
European
Western traveler
Why don't you come to America with me?
I cried at the dock
New York

The ships shake the salt shakers
Rome Prague London Nice Paris
Oxo-Liebig makes a frieze in your room
The books a stockade

The blunderbusses fire coconuts
Julie, or I Lost My Rose

Futurist

For a long time you wrote in the shade of a painting
You were dreaming of the Arabesque
O you the happiest of us all
Because Rousseau did your portrait
Among the stars
The sweet williams *oeillets du poète*

Apollinaire
1900—1911
For 12 years the only poet of France

December 1913

8. Mardi Gras

The skyscrapers are quartered
Way in the back I found Canudo pages uncut
For five cents
In a 14th Street bookshop
Religiously
Your improvisation on Beethoven's Ninth Symphony
New York is seen as the mercantile Venice of the western ocean

The Cross opens
Dances
There is no free commune
There are no Areopagites
There is no spiritual pyramid
I don't understand the word "Imperialism" very well
But in your attic
Among the wistitis the Indians the beautiful women
The poet came
Colored word

There are hours that sound
Montjoie!
Roland's Oliphant
My New York dump
The books
The telegrams
And the sun brings you today's beautiful body in newspaper clippings
These swaddling clothes

February 1914

9. Crackling

The rainbowesque dissonances of the Tower in its radio
Noon
Midnight
All over the world people say to each other, "Shit"

Sparks
Chrome yellow
We're in contact
The transatlantics are coming in from every direction
Going away
Every watch is set
And the bells are ringing
Paris-Midi announces that a German professor was eaten by cannibals
    in the Congo
Well done
This evening's *Intransigeant* includes poems for postcards
It's stupid when all the astrologers burglarize the stars
You can't see anymore
I question the sky
The Weather Bureau is forecasting bad weather
There is no futurism
There is no simultaneity
Bodin burned all the witches
There is nothing
There are no more horoscopes and you have to work
I'm upset
The Spirit
I'm going to take a trip
And I send this stripped-down poem to my friend R . . .

September 1913

10. News Flash

OKLAHOMA, *January 20, 1914*
Three convicts get hold of revolvers
They kill their guard and grab the prison keys
They come running out of their cells and kill four guards in the yard
Then they grab the young prison secretary
And get into a carriage waiting for them at the gate
They leave at top speed
While guards fire their revolvers in the direction of the fugitives

A few guards jump on horses and ride in pursuit of the convicts
Both sides exchange shots
The girl is wounded by a shot fired by one of the guards

A bullet shoots down the horse pulling the carriage
The guards can move in
They find the prisoners dead their bodies riddled with bullets
Mr. Thomas, former member of Congress who was visiting the prison,
Congratulates the girl

Copied telegram-poem in *Paris-Midi*

January 1914

11. Bombay Express

The life I've led
Keeps me from suicide
Everything leaps
Women roll beneath the wheels
Screaming
The jalopies are fanned out at the station entrances.
I have music under my fingernails.

I never have liked Mascagni
Nor art nor Artists
Nor barriers nor bridges
Nor trombones nor trumpets
I don't know anything anymore
I don't understand anymore . . .
Such a caress
That the map is trembling from it

This year or next year
Art criticism is as idiotic as Esperanto
Brindisi
Good-bye good-bye

I was born in that town
And my son too
He whose forehead is like his mother's vagina

There are thoughts that make buses jump
I no longer read books found only in libraries
Beautiful ABC of the world

Bon voyage!

Oh to sweep you away
You who laugh at bright red

April 1914

12. F.I.A.T.

I have torn hearing

I envy the way you lie there
Big steamship of factories
At anchor
On the outskirts of town

I wish I could be empty
Like you
After you gave birth
The *pneumatiques* fart silently in my back
I have electric knobs on my nerve endings

Your white modern nickel-plated room
The cradle
The few sounds of hospital
Sainte-Clothilde
I always have a fever
Paris-Addresses

To be in your place
Sharp turn!
It's the first time I've envied a woman
That I want to be a woman
To be a woman
In the universe
In life
To be
And to open oneself to the childlike future
I who am dazzled

Blériot headlights
Self-starter
See

My pen is frisky

Beat it!

April 1914

13. At the 5 Corners

To dare and make some noise
Everything is color movement explosion light
Life flowers at the windows of the sun
Which melts in my mouth
I'm ripe
And I fall translucent in the street

You said it, buddy

I don't know how to open my eyes?
Golden tongue
Poetry is in play

February 1914

14. Still Lifes
for Roger de La Fresnaye

Green
The heavy trot of the artillerymen passes over the geometry
I strip down
Soon I'd be nothing but steel
Without the square rule of the light
Yellow
Bugle of modernity
The American filing cabinet
Is as dry and
Cool
As the first fields are green
Normandy
And the architect's table
Is as strictly beautiful
Black
With a bottle of India ink
And some blue shirts
Blue
Red
Then there's also a liter, a liter of sensuality
And that latest style
White
Sheets of white paper

April 1914

15. Fantômas

You studied the Age of Louis XIV in *The History of the French Navy* by
   Eugène
Sue
Paris Duty Copies Deposited in la Librairie, 1835
4 vols. in-16 long royal
The finest flower of pure Catholicism
Moralist
Plutarch
Simultaneism is old hat

You took me to the Cape to Father Moche's to Mexico
And you took me back to Saint Petersburg where I had already been
It's right down there
You turn right to get the trolley
Your slang is alive just like the sentimental foolishness of your bawling
   heart
Alma Mater Humanity Holy Cow
But everything that is machinery staging scenery changes etc. etc.
Is directly plagiarized from Homer, his operettas

There is also one pretty page
        " . . . did you imagine, Monsieur Barzum, that I was calmly
   going to allow you to ruin my plans, to deliver my daughter to
   justice, did you think that? . . . Really! Despite your intelligent
   appearance, you were just an imbecile . . ."
And I could do worse than to quote the King of Thieves
Vol. 21, The Lost Train, p. 367.

We have a lot of other things in common
I was in jail
I spent ill-gotten fortunes
I know more than 120,000 different postage stamps and they give more
    pleasure than Number This and Number That in the Louvre
And
Like you
Industrial heraldist
I studied the trademarks registered at the International Office of
    International Patents

There are still some nice shots to take
Every morning from 9 to 11

March 1914

16. Titles

Shapes Sweats Tresses
The Leap of Being
Stripped
First Poem with No Metaphors
No Images
News
The New Spirit
Accidents in Fairyland
400 Open Windows
The Propeller of Gems of the Runs of Menses
The Stunted Cone
Moving on Your Knees
In the Dragnets
Across the Accordion of Sky and Telescoped Voices
When the Newspaper Seethes Like a Cooped-up Bolt of Lightning
Headline

July 1914

17. Mee Too Buggi

As among the Greeks it is believed that every well-bred man ought to
    know how to pluck the lyre
Give me the fango-fango
So I can press it to my nose
A sound soft and resonant
From the right nostril
There are descriptions of landscapes
The story of past events
A telling of distant lands
Bolotoo
Papalangi
The poet describes among other things the animals
The houses are turned over by enormous birds
The women have on too many clothes
Rhymes and measures lacking
If you don't count a little exaggeration
The man who cut off his own leg succeeded in a light and simple genre
Mee low folla
Mareewagee beats the drum at the entrance to his house

July 1914

18. The Head

The guillotine is the masterpiece of plastic art
Its click
Creates perpetual motion
Everyone knows about Christopher Columbus's egg
Which was a flat egg, a stationary egg, the egg of an inventor
Archipenko's sculpture is the first ovoidal egg
Held in intense equilibrium
Like an immobile top
On its animated point
Speed
It throws off
Multicolored waves
Colored zones
And turns in depth
Nude.
New.
Total.

July 1914

19. Construction

Color, color, and more colors . . .
Here's Léger who grows like the sun in the tertiary epoch
And who hardens
And who fixes
The still life
The earth's crust
The liquid
The steamy
Everything that grows dim
The cloudy geometry
The plumb line that retracts itself
Ossification
Locomotion
Everything is teeming
The mind suddenly comes alive and gets dressed in its turn like the
    plants and animals
Prodigiously
And now
Painting becomes this great thing that moves
The wheel
Life
The machine
The human soul
A 75 mm breech
My portrait

February 1919

The War in the Luxembourg

Cendrars, September of 1915, after the loss of his right arm.

This children's piece
is dedicated
to my
comrades
in the
Foreign Legion
Mieczyslaw Kohn, Pole,
killed at Frise;
Victor Chapman, American,
killed at Verdun;
Xavier de Carvahlho, Portuguese,
killed at Navarin Farm;
volunteers
who died
for France.
Blaise Cendrars
MCMXVI

The War in the Luxembourg

"One two, one two
And everything will go just right . . . "
They were singing
A wounded soldier kept time with his crutch
Beneath the bandage his eye
The smile of the Luxembourg
And the smoke from munitions factories
Above the golden foliage
Pale autumn summer's end
You can't forget anything
Only little children play war
The Somme Verdun
My big brother's in the Dardanelles
It's so beautiful
A rifle   ME!
Cries melodious voices
Cries   ME!
The hands reach out
I look like my daddy
They have cannons too
A little girl pretends she's the bicycle messenger
A hobbyhorse wheels around
In the basin the flotillas crisscross
The Paris meridian is in the fountain's spray
They mount an attack on the guard who has the only real saber
And he dies
Laughing
The sun hangs above the potted palms
A Military Medal
They applaud the zeppelin going by over near the Eiffel Tower
Then they raise the dead
Everyone wants to be dead

Or at least wounded   RED
Cut cut
Cut off the arm cut off the head   WHITE
They give everything
Red Cross   BLUE
The nurses are six years old
Their hearts are deeply moved
They take out their dolls' eyes to fix the blind
I can see! I can see!
The ones who were Turks are now stretcher-bearers
And the ones who were dead revive to take part in the marvelous
    operation
Now they're studying pictures in the newspaper
Photographs
They remember what they've seen in the movies
It gets more serious
They yell and whack better than Punch and Judy
At the height of the fray
Get 'em while they're hot
Everyone flees toward the waffles
They're ready.   D
It's five o'clock.   R
The gates are closing.   E
Time to go home.   A
It's evening.   M
They wait for the zeppelin that doesn't come   E
Tired   R
Gazing at the rocket stars   S
While the maid pulls you by the hand
And the mommies stumble on the big shadow cars

Tomorrow or another day
There's a trench in the sandpile
There's a little woods in the sandpile
Towns
A house
The whole country   The Sea

And quite possibly the sea
The improvised artillery moves around the imaginary barbed wire
A kite quick as a fighter plane
The trees shrink and the flowers fall out and turn like parachutes
The three veins of the flag swell up at every blast of the wind howitzer
You won't be swept away, little ark of sand
Children more prodigal than the engineers
They laugh and play tank poison gas submarine-facing-New-York-that-
    can't-get-through
I'm Australian, you're black, he washes up to play the-life-of-the-
    English-soldier-in-Belgium
Russian helmet
1 chocolate Legion of Honor is worth 3 uniform buttons
There's the general going by
A little girl says:
I love my new American mommy very much
And a little boy: Not Jules Verne but buy me another nice Sunday
    dispatch

IN PARIS
On Victory Day when the soldiers come home . . .
Everyone will want to see THEM
The sun will open up early like a candy store on Valentine's Day
It'll be springtime in the Bois de Boulogne or out toward Meudon
All the cars will be perfumed and the poor horses will eat flowers
In the windows the little girls orphaned by the war will all have
    beautiful patriotic dresses
Photographers straddling the limbs of chestnut trees along the
    boulevards will aim their shutters
There'll be a circle around the movie cameraman who'll swallow up the
    historic procession better than a sword swallower
In the afternoon
The wounded will hang their Medals on the Arch of Triumph and go
    home without limping
Then
That evening

The place de l'Etoile will rise up into the sky
The dome of the Invalides will sing out over Paris like an immense
    golden bell
And the voices of a thousand newspapers will acclaim "La Marseillaise"
Woman of France

Paris, October 1916

Unnatural Sonnets

Cendrars (*left*) and Francis Picabia, 1923.

to Jean COctO

what crimes are
not cOmmitted
in thy name!

Once upon a time there were pOets who spOke with rOund mOuths
Round as salami her beautiful eyes and smOke
Ophelia's hair Or the lyre Orpheus strOked
You belch up rOund hats to find a strOke-of-genius rhyme sharp as
    teeth that would nibble your lines
Open-mouthed
Since you like smOke rings why don't you repeat *smOke*
It's too easy or too hard
The 7 pawns and the Queens are there as commas
Oh POEtry
Ah! Oh!
COcOa
Since you like cowboys why don't you write *cowpOke*
It's a written grOan that'll make the French crOak
The English clOwn did it with his legs
The way AretinO made love
The Mind envies the circus poster and the alphabetical pOsitions of the
    Snake Man
Where are the pOets who spOke with rOund mOuths?

We have to loosen up their b O nes z enfant h

POETRY

Nov. '16

Académie Médrano

To Conrad Moricand

Dance with your tongue, Poet, do an entrechat
Once around the ring
                           on a tiny black basset hound
                                                   or old gray mare
Measure the lovely measures and fix the fixed forms
Which are the *BELLES LETTRES* you learn
Look:
                   The billboards are bored with you bite
                                   you with their colored teeth
                                   between your toes
The director's daughter has electric lights
The jugglers also fly through the air
              pael suoregnaD
      pihw eht fo kcarC
taht sserpxE
The clown is in the mixing barrel
                              ⎧ go to the box office
       Your tongue must ⎨   on nights when
                              ⎩ do the orchestra

No **Free Passes** are accepted.

November 1916

The Musickissme
To Erik Satie

What do we care about Venizélos
Only Raymond   •   let's put Duncan
   still tucks up old Greek clothes
Music with vegetable ears
Like an elephant's
Fish cry out in the Gulf Stream
Can juicier than a fig
And the Basque voice of the sea microphone
Music hall duet
With car accompaniment
Gong
The musical seal
50 measures of do-re do-re do-re do-re do-re
   do-re do-re do-re do-re do-re do-re do-re do-re
That's it!
And a diminished chord in A-flat minor
                    ETC.!
When it's pretty a pretty toy noisemaker
   dances the doorbell
Intermission
Over
Theme: Orchestra conductor CHARLIE CHAPLIN keeps time
Before
The top-hatted European and his corseted wife
Counterpoint: Dances
Before the bewildered European and his wife
Coda: Sings
Quod erat demonstrandum

Nov. 1916

Black African Poems

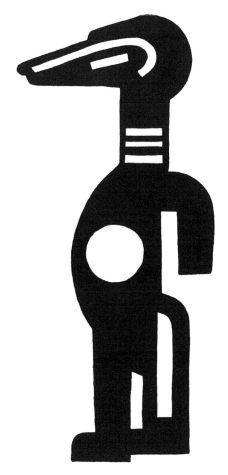

Fernand Léger sketch for *The Creation of the World*, a ballet
with scenario by Cendrars, 1923.

Dark Continent

Africa
Strabo thought so little of it
Mojos for general use
The women do all the work in this matrilineal society
One day a father had the idea of selling his son, who prevented it by
    selling *him* instead
These people are given to theft
Everything that meets the eye excites their greed
They grab things with their big toe and by twisting their knee bury them
    beneath their loincloths
They used to be subject to chiefs who had authority and who counted
    among their many rights that of spending the first night with every
    virgin who got married
They didn't bother with widows,
Adds the old author.
The marvelous island of Saint Borandion where chance had led a few
    travelers
It seems to appear and disappear from time to time.
The forests of Madeira burned for seven years.
Mumbo Jumbo idol of the Mandinkas
Gold Coast
The Governor of Guinea has a dispute with the natives
Lacking cannonballs he loads his cannons with gold
Toto Papo
It is only their interests that make them suffer the foreigner
On that coast European commerce and their licentiousness have
    created a new race of man that is perhaps the meanest of all
And there are nine types
The sacatra, the griff, the marabou, the mulatto, the quadroon, the
    half-breed, the mameluco, the quarteron, the half-caste
Happy the Bossum devoted to the domestic idol

1916

The Great Fetishes

I

A hardwood sheathing
Two embryonic arms
The man tears his belly
And worships his risen member

II

Who are you threatening
As you go off
Fists on hips
Barely in control
Almost fat

III

Wood knot
Head shaped like an acorn
Hard and refractory
Face stripped
Young god sexless and shamelessly jovial

IV

Envy has eaten away your chin
Covetousness lures you
You rise
The missing part of your face
Makes you geometric
Aborescent
Adolescent

Here's the man and the woman
Equally ugly equally nude
The man slimmer but stronger
Hands on his belly
Mouth like a piggy bank slot

VI

Her
The bread of her sex she bakes three times a day
And her belly stretched full
Pull
On her neck and shoulders

VII

I'm ugly!
By sniffing the smell of girls in my solitude
My head is swelling up and soon my nose is going to fall off

VII

I wanted to escape the chief's women
My head was shattered by the sun's stone
In the sand
All that's left is my mouth
Open like my mother's vagina
And crying out

IX

This one
Bald

Has only a mouth
A member that goes down to his knees
And feet cut off

X

Here's the woman I like best
Two sharp lines around a mouth shaped like a funnel
A blue forehead
Some white at the temples
And the gaze shining like a bugle

British Museum
London, February 1916

Kodak (Documentary)

Francis Picabia's frontispiece portrait of Cendrars for the first edition of *Kodak*.

WEST

I. Roof Garden

For weeks the elevators have hoisted hoisted crates crates of loam
At last
By dint of money and patience
The shrubbery is blooming
The lawn is a delicate green
A spring gushes out between the rhododendrons and camellias
On top of the building the building of bricks and steel
Evenings
The waiters in white serious as diplomats lean over the chasm which is
    the town
And the gardens are bright with a million little colored lights
I believe Madam murmured the young man in a voice vibrant with
    restrained passion
I believe we will be fine here
And with a large gesture he swept the large sea
The coming and going
The navigational lights of the giant ships
The gigantic Statue of Liberty
And the enormous panorama of the town cut with perpendicular bands
    of darkness and hard light
The old scientist and the two multimillionaires are alone on the terrace
Magnificent garden
Masses of flowers
Starry sky
The three elderly gentlemen stand in silence listening to the laughter
    and happy voices rising from bright windows
And to the murmured song of the sea at the end of the record

II. On the Hudson

The electric boat glides silently among the numerous ships anchored in
    the immense estuary and flying the flags of every nation in the world
The great clippers loaded with wood from Canada were unfurling their
    gigantic sails
The iron steamers were shooting torrents of black smoke
Dockhands of all races and nationalities were bustling around in the din
    of foghorns and whistles from factories and trains
The elegant launch is made entirely of teak
In the center rises a sort of cabin something like those on Venetian
    gondolas

III. Amphitryon

After the dinner served in the winter gardens among clumps of lemon
    trees of jasmine of orchids
There is a dance on the park lawn beneath bright lights
But the gifts sent to Miss Isadora are the main attraction
Of special interest is a pigeon blood ruby whose size and brilliance are
    unequaled
None of these young ladies own one to which it might be compared
Elegantly dressed
Skillful detectives mixing among the guests watch over that gem and
    protect it

IV. Office

Radiators and fans running on liquid air
Twelve telephones and five radios

Wonderful electric files contain endless industrial and scientific dossiers
   on every kind of business
The only place the multimillionaire feels at home is in this office
The big plate-glass windows overlook the park and the city
In the evening the mercury vapor lights shed their soft bluish glimmer
This is the origin of the orders to buy and sell which sometimes cause
   the Stock Markets of the entire world to crash

V. Girl

Light dress in crêpe de chine
The girl
Elegance and wealth
Hair a tawny blond where matched pearls shine
Calm and regular features that reflect frankness and kindness
Her big almost green sea-blue eyes are bright and bold
She has this fresh and velvety complexion with a special pinkness that
   seems to be the prerogative of American girls

VI. Young Man

He's the Beau Brummell of Fifth Avenue
Tie of gold cloth sprinkled with little diamond flowers
Suit a pink and violet metallic material
Ankle-boots in real sharkskin with each button a little black pearl
He sports fine asbestos flannel pajamas a glass suit a crocodile-skin vest
His valet soaps his gold pieces
He never has anything but perfumed brand-new bills in his wallet

VII. Work

Some crooks have just blown up the railway bridge
The coaches caught fire at the bottom of the valley
The injured swim in the boiling water from the disemboweled
    locomotive
Living torches run among the debris and spewing steam
Other coaches stay hanging 60 yards up
Men with flashlights and acetylene torches follow the trail down the
    valley
And the rescue is organized quietly and quickly
Under the cover of rushes of reeds of willows the waterfowl make a nice
    rustling noise
Dawn is long in coming
But already a team of a hundred carpenters called by telegraph and
    come by special train is busy rebuilding the bridge
Bang bang-bang
Pass me the nails

VIII. Trestle Work

Should you come to a river or a deep valley
You go over it on a wooden bridge until the company receipts allow
    them to build one of stone or iron
The American carpenters are unrivaled in the art of building them
They begin by laying a bed of hard rock
Then a first support goes up
Which supports a second then a third then a fourth
As many as are necessary to reach the height of the bank
On the last support two beams
On the two beams two rails

These daring constructions are reinforced by neither Saint Andrew's
    crosses nor T girders
They are held only by a few smaller beams and a few spikes that
    maintain the gauge of the trestles
And that's it
It's a bridge
A beautiful bridge

IX. The Thousand Islands

Around here the countryside is one of the most beautiful in North
    America
The immense sheet of lake is a blue that's almost white
Hundreds and hundreds of little green islands float on the calm surface
    of the clear water
The delicious cottages built in bright-colored brick give this landscape
    the appearance of an enchanted kingdom
Luxurious maple mahogany boats elegantly decked out with flags and
    covered with multicolored awnings come and go from one island to
    another
Any suggestion of fatigue of labor of poverty is missing from this
    gracious setting for multimillionaires

The sun disappears on the horizon of Lake Ontario
The clouds bathe their folds in vats of purple violet scarlet and orange
What a beautiful evening murmur Andrea and Frederika seated on the
    terrace of a medieval castle
And the ten thousand motorboats reply to their ecstasy

X. Laboratory

Visiting the greenhouses
The thermo-syphon maintains a constant temperature
The soil is saturated with formic acid with manganese and other
    substances which give the vegetation tremendous strength
In one day the leaves grow the flowers bloom and the fruits ripen
Thanks to an ingenious device the roots are bathed in an electric
    current which guarantees this monstrous growth
Anti-hail guns explode nimbus and cumulus
We go back to town across the barren waste
The morning is radiant
The dark purple heather and golden broom still haven't shed their petals
The seagulls trace big circles in the light blue sky

FAR WEST

I. Cucumingo

The San Bernardino hacienda
It was built in the middle of a lush valley fed by a multitude of small
    streams that run down from the surrounding mountains
The roofs are tile red in the shade of sycamores and laurels

Trout thrive in the streams
Immense flocks graze untended in the lush meadows
The orchards are thick with fruit pears apples grapes pineapples figs
    oranges
And in the truck gardens
Old World vegetables grow beside those of the tropics

Plenty of game here
The California quail
The rabbit known as the cottontail
The long-eared hare known as the jackass
The prairie hen the turtledove the partridge
The wild duck and wild goose
The antelope
It's true you still see wildcats and rattlesnakes
But there aren't any pumas anymore

II. Dorypha

On holidays
When the Indians and vaqueros get drunk on whiskey and pulque
Dorypha dances
To the sound of the Mexican guitar

Such exciting habaneras
That people come from miles around to admire her

No woman knows as well as she
How to drape the silk mantilla
And to fix her blond hair
With a ribbon
A comb
A flower

III. The Mockingbird

The heat is staggering
Balcony shaded with trumpet vines and purplish honeysuckle
In the big silence of the dozing countryside
You can hear
The gurgling of little rills
The distant mooing of big herds of grazing cattle
The song of the nightingale
The crystal-clear hissing of big bullfrogs
The hooting of the owl
And the call of the mockingbird in the cactus

IV. Mushroom Town

Toward the end of the year 1911 a group of Yankee financiers decide to
    build a town way out west at the foot of the Rocky Mountains
Not even a month goes by and there are three Union railroads although
    still no houses
Workers pour in from everywhere
As early as the second month three churches are built and five theaters
    are going full blast

Around a square that still has a few nice trees a forest of metal girders
    rings day and night with pounding hammers
Winches
Machines huffing and puffing
The steel skeletons of houses thirty stories high start lining up
Brick walls or often plain aluminum sheets fill in the interstices of the
    framework
In a few hours reinforced concrete is poured using the Edison method
Because of a sort of superstition no one wants to christen the town and a
    contest is announced with a raffle and prizes given by the town's
    biggest newspaper which is also looking for a name

V. Club

Although it's on the official map of the town this street still consists only
    of plank fences and piles of rubbish
The only way to get across the street is by hopping in zigzags over the
    mud and puddles
At the end of this unfinished boulevard lit by powerful arc lights is the
    Black Bean Club which is also a matrimonial agency
Wearing cowboy hats or wool caps with earflaps
Faces hard as nails
Men get out of the 60-horsepower cars they're breaking in and put their
    names on the list look through the photograph album
Choose their fiancées who are cabled to embark at Cherbourg on the
    Kaiser Wilhelm and who sail full steam ahead
Mostly German girls
A stable-boy in black wearing swansdown shoes opens the door with a
    glacial propriety and gives the newcomer a suspicious once-over
I drink a whiskey cocktail then another then another
Then a mint julep a mother's milk a prairie oyster a nightcap

VI. Squaw's Wigwam

When you go through the rickety door made of boards ripped from
    packing crates and with pieces of leather for hinges
You find yourself in a low room
Smoky
Smell of rotten fish
Stench of exquisitely rancid fat

Barbaric panoply
War bonnets of eagle feathers necklaces of puma teeth or bear claws
Bows arrows tomahawks
Moccasins
Seed and glass bead bracelets
You also see
Some scalping knives one or two old-fashioned carbines a flintlock
    pistol elk and reindeer antlers a whole collection of little embroidered
    tobacco pouches
Then three very old soft stone peace pipes with reed stems

Eternally bent over the hearth
The hundred-year-old proprietress of this establishment is preserved like
    a ham smoked and dried and cured like her hundred-year-old pipe
    and the black of her mouth and the black hole of her eye

VII. City of Frisco

It's an old hulk eaten away by rust
Twenty times in dry dock and the engine makes only 7 or 8 knots
And to economize they burn old half-used cinders and cast-off coal
They hoist some makeshift sails every time there's a puff of wind

With his scarlet face his bushy eyebrows his pimply nose Captain
    Hopkins is a real sailor
Little silver rings pierce his ears
This ship is loaded exclusively with the caskets of Chinese who died in
    America but who wanted to be buried in their native land
Oblong boxes red or light blue or covered with golden inscriptions
Now that's a type of merchandise illegal to transport

VIII. Vancouver

In the thick fog that packs the boats and docks you can barely hear the
    bell ringing ten o'clock
The docks are deserted and the town is fast asleep
You walk along the low and sandy coast where a glacial wind is blowing
    and the long Pacific waves are breaking
That pale spot in the murky shadows is the station for the Canadian
    Northern the Grand Trunk
And those bluish halos in the wind are steamers bound for the Klondike
    Japan and the East Indies
It's so dark I can barely make out the street signs as I lug my suitcase
    around looking for a cheap hotel

Everyone has embarked
The oarsmen are bent over the oars and the heavy boat loaded to the
    gunwales pushes into the high waves
From time to time a little hunchback at the tiller changes their course
Steering his way through the mist guided by a foghorn
They bump against the dark mass of the ship and Siberian huskies rise
    on the starboard quarter
Washed out in the gray-white-yellow
As if they were loading fog

ALEUTIAN ISLANDS

I.

Steep cliffs facing the icy polar winds
Inland there are fertile meadows
Reindeer elk musk-ox
The arctic fox the beaver
Fish in streams
A low beach has been used as a seal fur farm
At the top of the cliff they harvest eider nests whose feathers are worth a
    fortune

II.

Huge sturdy buildings where a rather large number of traders live
All the way around a little garden containing every kind of vegetable
    capable of withstanding the climate
Mountain ash pine arctic willow
Border of heather and alpine plants

III.

Bay scattered with small rocky islands
The seals sunbathe in groups of five or six
Or stretch out on the sand
When they play they give a kind of guttural grunt like barking
Next to the Eskimo hut there is a lean-to where the skins are prepared

R I V E R

Mississippi

Right here the river's almost as wide as a lake
The yellowish muddy water rolls between two marshy banks
Aquatic plants extending the acreage of the cotton fields
Here and there appear the towns and villages lurking back in some little
    bay with their factories with their tall black chimneys with their long
    piers on pilings running way out into the water

Overwhelming heat
The ship's bell rings for lunch
The passengers sport checked suits blinding ties sunset-red vests like
    flaming cocktails and Louisiana hot sauce

You see a lot of crocodiles
The young ones frisky and wriggling
The big ones their backs covered with greenish moss just drifting along

The luxuriant vegetation indicates the approach of the tropical zone
Gigantic bamboos palm trees tulip trees laurels cedars
The river itself is now twice as wide
Dotted with floating islands from which our boat scares up clouds of
    waterfowl
Steamboats sailboats barges boats of all kinds and enormous rafts
A yellow steam rises from the overheated river

Now there are hundreds of crocs thrashing around us
You hear the dry snapping of their jaws and you see very clearly their
    wild little eyes
The passengers get a kick out of firing into them with hunting rifles
When a sharpshooter kills or mortally wounds one
Its fellows rush to tear it
To pieces
With small cries rather like the wailing of a newborn baby

THE SOUTH

I. Tampa

The train has just stopped
Just two passengers get off on this broiling end-of-summer morning
Both are dressed in khaki suits and pith helmets
Both are followed by a black servant who carries the baggage
Both glance absentmindedly at the distant houses that are too white at
    the sky that is too blue
You see the wind raising swirls of dust and flies pestering the two mules
    harnessed to the only coach
The driver is asleep his mouth open

II. Bungalow

It's small but quite comfortable
The flooring is held up by bamboo posts
Vanilla plants climbing all over
Angola peas
Jasmine
Above which burst magnolia and poinciana flowers

The dining room is designed with the sense of luxury characteristic of
    Carolina Creoles
Big chunks of ice in yellow marble vases keep the room deliciously cool
The plates and crystal sparkle
And behind each guest stands a black servant

The diners take it slow and easy
Stretched out in rocking chairs they surrender to the softening climate
At a signal from his master old Jupiter brings out a little lacquered stand

A bottle of sherry
An ice bucket
Some lemons
And a box of Havana cigars

No one spoke
The sweat was streaming down their faces
It was absolutely still
In the distance the loud croaking laughter of the bullfrog which
    abounds in these parts

III. Vomito Negro

The pretty gardens and woods are all behind us
It's a bare and dismal plain with an occasional
Stand of bamboo
A stunted willow
A windblown eucalyptus
Then marshland
You see this yellowish smoke
This gray fog along the ground continually quivering
With thousands of mosquitoes and the yellow breath of the rotting muck
    There are some places where even the blacks can't live

On this side the bank is lined with big mangroves
Their tangled roots plunge into the sludge and are covered with clusters
    of poisonous oysters

The mosquitoes and poisonous insects form a thick cloud over the
    stagnant water
Beside harmless bullfrogs you see incredibly fat toads
And the famous hoop snake which chases its victims as friskily as a dog
There are stagnant pools teeming with slate-colored leeches
Hideous scarlet crabs playing around sleeping caymans

In the spots where the ground is hardest you meet gigantic ants
Thousands of them all voracious

On these stinking waters in the poisonous muck
Flowers bloom with a stunning scent a heady and persistent smell
Bursts of blue and purple
Chrome leaves
Everywhere
The black water is carpeted with flowers next to which will protrude the
    flat head of a snake

I walked through a thicket of big mimosas
They parted in front of me as I went
Their branches moved aside with a small swish
Because these trees have a sensitivity almost a nervous system
Among the jalap vines full of talking blossoms
Big pink and gray birds on long thin legs feasting on crusty lizards fly off
    with a great beating of wings as we approach
Then giant butterflies the color of sulfur of gentian of heavy-duty oil
And really big caterpillars

IV. Spanish Ruin

The nave is in the 18th-century Spanish style
It is all cracked
The damp vault is white with saltpeter and still bears some traces of gold
    leaf
The lantern beams fall on a mildewed painting in the corner
It is a Black Madonna
Thick moss and poisonous striped dotted beaded mushrooms cover the
    stone floor of the sanctuary
There is also a bell with some Latin inscriptions

V. Golden Gate

The old grillwork provided a name for the establishment
Iron bars thick as a wrist which separate the drinkers from the counter
    where bottles of every kind of alcohol are lined up
Back when gold fever was at its height
When women from Chile or Mexico were auctioned off right and left
    by slave traders
All the bars had grillwork like this
And the bartenders came with a drink in one hand and a pistol in the
    other
It was not uncommon to see a man killed because of a drink
It's true the grillwork has been left there for show
Just the same the Chinese come in for drinks
Germans and Mexicans
And also a few Kanaks off little steamboats loaded with mother-of-pearl
    copra tortoise shell
Chantcuses
Atrocious makeup bank tellers outlaws sailors with huge hands

VI. Oyster Bay

Canvas tent and bamboo chairs
Now and then on these deserted beaches you see a hut with a palm roof
    or the skiff of a Black pearl diver

Now the country is completely different
As far as the eye can see
The beaches are covered with shining sand
Two or three sharks are sporting in the wake of the yacht
Florida slips below the horizon

You take a golden Regalia from the ebony end table
You break it off with your fingernail
You light it voluptuously
Smoke smoker smoke smoke spirals away

THE NORTH

I. Spring

The Canadian springtime is the most invigorating and powerful in the
  world
Beneath the thick blanket of snow and ice
Suddenly
Generous nature
Tufts of violets pink white and blue
Orchids sunflowers tiger lilies
Down the venerable avenues of maple black ash and birch
The birds fly and sing
In shrubs budding again with new and tender shoots
The happy sunlight is the color of anise

Woods and farmlands stretch away from the road for over five miles
It's one of the biggest pieces of property in Winnipeg
On it rises a solid stone farmhouse something like a manor house
This is where my good friend Coulon lives
Up before daybreak he rides from farm to farm on his big bay mare
The earflaps of his rabbitskin hat dangle on his shoulders
Dark eyes and bushy brows
Very chipper
Pipe on his chin

The night is foggy and cold
A hard west wind bends and sways the firs and larches
A small glow is spreading
An ember crackles
It smolders and then burns through the brush
Clumps of resinous trees thrash around in the wind
Wham wham huge torches burst
The fire moves along the horizon with a majestic slowness

Black trunks and white trunks turn blood red
A dome of chocolate smoke out of which a million burning bits and
    sparks are flying spinning upward and sideways
Behind this curtain of flame you can see massive shadows twisting and
    crashing to the ground
Resounding axes chopping
An acrid haze spreads over the incandescent forest which a gang of
    lumberjacks are circumscribing

II. Country

Magnificent landscape
Green forests of fir beech chestnut cut with ripe fields of wheat oats
    buckwheat hemp
Everything breathing abundance
And it's absolutely deserted
Every great once in a while you run into a farmer driving a cartload of
    fodder
In the distance the birches are like columns of silver

III. Hunting and Fishing

Wild duck pintail teal goose lapwing bustard
Grouse thrush
Arctic hare snow partridge ptarmigan
Salmon rainbow trout eel
Gigantic pike and crawfish that taste particularly exquisite

Carbine across the back
Bowie knife in the belt
The hunter and the redskin are bent beneath the weight of the game
Strings of wood doves red-legged partridge

Wild peacock
Wild turkey
And even a big reddish-brown and white eagle brought down from the
  clouds

IV. Harvest

A six-cylinder and two Fords out in the field
All around and as far as you can see the slightly tilted sheaves form a
  checkerboard of wavering rhomboids
Not a tree
From the north the chugging and clatter of the thresher and hay wagon
And from the south the twelve empty trains coming to load the wheat

ISLANDS

I. Chow

The little port is very busy this morning
Coolies—Tagals Chinese Malays—are unloading a big junk with a
  golden stern and sails of woven bamboo
The cargo is china from the big island of Japan
Swallows' nests harvested in the caves of Sumatra
Sea cucumbers
Ginger preserves
Pickled bamboo shoots
All the merchants are very excited
Mr. Noghi pretentiously dressed in an American-made checked suit
  speaks very fluent English
Which is the language these gentlemen use in their arguments
Japanese Kanaks Tahitians Papuans Maoris and Fijians

II. Brochure

Visit our island
It is the southernmost island of the Japanese possessions
Our country isn't as well known in Europe as it should be
It merits greater attention
The fauna and flora are highly varied and have heretofore hardly been
  studied
You will find picturesque views everywhere
And in the interior
Ruins of Buddhist temples which of their type are pure marvels

III. The Red-Crested Adder

Using the hypodermic needle he administers several injections of
    Doctor Yersin's serum
Then he enlarges the arm wound making a cruciform incision with the
    scalpel
He makes it bleed
Then he cauterizes it with a few drops of lime hypochlorite

IV. Japanese House

Bamboo stalks
Thin boards
Paper stretched across frames
There is no real heating system

V. Little Garden

Lilies chrysanthemums
Cycads and banana trees
Cherry trees in bloom
Palm trees orange trees and wonderful coconut palms loaded with fruit

VI. Rock Garden

In a basin filled with Chinese goldfish and fish with hideous mouths
A few have little silver rings through their gills

VII. Light and Delicate

The air is balmy
Amber musk and lemon flowers
Just being alive is true happiness

VIII. Keepsake

The sky and the sea
The waves come in to caress the roots of the coconut palms and the big
    tamarinds with metallic leaves

IX. Fishy Cove

The water is so calm and so clear
In its depths you can see the white bushy coral
The prismatic sway of suspended jellyfish
The fish darting pink yellow lilac
And beneath the waving seaweed the azure sea cucumbers and the
    green and violet sea urchins

X. Hatuara

She doesn't know anything about European styles
Her frizzy blue-black hair is swept up Japanese-style and held in place
    by coral pins
She is naked under her silk kimono
Naked to her elbows

Strong lips
Drowsy eyes
Straight nose
Skin like light copper
Small breasts
Opulent hips

The way she moves is alive and direct
The young look of a charming animal

Her specialty: the grammar of walking

She swims the way you write a 400-page novel
Strong
Proud
Smooth
Beautiful sustained prose
She catches tiny fish which she holds inside her mouth
Then she dives straight down
Gliding between the corals and multicolored seaweed
Soon to reappear
Smiling
Holding two big sea bream with silver bellies

So proud of her brand-new blue silk dress her houseshoes with gold
    embroidery her pretty coral necklace given to her just this morning
She brings me a bucket of spiny and weird crabs and some of those
    tropical jumbo shrimp known as carrack that are as long as your hand

XI. Softened

Garden overgrown like a clearing in the woods
Along the shore drifts the eternal humming of the wind in the leaves of
    the filaos
A straw hat on my head and a big paper parasol over that

I contemplate the games of the gulls and cormorants
Or I examine a flower
Or some rock
Every time I move I scare the palm squirrels and palm rats

Through the open window I see the entire length of a steamer of
    medium tonnage
Anchored about a mile off and already surrounded by junks sampans
    and boats loaded with fruit and local products
At last the sun sets

The air is crystal clear
The same nightingales are singing like mad
And the big vampire bats glide silently across the moon on velvet wings

A young girl goes by completely nude
On her head one of those old helmets collectors are so crazy about these
    days
In her hand a big bouquet of pale flowers which give off a powerful
    scent reminding you of both tuberose and narcissus
Suddenly she stops at the garden gate
Some glowing bugs alight on the horn which forms the top of the
    helmet and the apparition becomes incredible

Night sounds
Dead branches breaking
Sighs of animals in heat
Crawling
Humming of insects
Birds in their nests
Whispering voices

The gigantic plane trees are pale gray in moonlight
Light lianas sweep down from their tops and are gently blown by an
    invisible mouth

The stars melt like sugar

RIVER

The Bahr el Zeraf

There isn't any tall grass along the banks
Great flat stretches of lowlands fade away into the distance
Islands almost flush with the water level
Big crocs warming in the sun
Thousands of big birds cover the muddy or sandy banks

The country changes
Now there is some light brush with a sprinkling of stunted trees
There are some beautifully colored small birds and coveys of guinea
    hens
Now and then in the evening a lion roars and his silhouette is seen on
    the west bank
This morning I killed a varanian a yard and a half long

Still the same landscape of flooded plains
The Arab pilot has spotted some elephants
Everyone is excited
We go up to the upper deck
For each of us it's the first appearance of the emperor of animals
The elephants are about three hundred yards off two big ones a
    medium-sized one three or four babies
During lunch ten big fat hippo heads are seen swimming ahead of us

The mercury hardly moves
Around 2 in the afternoon it's usually 90 to 100°
The dress is khaki good shoes leggings and no shirt
One does justice to the good cooking on board and the bottles of brown
    Turin
In the evening one simply adds a white jacket
Kites and vultures graze us with their wings

After dinner the boat moves out into the middle of the river to elude the
    mosquitoes as much as possible
The banks drift by covered with papyrus and gigantic euphorbia
The trip follows its slow meandering way down the river
We see a lot of rather tame antelope and gazelles
Then an old water buffalo but no rhinoceros

ELEPHANT HUNT

I.

Infernal terrain
Tall forest on a marsh with a tangle of tropical creepers and an
    underlevel of low palms with foliage of enormous diameter
Quills sticking out
Around 12:30 we hear a herd of the big animals we're after
Every step is off balance
The approach is slow
I got a quick look and they fled

II.

Night
There are elephants in the plantations
The strident noise of branches broken ripped off is succeeded by the
    duller sound of big banana trees turned over with a slow push
We're coming right up on them
Climbing a rise I see the front of the nearest animal
With the moonlight coming straight down on him he's a handsome
    elephant
His trunk in the air the end of it pointed toward me
He's caught my scent there's not a moment to lose
The shot
Immediately a new bullet goes into the Winchester's breech
Then I light my pipe
The huge animal looks as if it's sleeping in the blue clearing

III.

We come to a clay terrain
After their mud bath the animals went through some particularly heavy
    thickets
At fifteen yards you still can't see anything but vague masses so you can't
    get any idea of either their size or their tusks
I've rarely heard so clearly the intestinal noises of the elephants their
    snorting the sound of branches breaking
All of that comes after long silences during which you'd hardly believe
    they were so near

IV.

In the camp we can hear the elephants in the forest
I keep one man with me to carry the big Kodak
At twelve yards I can barely make out a large animal
I think I see a little one next to it
They're in the boggy water
I hear them literally gargling
The sun shines straight down on the head and breast of the large female
    now irritated
What an interesting photo the cool-headed man beside me was able to
    take

V.

The terrain is just impossible
Passable only if you follow the paths tramped out by the elephants
    themselves

Paths littered with obstacles fallen trees
Creepers these powerful animals step over or simply brush aside with
their trunks
Never breaking or pushing them down so they'll never be in the way
again
They are like the natives who also don't clear away obstacles even on the
most beaten paths

VI.

We cut across the trail of a big male again
He leads us due west all the way across the big plain
Goes through five hundred yards of forest
Circles around for a while in an open space we hadn't known about
Then goes back into the woods
Now the animal is perfectly still only a snort gives him away from time
to time
At ten yards I vaguely see something
Can it be the animal?
Yes look a huge white tooth
At that moment a torrential rain starts falling with a heavy darkness
The film is ruined

VII.

Sometimes the elephant trails twist and crisscross
Tight between walls of thorny bushes
The stuff is impenetrable you can't even see through it
It's from three to six yards high
Along the paths the lianas descend to one two three feet from the
ground
Then rise again assuming the oddest shapes
The trees are all enormous the collar of their aerial roots is from four to
five yards above the ground

VIII.

We hear a herd
It's in the clearing
The grass and undergrowth grow five or six yards high
There are also a few limited bare spots
I have my three men stay put each one aiming his Bell & Howell
And I move in alone with my little Kodak to ground where I can walk
    silently
There is nothing funnier to see going down going back up
Turning every which way
The elephants' trunks
While their heads and entire immense bodies remain hidden

IX.

I approach in a semicircle
Raising his enormous head decked out with large tusks
Stirring the air with his big ears
His trunk turned toward me
He sniffs the wind
A photo and a bullet are shot
The elephant takes the shock without flinching
I do it again quick
He rolls headfirst onto the ground with a tremendous death rattle
Then I fire a shot toward the heart then two in the head
The powerful rattle continues but finally the life's gone out of him
I noted the position of the heart and its measurements which are 22 by
    16 inches

X.

I see the beautiful animal for just an instant
Now I hear him rolling in the mud heavily regularly
He crumples the branches in his way
It's a grandiose music
He is against me and I see nothing absolutely nothing
Suddenly his huge head crashes through the underbrush
Full face
At six yards
Right over me
The elephant does a quick backward walk
At that moment the rain starts falling so loudly that it drowns out the
    sound of his steps

XI.

On a big plain to the north
At the edge of a forest a big female a little male and three young
    elephants of different sizes
The height of the grass keeps me from photographing them
From the top of a termite hill I watch them a long time through my
    Zeiss field glasses
The elephants seem to be having their dessert with an amusing delicacy
    of touch
When they smell us they clear out
The bush opens up to make way for them and closes again like a
    curtain over their gigantic forms

MENUS

I.

Truffled green turtle liver
Lobster Mexican
Florida pheasant
Iguana with Caribbean sauce
Gumbo and palmetto

II.

Red River salmon
Canadian bear ham
Roast beef from the meadows of Minnesota
Smoked eel
San Francisco tomatoes
Pale ale and California wine

III.

Winnipeg salmon
Scottish leg of lamb
Royal Canadian apples
Old French wines

IV.

Kankal oysters
Lobster salad celery hearts
French snails vanillaed in sugar
Kentucky fried chicken
Desserts coffee Canadian Club whiskey

V.

Pickled shark fins
Stillborn dog in honey
Rice wine with violets
Cream of silkworm cocoon
Salted earthworms and Kava liqueur
Seaweed jam

VI.

Canned beef from Chicago and German delicatessen
Crayfish
Pineapples guavas loquats coconuts mangoes custard apple
Baked breadfruit

VII.

Turtle soup
Fried oysters
Truffled bear paws
Lobster Javanese

VIII.

River crab and pimento stew
Suckling pig ringed with fried bananas
Hedgehog ravensara
Fruit

Traveling 1887–1923

Travel Notes

The SS *Gelria*, on which Cendrars returned from Brazil in
September of 1924.

I. THE *FORMOSA*

This notebook is dedicated
to
my good friends in São Paulo
Paulo Prado,
Mario de Andrade, Sergio Millet,
Justo de Almeida, Couto de Barros,
Rubens de Moraes, Luiz Aranha,
Oswaldo de Andrade, Yan,
and
to my friends in Rio de Janeiro
Graça Aranha,
Sergio Buarque de Hollanda, Prudente
de Moraes, Guillermo de Almeida, Ronald
de Carvalho, Americo Faco,
not forgetting
the inimitable and dear
Leopold de Freitas
of Rio-Grande-do-Sul.

On the 7:40 Express

It's been years since I stopped taking the train
I've gone by car
Took the plane
A boat trip and I'm taking an even longer one again

Suddenly here I am tonight with the sound of the railroad that used to
    be so familiar
And it seems I understand it better now

Dining car
You can't see anything outside
It's pitch black
The crescent moon doesn't move when you look at it
But sometimes it's on the left, sometimes on the right side of the train

The express does 70
I can't see anything
This dull shrillness that makes my ears ring—the left one aches from
    it—going through a stone underpass
Then the cataract of a metal bridge
The hammered harp of the switches the slap of a station the left and
    right hook to the jaw of a furious tunnel
When the train slows down for flooding you hear a water-slide sound
    and the hot pistons of the hundred tons among the noise of dishes
    and brakes

Le Havre bus elevator
I open the hotel room shutters
I lean over the docks and the great cold glimmering of a starry night
A tickled woman chuckles on the pier
An endless chain coughs whines strains

I fall asleep with the window open on this barnyard noise
As if in the country

Waking Up

I always sleep with the windows open
I slept like a man alone
The foghorns and compressed air whistles didn't bother me much

This morning I lean out the window
I see
The sky
The sea
The dock where I arrived from New York in 1911
The pilot shack
And
To the left
Smokestreams chimneys cranes arc lamps against the light

The first trolley shudders in the icy dawn
Me I'm too hot
Good-bye Paris
Hello sun

You Are More Beautiful Than the Sky and the Sea

When you love it's time to leave
Leave your wife leave your child
Leave your boyfriend leave your girlfriend
Leave your mistress leave your lover
When you love it's time to leave

The world is full of black men and women
Women men men women
Look at all the nice stores
That cab that man that woman that cab
All that lovely merchandise

There's air there's wind
The mountains the water the sky the earth
The children the animals
The plants and the coal

Learn to sell to buy to sell again
Give take give take
When you love it's time to know
How to sing to run to eat to drink
To whistle
And to learn to work

When you love it's time to leave
Don't snivel as you smile
Don't wedge yourself between two breasts
Breathe walk leave get out

I take a bath and I look
I see the mouth I know
The hand the leg the   the eye
I take a bath and I look

The whole world is always out there
Life full of surprises
I come out of the drugstore
I've just stepped off the scale
I weigh my 176 pounds
I love you

Letter

You said to me if you write me
Don't just use the typewriter
Add a line in your own hand
A word a nothing oh a little something
Yes yes yes yes yes yes yes yes

But my Remington is beautiful
I really love it and the work goes well
My writing is sharp and clear
It's very easy to see that I did the typing

There are white spaces only I know how to make
See how my page looks
Still to please you I add in ink
Two or three words
And a big blot of ink
So you can't read them

Moonlight

The ship tangos from side to side
The moon the moon makes circles in the water
As the mast makes circles in the sky
Pointing with its finger to the stars

A young girl from Argentina leaning over the rail
Dreams of Paris while gazing on the lighthouses that outline the coast of
    France
Dreams of Paris which she's hardly seen and misses already

These turning fixed double colored intermittent lights remind her of the
    ones she saw from her window over the Boulevards and which
    promised her she'd come back soon
She dreams of going back to France soon and living in Paris
The sound of my typewriter keeps her from going all the way with her
    dream
My beautiful typewriter that rings at the end of each line and is as fast
    as jazz
My beautiful typewriter that keeps me from dreaming portside or
    starboard
And makes me go all the way with an idea
My idea

La Pallice

La Pallice and the Ile de Ré are set on the water and painted
Minutely
Like those awnings on little Breton bistros around the Gare
    Montparnasse
Or those ghastly watercolors sold on the boulevard de la Madeleine by a
    hirsute dauber dressed in velvet whose hands have been gnarled since
    birth who paints with his elbows and lays his spiel on you through his
    harelip
Real true-ism

Bilbao

We arrive in Bilbao harbor well before dawn
A cove with low mountains and hills backlit black velvet pierced with
    the lights of the town
The good simple composition of the setting reminds me and at the risk
    of sounding like an idiot since I am in Spain I repeat reminds me of
    a scene by Picasso

There are little two-man boats with a very small triangular sail already
    taking to the open sea
Two porpoises turn cartwheels in the air
As soon as the sun rises from behind the mountains
This simple scene
Is invaded
By an onslaught of colors
From indigo to purple
That transform Picasso into a German expressionist
Extremes meet

La Coruña

A compassionate lighthouse like a giant madonna
From outside it's a pretty little Spanish town
On shore it's a dungheap
Where two or three skyscrapers are growing

Villa García

Three fast cruisers a hospital ship
The English colors
Shining optical signals
Two carabineros sleep in deck chairs
Finally we leave
In the sweet breeze

Pôrto de Leixões

We arrive late and it's Sunday
The port is a raging river

The poor emigrants waiting for the authorities to come on board are
    knocked around in poor little skiffs which climb up on each other
    without sinking
The port has one bad eye the other poked out
And an enormous crane tilted like a long-range gun

Along the Coast of Portugal

From Le Havre all we've done is follow the coastline like ancient
    navigators
The sea off Portugal is covered with boats and trawlers
It's a constant blue with a deep-sea transparency
It's a nice warm day
The sun is beating down
Innumerable green microscopic algae float on the surface
They manufacture food that allows them to multiply quickly
They are the inexhaustible provender that the legion of infusoria and
    delicate marine larvae stream toward
All sorts of animals
Worms starfish sea urchins
Tiny crustaceans
Seething little world near the surface of the water shot through with
    light
Gluttons and epicures
Then come the herrings the sardines the mackerels
Pursued by the white tunas the bluefin tunas the bonitos
Which are pursued by the porpoises the sharks the dolphins
It's a clear day the fishing's good
When it gets overcast the fishermen are unhappy and they make their
    lamentations heard all the way up to the podium in parliament

En Route to Dakar

The air is cold
The sea is steel
The sky is cold
My body is steel
Good-bye Europe which I leave for the first time since 1914
I am no longer interested in you not even the emigrants in steerage the
    Jews Russians Basques
Spaniards Portuguese and German saltimbanques who miss Paris
I want to forget everything no longer speak your languages and sleep
    alongside black men and women and Indian men and women
    animals and plants
And take a bath and live in the water
And take a bath and live in the sun with a big banana tree
And love the big buds of that plant
To segment my own self
And become hard as a rock
Drop straight down
Sink to the bottom

35°57′ North Latitude
15°16′ West Longitude

It happened today
I'd been waiting for it to happen ever since we set sail
The sea was beautiful with a heavy groundswell that made us roll
The sky had been overcast since morning
It was four o'clock in the afternoon
I was playing a game of dominoes
Suddenly I yelled and ran out on deck

That's it that's it
The ultramarine blue
The sky a blue topgallant sail
Warm air
No one knows how it happened or how to define it
But everything increases one degree in tonality
The evening gave me four proofs
The sky was now pure
The setting sun like a wheel
The full moon like another wheel
And the stars bigger and bigger

That point lies between Madeira on the starboard and Casablanca on
    the portside
Already

Within Sight of the Island of Fuerteventura

Everything has gotten even bigger since yesterday
The water the sky the purity of the air
The Canary Islands look like the shores of Lake Como
Trails of clouds like glaciers
It's starting to get hot

On Board the *Formosa*

The sky is dark streaked with leprous bands
The water is dark
The stars grow even larger and melt like weeping tapers
Here's what's happening on board

On the fo'c'sle four Russians have sat down inside a bundle of ropes and
    are playing cards by the glimmering light of a Chinese lantern

On the open deck forward the Jews in the minority as they are at home
in Poland are huddled together and give way to the Spaniards who
are playing the mandolin singing and dancing the *jota*

In the deckhouse the Portuguese emigrants are doing a peasant round a
dark man is clicking two long castanets made of bone and the couples
break the round go around turn around bang their heels while a
woman's shrill voice rises

The passengers in first class almost all of them watch and envy these
folk games

In the salon a pretentious German woman is playing the violin very
artsy-fartsy and very artsy-fartsy a pretentious French girl
accompanies her on the piano

On the promenade deck a mysterious Russian walks back and forth an
officer of the guard incognito grand duke Dostoyevskian character I
baptized Dobro-Véchter he's a sad little fellow tonight he was taken
with a certain nervous agitation he put on patent-leather pumps a
suit with tails and an enormous bowler like my father wore in 1895

In the smoking lounge they are playing dominoes a young doctor who
looks like Jules Romains and who is on his way to upper Sudan a
Belgian arms manufacturer who is getting off at Pernambuco a
Dutchman his forehead cut into two hemispheres by a deep scar he's
the director of the municipal pawnshop in Santiago de Chile and a
young artiste from Ménilmontant street girl busy with a thousand
car deals she even offers me a lead mine in Brazil and an oil well
in Baku

On the sterncastle the very clean and carefully combed German
emigrants sing severe hymns and sentimental songs with their wives
and children

On the deck aft there are loud discussions and squabbles in every
eastern European tongue

In the pantry the men from Bordeaux are playing manille and at his
   post the radio operator is telling off Santander and Mogador

Ocean Letter

The ocean letter is not a new poetic genre
It's a practical message with a descending rate and a lot cheaper than a
   radiogram
It's often used on board to conclude a deal you didn't have time to settle
   before you left or to give some final instructions
It's also a sentimental messenger that goes from me to you to say hello
   between two ports of call as far away from each other as Leixões and
   Dakar with you knowing I've been at sea for six days and so not
   expecting to hear from me
I'll use it again as we cross the South Atlantic between Dakar and Rio
   de Janeiro to send messages back because that's the only direction you
   can send them
The ocean letter was not invented for writing poetry
But when you travel when you do business when you're on board when
   you send ocean letters
It's poetry

Off Río de Oro

The cormorants are following us
They have a much stronger flight pattern than the gulls they are much
   larger birds they have prettier white feathers edged with brownish
   black or all black like sea crows
We come across six little sailboats loaded with salt running between
   Dakar and the grand Canaries

In Sight of Cape Blanc

The air is warm but not too warm
The sunlight filters down through the humid and cloudy atmosphere
The unchanging temperature is rather high
It must be the position of the planet Venus at this very moment
These are the best conditions for lazing around

Dakar

At last we skirt and go around the Two Breasts that emerged this
    morning and got bigger on the horizon
We go around them and enter Dakar harbor
When you turn around
You see a red breakwater a blue sky and a dazzling white beach

Gorée

A Mediterranean medieval castle
And behind it a flat little island Portuguese ruins and bungalows of a
    modern yellow very *salon d'automne*

Only colonial functionaries live in this former den of slave traders
    functionaries who can't find a place to live in Dakar where there's
    also a housing crisis
I visited dungeons scooped out of the red basalt you still see the chains
    and collars that used to restrain the blacks
Gramophone songs used to go that far down

Artificial Eggs

Waiting to go ashore we are drinking cocktails in the smoking lounge
A banker tells us all about an artificial egg factory on the outskirts of
    Bordeaux
The egg white is made with the hemoglobin of horse blood
The yolk is made with powdery cornmeal and light oils
This mixture is poured into round molds which go in the refrigerator
This produces a yellow ball which is dipped in a colloid so that a light
    film is formed around it
Around this product they put the hemoglobin whipped like cream and it
    all goes back in the fridge where the artificial egg white jells in the
    very low temperature
New colloid bath then by a very simple procedure they obtain a chalky
    precipitate which forms the shell
That reminds me that in Düsseldorf before the war I saw some
    machines for polishing seasoning and tinting coffee beans
And thus giving low-quality coffees the look of coffee beans from
    Jamaica Réunion Borneo Arabia etc.

The Mumus

Oh these black women you meet around the black village at the shops
    where percale is measured out for trade
No other women in the world possess that distinctiveness that nobility
    that bearing that demeanor that carriage that elegance that
    nonchalance that refinement that neatness that hygiene that health
    that optimism that obliviousness that youthfulness that taste
Not the English aristocrat in Hyde Park in the morning
Not the Spanish girl promenading on Sunday evening
Not the beautiful Roman girl on the Pincio
Not the most beautiful farm girls of Hungary or Armenia

Not the refined Russian princess who formerly went along the banks of
the Neva in her sleigh
Not the Chinese girl in a flower boat
Not the beautiful secretaries of New York
Not even the most Parisian of Parisians
Please God my whole life let these few evanescent shapes stroll along in
my brain

Each lock of their hair is a little tress of equal length anointed painted
shining
On the crown of their heads they wear a little leather or ivory ornament
held by threads of colored silk or little strings of bright pearls
That coiffure represents months of work and they spend their whole
lives doing it and redoing it
Rows of little gold coins pierce the cartilage in their ears
Some of them have colored incisions on their faces under the eyes and
on the neck and they all make themselves up with a prodigious
artfulness
Their hands are covered with rings and bracelets and all have painted
fingernails as well as palms
Heavy silver bracelets jingle at their ankles with rings on their toes
Their heels are painted blue
They wear mumus of different lengths one on top of the other they're
all colored prints and different embroideries they eventually bring
together a surprising ensemble in very good taste with the orange the
blue the gold or the white predominant
They also wear belts and heavy mojos
Others several heavenly turbans
Their most prized possession is their impeccable teeth that they polish
like brass on an expensive yacht
Their bearing is something like a fine sailboat's
But there is no way to describe the supple proportions of their bodies or
express the deliberate nonchalance of the way they walk

Bijou-Concert

No
Never again
I'll never drag my ass into another one of these colonial dives
I want to be this poor black man I want to be this poor black who stands
    in the doorway
Because the beautiful black girls would be my sisters
And not
And not
These stinking French Spanish Serbian German bitches who furnish
    the leisures of gloomy functionaries dying to be stationed in Paris and
    who don't know how to kill time
I want to be that poor black man and fritter my time away

The Vultures

The black village is less shabby and less dirty than the slums of Saint-
    Ouen
The vultures that fly over it swoop down sometimes to clean it up

In the Tropics

In these waters the flow of the waves covers the rocks with an abundant
    flowering of animal life
Sponges of all kinds
Polyps that look so much like plants that they're called
"Sea lilies" when they look like living flowers attached to the bottom of
    the sea by their peduncles

"Ocean palms" when they spread out at the top of a stem that can get as
    long as 17 yards their tuft of arms like leaves on a date palm
Some have five arms others ten of them that look like rose-colored
    feathers and they swim by waving them
Innumerable mollusks drag their shells over the reefs in an infinite
    variety
The long ones whose shells have numerous spiral twists have been
    joined by the flattened ones with round mouths
The shell swollen and shiny
The one with a long opening flared notched or stretched into a canal
And the mollusk that flies through the water with the help of two large
    wings which hang from its feet that flies in the ocean the way
    butterflies fly in the air

Ornithichnites

The birds that had followed us all the way from Le Havre are
    disappearing
On the other hand up front there are schools of flying fish the wind
    throws up on deck
They are little tiny creatures that smell horrible
Their membrane is sticky

Blues

The sea is like a blue blue blue sky
Up above the sky is like Lake Leman
Delicate blue

Sunsets

Everyone talks about sunsets
All travelers are happy to talk about the sunsets in these waters
There are hundreds of books that do nothing but describe sunsets
The tropical sunsets
Yes it's true they're wonderful
But I really prefer the sunrises
Dawn
I wouldn't miss one for the world
I'm always on deck
In the buff
And I'm always the only one there admiring them
But I'm not going to describe them the dawns
I'm going to keep them for me alone

Starry Nights

I spend the greater part of the night on deck
The familiar stars of our latitudes lean lean over the sky
The North Star descends further and further on the northern horizon
Orion—my constellation—is at the zenith
The Milky Way like a luminous slit grows larger every night
Ursa Major is a patch of fog
The south is darker and darker up ahead
And I can't wait for the Southern Cross to appear in the east
To help me wait Venus has doubled in size and quintupled in brightness
    like the moon she makes a trail across the water
Tonight I saw a big shooting star

White Suit

I stroll on deck in the white suit I bought in Dakar
On my feet the espadrilles bought in Villa García
I hold in my hand the Basque beret I brought from Biarritz
My pockets are filled with Caporal Ordinaires
From time to time I sniff my wooden cigarette case from Russia
I jingle the coins in my pocket and a pound sterling in gold
I have my big Calabrian handkerchief and some wax matches the big
    kind you find only in London
I'm clean washed scrubbed more than the deck
Happy as a king
Rich as a multimillionaire
Free as a man

Cabin No. 6

I live here
I should always live here
I deserve no praise for staying shut in and working
Besides I don't work I write down everything that goes through my head
Well not really everything
Because tons of things go through my head but don't get out into the
    cabin
I'm living in a breeze the porthole wide open and the fan whirring
Not reading

Baggage

To think that people travel with tons of luggage
Me I brought only my steamer trunk and already I find it's too much I
    have too many things
Here's what's in my trunk
The manuscript of *Moravagine* that I should finish on board and in
    Santos mail back to Grasset
The manuscript of *Le Plan de l'Aiguille* that I should finish as soon as
    possible and send to Au Sans Pareil
The manuscript of a ballet for the Swedish Ballet's forthcoming season
    that I wrote on board between Le Havre and La Pallice where I sent it
    to Satie
The manuscript of *Coeur du Monde* that I'll send bit by bit to Raymone
The manuscript of *Equatoria*
A big packet of African tales that will form the second volume of my
    Anthology
Several business files
The two big volumes of the Darmesteter dictionary
My portable Remington the latest model
A package of some small items that I must deliver to a woman in Rio
My babouches from Timbuktu that bear the mark of the big caravan
Two pairs of incredible clodhoppers
One pair of patent leather shoes
Two suits
Two overcoats
My heavy Mont Blanc sweater
Various little toiletries
A tie
Six dozen handkerchiefs
Three shirts
Six pairs of pajamas
Pounds of white paper
Pounds of white paper

And a mojo
My trunk weighs 115 pounds without my gray hat

Orion

It's my star
It's in the form of a hand
It's my hand gone up into the sky
During the entire war I saw Orion through a lookout slit
When the zeppelins came to bomb Paris they always came from Orion
I have it above my head today
The main mast pierces the palm of that hand which must hurt
As my amputated hand hurts me pierced as it is by a continual stabbing
    pain

The Equator

The ocean is dark blue the blue sky is pale next to it
The sea swells all around the horizon
It's as if the Atlantic were going to spill over into the sky
All around the steamer it's a vat of pure ultramarine

Crossing the Line

Of course I have been baptized
It's my eleventh baptism of the line
I got dressed up like a woman and we had a great time
Then we drank

I Swim

Up to the line it was winter
Now it's summer
The captain had a swimming pool set up on the upper deck
I dive I swim I float
No more writing
It's good to be alive

San Fernando de Noronha

I send a telegram to Santos to announce my arrival
Then I go back up and into the pool
As I was swimming along on my back and spouting Mr. Mouton the
    radiotelegrapher on board tells me he's in contact with the *Belle Isle*
    and asks me if I don't want to send an ocean letter (to Madame
    Raymone he adds with a nice smile)
I send an ocean letter to say it's good to be alive
And I get back in the water
The cool water
The salt water

Amaralina

This radiogram tells me they'll be meeting me in Santos with a car
It's depressing to get there so quickly
Just six more days at sea
It's depressing
I don't ever want to get there I want to blow up Western Union

The Blowers

We're on a level with Bahia
I saw a first bird
An English freighter
And three blowers on the open sea
I also saw a big dorado

Sunday

It is Sunday on the water
It's hot
I'm in my cabin as if trapped in melting butter

The Pitch Post

For several days now we've been in the area of the post
I'm quite aware that it's always been written down as the pitch *pot*
But here on board they say the pitch *post*
The post is a pitch-black post in the middle of the ocean where all ships
    come to a stop just to "post" a letter
The post is a black post coated with tar where they used to tie sailors
    who had been hanged or flogged
The post is a black post the cat-o'-nine-tails comes to rub up against
Certainly when the storm is upon you it's as if you were in a pot of
    pitch
But when the storm is gathering you see a black bar in the sky that bar
    darkens advances threatens and rams the sailor the sailor who lacks a
    clear conscience thinks of the pitch post

Anyway even if I'm wrong I'll write pitch *post* and not pitch *pot* because
   I like popular speech and nothing will convince me that this term is
   not in the process of changing
And all the men on the *Formosa* will back me up

Pedro Alvarez Cabral

The Portuguese Pedro Alvarez Cabral had embarked at Lisbon
In the year 1500
To make for the East Indies
Contrary winds carried him to the west and Brazil was discovered

Lands

A freighter points to Pernambuco
In the barman's opera glasses it's an English steamer all covered with
   white canvas
To the naked eye it seems pushed down into the water and broken across
   the middle like that series of American freighters built during the war
This subject is being hotly debated when I sight the coast
It's a rounded landmass surrounded by chromium mist topped with
   three pearly plumes
Two hours later we see some triangular mountains
Black and blue

Eggs

The coast of Brazil is strewn with round bare little islands we've been
   sailing through for two days
They're like speckled eggs laid by some gigantic bird

Or like volcanic dung
Or like vulture sphincteroids

Butterfly

It's odd
For two days now that we've been in sight of land not a single bird has
     met us or followed in our wake
On the other hand
Today
At dawn
As we were entering the Bay of Rio
A butterfly as big as your hand came fluttering all around the steamer
It was black and yellow with big streaks of faded blue

Rio de Janeiro

Everyone is on deck
We're in among the mountains
A lighthouse goes dark
They're looking everywhere for the Sugarloaf and ten people find it in a
     hundred different directions so much do these mountains look alike
     in their pyroformity
Mr. Lopart shows me a mountain with its profile against the sky like a
     cadaver stretched out with its silhouette looking like Napoleon on his
     deathbed
I think it looks more like Wagner a Richard Wagner puffed up with
     pride or overwhelmed with fat
Rio is now quite near and you can make out houses on the beach
The officers compare this panorama to that of the Golden Horn
Others talk about the revolt of the forts
Others unanimously deplore the construction of a big tall square
     modern hotel that disfigures the bay (the hotel is very beautiful)

Still others vehemently protest the leveling of a mountain
Leaning over the starboard rail I look at
The tropical vegetation of a deserted little island
The huge sun that cuts through the huge vegetation
A little boat with three fishermen
These men moving slowly and methodically
Who work
Who fish
Who catch the fish
Who do not even look at us
Absorbed in their craft

In Port

They have run up the colors
The yellow to ask for Health
The blue to ask for the police
The red and white to ask for customs
The starry one of Chargeurs Réunis
And the blue white and red
And the Brazilian
There are two others I don't recognize
The passengers admire the crestfallen buildings of the Exposition
Motorboats ferryboats come go and big lateen sailboats very slow like on
    Lake Geneva
The sun beats down
An eagle drops

The Gangway

Finally we're dockside a modern rectilinear dock equipped with cranes
    from Duisburg

Handkerchiefs wave
Hands signal
Blank-booboo-booboo-blank has already forgotten me
She sees in the crowd a big-shot tall bronze very chic and indolent
    whom I really think I've met before in Paris
She's touched it's beautiful then signals to him to hire a porter and yells
    and waves that she has five trunks and many many other bags big
    ones and small ones
Me I even know what she has in those trunks because I locked them for
    her this morning while she was almost having a nervous breakdown
So long kiddo now she goes down the gangway on the arm of her guy
    who is as sleek as a roebuck disturbing and attractive
Like all princely mixtures of black and white blood
I think of the big Creole mojo he carries in his pants
A voice rises from the dock Is Monsieur Blaise Cendrars on board?
Here!
Twelve hats wave
I disembark
And am photographed
"Up here please. . . . Up here. . . ."

Banquet

One hour by taxi along the beach
Speed horn introductions laughter young people Paris Rio Brazil France
    interviews introductions laughter
We go out to Press Grotto
Then we go back for lunch in town
The hors d'oeuvres haven't arrived and already the newspapers are
    talking about me and printing the photo taken a few hours ago
Good local cuisine Portuguese wines and *pinga*
At two on the dot I'm back on board
A nice young poet pukes on the deck I take him back down to the dock
    where his friend starts puking too

The others weren't able to keep up
I go up and dive into the pool while the *Formosa* gets under way
Long live water

Beautiful Evening

Evening descends on the American coast
Not a fish not a bird
A continuous chain of even mountains all covered with luxuriant
    growth
The sea is smooth
The sky too
I think of the two friends I made on board and who have just left me at
    Rio
Mr. Lopart stockbroker from Brussels nice charming who held his own
    with me at the table or evenings in the smoking lounge with a bottle
    of whiskey
And Booboo-blank-blank-booboo she was the best pal you could have I
    swam for hours with her mornings and evenings
The three of us made a wonderful group laughing so hard we cried
We drove everyone on board up the wall scandalized the officials and
    soldiers (officers) on official business
I haven't laughed so hard for ten years laughed for twenty straight days I
    was sick from laughing and I gained twelve pounds
Good-bye good friends see you soon we'll meet again on board going
    back to France or some other time in Paris or in Brussels or
    somewhere on a train crossing the Andes or on board the *Empress*
    steering a course toward Australia we'll always have the same
    bartender because it's a small world for such happy friends
See you soon

Dead of Night at Sea

The mountainous coast is floodlit by the full moon traveling with us
The Southern Cross is to the east and the south remains all dark
The heat is stifling
Big pieces of wood float in the opaque water
The two German acrobat girls stroll along the deck three-quarters naked
They need a cool breeze
The little Portuguese doctor who is traveling with the emigrants from
    his country as far as Buenos Aires winks as he walks past me
I see him disappear with the two German girls into a big unoccupied
    cabin
Two ships go by to starboard then three to port
All five are lit up as if for a party
It's as if we're docked at Monte Carlo and the virgin forest grows right
    down to the sea
Pricking up my ears and straining all my faculties I hear something like
    the rustling of leaves
Or perhaps my sorrow at getting off tomorrow
After a long quarter of an hour I perceive the quavering song of an
    emigrant on the forecastle where linen is drying in the moonlight
    and waving to me

Paris

I stayed on deck all night listening to the messages coming in over the
    wireless and deciphering various bits
And translating them as I squinted at the stars
A new star shone as high as my nose
The tip of my cigar
I was thinking absentmindedly about Paris

And each star in the sky was replaced at times by the face of someone I
     know
I saw Jean like an elfish torch Erik's twinkling eyes the steady look of
     Fernand and the eyes of a hundred cafés around Sanders
Eugenia's round spectacles and Marcel's
Mariette's piercing glance and the drooping eyes of the guy from
     Gascony
From time to time Francis and Germaine went by in a car and Abel was
     handling a production and being sad
Then the wireless started up again and I looked at the stars
And the new star shone again at the tip of my nose
It lit me up like Raymone
So close so close

Dawn

At dawn I went down among the machines
For the last time I listened to the deep breathing of the pistons
Leaning on the fragile nickel-plated handrail I felt for the last time the
     dull vibration of the drive shafts sink into me with the musty smell of
     the overheated oil and the tepidness of the steam
We had one more drink me and the chief mechanic that sad quiet man
     who has such a beautiful childlike smile and who never indulges in
     small talk
As I was leaving the engine room the sun naturally was leaving the sea
     and already getting hot
There was not one cloud in the purple sky
And as we swung toward Santos our wake described a big arc glistening
     on the unmoving sea

Islands

Islands
Islands
Islands where no one'll ever land
Islands where no one'll ever stop
Islands overgrown
Islands crouched like jaguars
Islands that are silent
Islands that do not move
Islands that are unforgettable and nameless
I throw my shoes overboard because I really would like to go right over
    to you

Arriving in Santos

We go between mountains that close again behind us
Now you can't tell where the open sea is
Here's the pilot climbing the ladder he's a half-breed with big eyes
We enter an inner bay which ends in a strait
To the left is a dazzling beach with cars driving along and to the right
    the hard mute tropical growth falls into the sea like a Niagara of
    chlorophyll
When we've passed a little Portuguese fort pleasant like a chapel in the
    suburbs of Rome and with cannons like armchairs good for sitting in
    the shade we wind along the muddy waters of the strait
The banks are low
The one on the left planted with mangoes and gigantic bamboo trees
    around the red-and-black or blue-and-black shanties of the black
    people
The one on the right desolate marshy filled with prickly palms
The sun is staggering

Portside

The port
Not one sound of a machine not a whistle not a horn
Nothing moves there's not a single person
No smoke rises not a single puff of steam
Sunstroke of an entire port
Only the cruel sun and the heat falling from the sky and rising from the
    water the astounding heat
Nothing moves
Still there's a town there some activity an industry
Twenty-five freighters from ten nations are anchored and loading coffee
Two hundred cranes work silently
(In the spyglass you can make out the sacks of coffee moving along on
    conveyer belts and loading hoists
The town is hidden behind the flat sheds and the big rectilinear
    corrugated-iron warehouses)
Nothing moves
We wait for hours
No one comes
No boat leaves the dock
Our steamer seems to melt minute by minute and to drip slowly in the
    thick heat to buckle and sink straight to the bottom

Starboard

A frigate is suspended in the air
It's a bird of sovereign elegance with wings at variable angles and
    streamlined like a glider
Two big scaly backs emerge from the muddy water and plunge back into
    the ooze
Bunches of bananas float downstream

Since we've been here three new freighters have loomed up behind us
    silent and tired
The heat is crushing them

Life

The *Formosa* swings on her anchor and we turn imperceptibly
A launch separates from the shore
It's a canoe carved out of a tree trunk
It carries two little black boys
One is lying motionless on his back
The other crouched in the front paddles along casually
The sun plays on the two sides of his paddle
They go slowly around the ship and then return to shore

Guarujá Beach

It's two o'clock we're finally docked
I noticed a bundle of men in the shadow the foreshortened shadow of a
    crane
Medical certificates passport customs
I disembark
I'm not sitting in the car that carries me but in the thick soft heat stuffed
    like upholstery
My friends who have waited since seven this morning on the sunny
    dock have just barely enough strength left to shake my hand
The whole town resounds with young horns saying hello to each other
Young horns that revive us
Young horns that make us hungry
Young horns that take us to lunch at Guarujá Beach
To a restaurant filled with slot machines with electric shooting galleries
    mechanical birds automatic machines that read your palm
    gramophones that tell your fortune and where you eat that good old
    Brazilian cooking tasty spicy Indian black

Banana Plantation

Before catching the train we go for one more drive
We go through dusty banana plantations
The stinking slaughterhouses
A rundown suburb and a flourishing scrub
Then we skirt a mountain of red earth where cubical houses spattered
    in red and dark blue are piled up wooden houses built on abandoned
    placers
Two midget goats graze on the rare plants that grow alongside the road
    two midget goats and a little blue pig

Mictorio

The *mictorio* is the station toilet
I'm always curious to see it when I arrive in a new country
The john in the station in Santos is a little nook where an immense
    earthenware pot which reminds me of the big jars among the vines
    in Provence where an immense earthenware pot is buried up to
    the neck
A big thick dark wooden sausage sits like a crown on the edge and serves
    as a seat
It must be rather uncomfortable and too low
The exact opposite of the tanks of the Bastille which are too high

The Bastille Tanks

The Bastille tanks are still used in the brig at the Reuilly barracks in
    Paris
They're stoneware pots shaped like an inverted funnel over four feet
    high
They sit in the middle of each cell the widest part on the ground and
    the small end the narrowest part in the air
It is in this sort of trumpet mouthpiece which is a lot higher that the
    soldier doing time must manage to do his duty
Without letting anything drop outside unless he wants to do a double
    stretch
It's the torment of Tantalus backward
At the beginning of the war I knew soldiers who for this reason spent
    months in the brig doing a one-day stretch and ended up being
    court-martialed for being hardheads
They used to say that those tanks were formerly the tanks of the old
    Bastille prison

São Paulo Railway Co.

The express is getting up steam
We move into a Pompeian Pullman which looks like the comfortable
    cars of the Egyptian railways
We're sitting around a bridge table in big wicker chairs
There's a bar at the end of the car where I drink my first Santos coffee
Leaving we pass a convoy of white cars bearing the inscription
Caloric Co.
You're telling me
I'm suffocating

Landscape

The ground is red
The sky is blue
The vegetation is a dark green
This landscape is cruel hard sad despite the infinite variety of shapes
    growing
Despite the leaning gracefulness of the palm trees and the bouquets
    bursting from big flowering trees flowers of Lent

On the Train

The train goes rather fast
The switch signals and grade crossings work like they do in England
Nature is a much darker green than at home
Bronzed
Closed
The forest has an Indian face
Whereas our fields are predominantly yellow and white
Here it's heavenly blue in the flowering *campos*

Paranapiaçaba

The Paranapiaçabas are the Serra do Mar
It's here the train is hoisted by cables and crosses the rugged mountain
    in several sections
All the stations are suspended in the void
There are a lot of waterfalls and great work projects had to be
    undertaken to shore up this crumbling mountain

Because the Serra is a rotting mountain like Les Rognes above
    Bionnasay but les Rognes covered with tropical forests
The weeds that grow on the slopes of the ditch between the tracks are all
    rare plants that you see in Paris only in the shop windows of the best
    horticulturists
In a station three indolent half-breeds were in the process of hoeing
    them up

Telegraph Line

You see that telegraph line at the bottom of the valley with its path
    cutting straight up through the forest on the mountainside over there
All the poles are iron
When it was put in they were wooden
After three months they grew branches
So they were torn out turned upside down and replanted headfirst the
    roots in the air
After three months they grew new branches they took root and started to
    live again
The whole thing had to be torn out and to make a new line iron poles
    had to be brought in from Pittsburgh at great expense

Openings

Glimpses of the sea
Waterfalls
Long-haired mossy trees
Heavy rubbery leaves shining
A sun glaze
A highly polished heat
Glistening
I stop listening to the lively conversation of my friends sharing the news
    I brought from Paris

On both sides of the train up close or on the other side of the distant
   valley
The forest is there and looking at me and disturbing me and attracting
   me like a mummy's mask
I look
Not the shadow of an eye

Furrowed Face

The leaves of the forest the leaves
This leaning architecture detailed like the facade of a cathedral with
   niches and embellishments perpendicular masses and delicate shafts

Piratininga

When you go over the crest of the Serra and emerge from the mist that
   hoods it the land evens out
It ends up being just a vast wavy plateau lined by blue mountains to the
   north
The ground is red
This plateau offers short trees in little clumps that cover a small stretch
   quite close to each other often touching at some point and scattered
   over an almost perfectly flat grassy area
It's hard to say whether there is more woods or pasture
It makes a sort of inlay of two nuances of very different and distinct
   greens
The grass a delicate color
The woods a dark shade

Botany

The araucaria catches your eye
You admire its gigantic size
Especially its branches
Which rise at different stages
Like a candelabrum
And all end at the same level to form a perfectly even plateau
You also see the great groundsel tree with golden yellow flowers the
    myrtle
The turpentine tree
The very common composite they call *Alecrim do campo* wild rosemary
And the small tree with trifoliate leaves no. 1204a
But what I like best is not being able to put a name on hundreds of
    plants each more beautiful than the other
And which I know nothing about
And which I see for the first time
And which I admire

Ignorance

I no longer listen to all the beautiful stories they tell me about Brazil's
    future past or present
Through the doorway of the train now picking up speed I see
The big *pteris caudata* fern
That there's not a single bird
The masonry of big anthills
That the lilies here form impenetrable thickets
The savannahs are sometimes dry grass and undergrowth sometimes a
    few trees here and there almost always twisted and stunted
That the castor oil plant grows several yards high

There are a few animals in the fields longhorn steers skinny horses that
    move like mustangs and zebu bulls
That there is no trace of culture
And that's all I know about what I see
Forms
Forms of vegetation
Palm trees cacti what do you call those broomsticks topped with pink
    tufts that apparently are an aphrodisiac fruit

São Paulo

Finally here are some factories a suburb a nice little trolley
Electric lines
A street crowded with people doing their evening shopping
A natural gas tank
Finally we pull into the station
São Paulo
I feel like I'm in the station in Nice
Or getting off at Charing Cross in London
I find all my friends
Hello
It's me

Le Havre–São Paulo, February 1924

II. SAO PAULO

Up

The night is almost over
Day begins to break
A window opens
A man leans out humming
He's in shirtsleeves and looks out over the world
The wind murmurs softly like a buzzing head

The City Wakes Up

The first trolleys go by filled with workers
A man is selling newspapers in the middle of the square
He's jumping around in the big sheets of paper that are flapping their
    wings and he's doing his own solitary kind of ballet to the music of
    his guttural cries . . . STADO . . . ERCIO . . . EIO
Horns answer him
And the first cars go speeding past

Electric Horns

Here they never heard of the League of Silence
As in all new countries
The joy of living and making money is expressed by the voices of horns
    and the backfiring of wide-open mufflers

Small Fry

The sky is a harsh blue
The wall across is a harsh white
The harsh sun is beating down on my head
A black woman on a little terrace is frying tiny fish on a portable stove
    made out of an old cookie tin
Two little black kids chew on a stalk of sugarcane

Landscape

The high-gloss wall of the PENSION MILANESE is framed by my
    window
I see a slice of São Joao Avenue
Trolleys cars trolleys
Trolleys-trolleys trolleys trolleys
Yellow mules harnessed in threes pull tiny empty carts
Above the avenue's pepper trees the giant sign of the CASA TOKYO
    stands out
The sun is spilling varnish

São Paulo

I adore this city
São Paulo is after my own heart
No tradition here
No prejudice
Ancient or modern
All that matters is this furious appetite this absolute confidence this
    optimism this daring this work this labor this speculation which

builds ten houses per hour in all styles ridiculous grotesque beautiful
   big small northern southern Egyptian Yankee cubist
With no other concern than to follow the statistics foresee the future the
   comfort the utility the increment value and to attract a large
   immigrant population
All countries
All peoples
I love that
The two or three old Portuguese houses that remain are blue china

III.

Leaving

For the last time I take the *caminho do Mar*
But I don't enjoy it because of Oswald who has the blues
And who's being dark and gloomy
La Serra's in the mist
The car backfires
The motor missing

At the Pier

Good-bye my good friends Good-bye
Hurry back to São Paulo before nightfall
We talk one last time about machine guns about revolution
Now I'm alone on board this big Dutch ship filled with Germans
    Dutchmen Argentinians childish shining all made up and 2–3
    phony Englishmen
The Spanish emigrants are going back home
They made a little money they can afford the return ticket and they
    seem really happy
One couple is dancing to the sound of an accordion
Another *jota*

Cabin 2

It's mine
It's all white
I'm going to like it
All alone

Because I have a lot of work to do
To make up for 9 months in the sun
The 9 months in Brazil
The 9 months with Friends
And I must work for Paris
That's why I already like this jam-packed ship where I see no one to
    chat with

At Dinner

I gave the chief steward a big tip for a little corner table of my own
I will meet no one
I look at the others and I eat
Here's the first European menu
I admit it's a pleasure to eat these European dishes
Soup Pompadour
Beef tenderloin à la bruxelloise
Partridge on toast
Taste is the most atavistic most reactionary most nationalistic sense
Analytic
At the antipodes of love of touching of touching of love in full
    evolution and universal growth
Revolutionary
Synthetic

Delay

It's almost two in the morning and we still haven't left
They never stop loading coffee
The sacks go go and go up the never-ending hoists and drop to the
    bottom of the hold like the bloated pigs of Chicago
I'm sick of it
I'm going to bed

Waking Up

I'm naked
I've already taken my bath
I rub on some cologne
A sailboat is buffeted across my porthole
It's cold this morning
There's some fog
I straighten my papers
I set up a schedule
My days will be busy
I don't have a minute to lose
I write

The Breeze

Not a sound not a jolt
The *Gelria* holds the sea admirably
On this first-class steamer with its gypsy orchestras in every nook and
    cranny everyone gets up late
The morning belongs to me
My manuscripts are spread out on my bunk
The breeze leafs through them with a listless finger
Presences

Rio de Janeiro

A bright light inundates the atmosphere
A light so colored and so fluid that the objects it touches

The pink rocks
The white lighthouse above them
The semaphore signals seem liquefied by it
And now I know the names of the mountains that surround this
    marvelous bay
The Sleeping Giant
La Gavea
Bico de Papagaio
Corcovado
Sugarloaf which Jean de Lery's shipmates called the Butter Pot
And the strange needles of the Organs chain
Hello You

Dinner in Town

Mr. Lopart wasn't in Rio he had left Saturday on the *Lutetia*
I had dinner in town with the new director
After signing the 24 F/N Grand Sport type contract I took him to a little
    joint in the port
We ate grilled shrimp
Dorado tongues with mayonnaise
Armadillo
(Armadillo meat tastes like the reindeer meat Satie likes so much)
Local fruit mommas bananas oranges from Bahia
Each of us drank his own bottle of Chianti

The Morning Is Mine

The sun rises at quarter to six
The wind is a lot cooler
Mornings the deck is mine until 9 o'clock
I watch the sailors mopping the spar deck

The high waves
A Brazilian steamer we're catching up with
A one and only black and white bird
When the first women appear with the wind blowing against them and
    the little girls with their dresses blown up showing their little bottoms
    with goose pimples I go back down to my cabin
And get back to work

Writing

My machine clacks in time
It rings at the end of each line
The gears roll their *r*'s
From time to time I lean back in my wicker chair and release a big fat
    puff of smoke
My cigarette is always lit
Then I hear the sound of the waves
The gargling water strangled in the pipes under the sink
I get up and plunge my hand in cold water
Or I put on some cologne
I've covered the wardrobe mirror so I can't see myself writing
The porthole is a disk of sun
When I think
It vibrates like the skin on a drum and talks loudly

Bad Faith

That damned chief steward I'd given a big tip to so I could be alone
    comes to find me like an alley cat
He begs me on behalf of the captain to come join them at the head
    table
I'm furious but I can't refuse

At dinner it so happens the captain is a very nice man
I'm between an embassy attaché at the Hague and an English consul at
    Stockholm
On the other side there is the leading light in bacteriology and his wife
    who is a soft gluttonous woman with totally white skin and dull
    round eyes
My antimusical paradoxes and culinary theories shake the table with
    indignation
The attaché at the Hague dips his monocle in the bouillon
The Stockholm consul chokes and turns green like striped pajamas
The bacteriological light pulls a face even longer than his pointed
    ferretlike head
His wife chortles and wrinkles from the center toward her edges so that
    her whole face ends up looking like a navel on a potbelly
The captain winks maliciously

Tuxedo

Only the seedy have no tuxedo on board
Only the too well-bred have tuxedos on board
I put on a nice suit of English tweed and the sea is a blue as smooth as
    my tropical-blue suit

Night Rises

I watched very closely how it happened
When the sun has gone down
It's the sea that gets darker
The sky stays bright for quite a while
The night rises from the water and slowly encircles the entire horizon
Then in its turn the sky slowly darkens
There is a moment when it is completely dark

Then the darkness of the water and the darkness of the sky recede
An eburnean transparency appears with reflections in the water and
    dark pockets in the sky
Then the Coal Sack beneath the Southern Cross
Then the Milky Way

Crossing with Nothing Happening

Holland Holland Holland
Smoke fills the smoking lounge
Gypsies fill the orchestra
Armchairs fill the sitting room
Families families families
Holes fill the stockings
And the women knitting knitting

Heat

It's six days from La Plata to Pernambuco on a fast transatlantic steamer
You often see the coast but not a single bird
Like in the middle of the immense state of São Paulo where you drive
    all day down dusty roads
Without scaring up a single bird
That's how hot it is

Cape Fria

I heard tonight a child's voice through my door
Soft
Rising and falling

Pure
It did me good

Incognito Unveiled

For several days I totally mystified my companions at table
They wondered what on earth I might be
I talked bacteriology with the leading light
Women and nightclubs with the captain
Kantian theories of peace with the attaché at the Hague
The freight business with the English consul
Paris movies music banking vitalism aviation
This evening at dinner as I was complimenting her the wife of the
    leading light said It's true
This gentleman is a poet
Clunk
She found out from the jockey's wife in second class
I can't be mad at her because her glutton navel smile is funnier than
    anything on earth
I would actually like to know how she manages to wrinkle up that
    chubby round face

Nannies and Sports

There are several nannies on board
Some dry nurses and some not so dry
When they're playing quoits on deck
Every time the young German bends over she shows two little breasts
    snuggled down at the bottom of her bodice
Every man from first-class passenger to deckhand knows this game and
    they all walk down the portside to see these two round things in their
    nest

They must be talking about it as far down as the storeroom
At the end of a bench
In a dark corner
A baby clings to and squirts a big black breast abundant and gummy as
    a bunch of bananas

Dangerous Life

Today I am perhaps the happiest man in the world
I have everything I don't want
And the only thing in life I do want is what every turn of the propeller
    brings me closer to
And maybe I will have lost everything when I get there

Misprints

Spelling errors and misprints make me happy
Some days I feel like making them on purpose
That's cheating
I really love mispronunciations hesitations of the tongue and the accents
    of all local dialects

The Day Will Come

The day will come
Modern technology can't handle it anymore
Each crossing costs the voters a million
With planes and dirigibles it will cost ten million
Underwater cables my first-class cabin the wheels the port projects the
    big industries eat money
All the prodigious activity which is our pride

Machines can't handle it anymore
Bankruptcy
On his dungheap Job still uses his electric face massager
That's nice

Sunset

We can see the coastline now
The sunset was extraordinary
In the flaming evening
Enormous clouds perpendicular and insanely tall
Chimeras griffins and a big winged victory stayed all night just above
    the horizon
At daybreak the whole flock found itself reunited pink and yellow over
    Bahia laid out like a checkerboard

Bahia

Lagoons churches palm trees cubical houses
Big boats with two upside down rectangular sails which look like
    immense puffed-out pant legs
Little boats with shark fins bounding among groundswells
Big perpendicular inflated clouds colored like pottery
Yellow and blue

Hic Haec Hoc

I bought three wistitis which I have baptized Hic Haec Hoc
Twelve hummingbirds
A thousand cigars
And a Bahian's hand as big as a foot

With that I take away with me the memory of the most beautiful burst
    of laughter

Pernambuco

Victor Hugo called it Fernandbouc of the Blue Mountains
And an old author I'm reading Ferdinandburg of the Thousand
    Churches
In Indian this name means Mouth-from-Ear-to-Ear
Here's what you see today when you arrive from the open sea and put in
    for an hour and a half
Sandy lowlands
A jetty of reinforced concrete and a tiny crane
A second jetty of reinforced concrete and an immense crane
A third jetty of reinforced concrete on which they're building
    warehouses of reinforced concrete
A few cargo ships tied up
A long series of numbered huts
And behind that some domes two three clock towers and an
    astronomical observatory
Also the tanks of the American Petroleum Co. and the Caloric
Sun heat and corrugated iron

Adrienne Lecouvreur and Cocteau

I bought two more very small wistitis
And two birds with feathers like moiré paper
My little monkeys have rings in their ears
My birds have gilded claws
I baptized the smaller monkey Adrienne Lecouvreur and the other Jean
I gave a bird to the daughter of the Argentinian admiral who is on board
She's a stupid girl who squints out of both eyes

She gives a footbath to her bird to remove the gilt from its claws
The other one is singing in my cabin in a few days it will imitate these
    familiar sounds and will ding like my typewriter
When I write my little monkeys watch me
I amuse them enormously
They think they have me in a cage

Heat

The heat in my cabin is killing me but I can't air it out for fear of
    exposing my little family of little animals to the draft
Too bad
I stay in my cabin
I suffocate and I write I write
I write to please them
These little animals are really nice and so am I

Sharks

They call me
There are sharks in our wake
Two or three monsters which veer up white out of the water when hens
    are thrown out to them
I buy a sheep and throw it overboard
The sheep swims the sharks are scared I've been had

Steerage

I spent the evening in steerage and in the crew's quarters
There's a real menagerie on board

Waxbills parrots monkeys an anteater a *cachorro do mato*
Naked kids
Women with a strong smell

A Line

A line that fades away
Good-bye
It's America
Above is a crown of clouds
In the coming night an absolutely flawless star
Now we'll steer a course to the east and starting tomorrow the
    swimming pool will be set up on the upper deck

The Carpenter

Hic Haec Hoc are in the carpenter's room
I'm keeping in my cabin only the bird and the monkeys Adrienne and
    Cocteau
The carpenter's is filled with parrots monkeys dogs and cats
Him he's a guy who smokes his pipe
He has the gray eyes of a white wine drinker
When you talk he replies with a great sweep of his plane that makes
    curls of wood
Fly off ·
I nickname him Robinson Crusoe
Then he deigns to smile

I Told You So

I had said so
When you buy monkeys
You must take the really lively ones that almost scare you
And never pick a sweet sleepy monkey that snuggles up in your arms
Because these are drugged monkeys that will be ferocious the day after
    tomorrow
And that's what just happened to a girl who got bitten on the nose

Christopher Columbus

What I lose sight of today by heading east is what Christopher
    Columbus discovered by heading west
It's in these waters that he saw that first bird black and white which
    made him fall to his knees and thank God
With such feeling
And to improvise that Baudelairian prayer which can be found in his
    log-book
Where he asks forgiveness for lying to his mates every day by giving
    them a false position
So they couldn't find their way back

Laughing

I laugh
I laugh
You laugh
We laugh

Nothing else matters
But this laughing we love
You just have to know how to be stupid and happy

The Captain Is a Terrific Guy

All the same the captain's a terrific guy
Yesterday he had the pool set up just for me
Today without a word and simply to please me
He swung the ship around
And skirted Fernando de Noronha so closely I could have almost picked
    a bouquet

Fernando de Noronha

From far off it looks like a sunken cathedral
Up close
It's an island with colors so intense that the green of the grass is
    completely gold

Grotto

There is a grotto that goes all the way through the island

Peak

There's a peak whose name no one could tell me
It looks like the Matterhorn and it's the last pillar of Atlantis

What a feeling when I look through the spyglass and think I've
    discovered the traces of a ridge of Atlantis

Beach

In a bay
Behind a promontory
A beach with yellow sand and mother-of-pearl palm trees

Penal Colony

A white wall
High as a cemetery's
In gigantic letters it bears the inscription you can easily make out with
    the naked eye
"Caught Arms"

Civilization

There are some traces of farming
A few houses
A radio post two pylons and two Eiffel Towers under construction
An old Portuguese port
A calvary
With the spyglass I make out a naked man on the prison wall waving a
    white rag
The nights are absolutely beautiful with no moon with immense stars
    and the heat that will only get hotter
As the churning propellers turn the dark water more and more
    phosphorescent in our wake

Passengers

They're all there in their deck chairs
Or playing cards
Or having tea
Or being bored
There is however a little group of sporty types who play shuffleboard
Or deck tennis
And another little group that goes swimming in the pool
At night when everyone is asleep the empty chairs lined up on deck
    look like a collection of skeletons in a museum
Dried-up old women
Chameleons dandruff fingernails

The Blue Bird

My blue bird has an all-blue breast
Its head is a bronzed green
It has a black spot under its throat
Its wings are blue with tufts of little golden yellow feathers
At the tip of its tail there are some traces of vermilion
Its back is striped black and green
It has a black beak rosy claws and two jet-black little eyes
It loves to take a dip eats bananas and has a call like a tiny blast of steam
It's called Sevencolors

Why

The bird whistles
The monkeys look at it

Mastery
I smile while I work
Whatever happens to me is all the same to me
And everything I do is a matter of complete indifference
My eyes follow someone who isn't here
I write with my back turned toward where we're going
Sun in the fog
Speed up
Slow down
Yes

Birds

The guanoey rocks are covered with birds

Jangada

Three naked men on the open sea
In a *jangada* they hunt the sperm whale
Three white beams a triangular sail one outrigger

Wake

The sea continues to be sea blue
The weather continues to be the most beautiful I have ever seen at sea
This crossing continues to be the calmest and most uneventful you
    could possibly imagine

Dance

An American couple dances apache dances
The Argentinian girls gripe about the orchestra and heartily despise the
    young men on board
The Portuguese burst into applause when a Portuguese song is played
The French have their own group laugh loudly and make fun of
    everyone
Only the little maids want to dance in their pretty dresses
To the horror of some and the amusement of others I ask the black wet
    nurse to dance
The American couple dances apache dances again

Pedometer

When you pace back and forth on deck . . .

Why Do I Write?

Because . . .

1924

South American
Women

Drawing by Tarsila do Amaral, Brazilian artist and friend of
Cendrars.

I.

The road rises in hairpins
The car climbs rough and powerful
We climb in a roar like an airplane approaching its greatest height
Each turn throws her against my shoulder and when we swerve in the
    void she unconsciously clutches my arm and leans over the precipice
At the *serra's* top we skid to a stop before the gigantic fault
A monstrous close-up moon is rising behind us
"Lua, lua!" she murmurs
In the name of the moon, tell me, how does God authorize these
    gigantic constructions that allow us to get across?
It's not the moon, sweetheart, but the sun, precipitating the fog, that
    made this enormous gash
Look at the water down there rushing through the fallen rocks and into
    the generator pipes
That station sends electricity as far as Rio

II.

Libertines of both sexes
Now we can admit
There are a few of us around the world
Perfect health
We also have the most beautiful women in the world
Simplicity
Intelligence
Love
Sports
We have also taught them how to be free
The children grow up with dogs horses birds among pretty maids all
    round and mobile like sunflowers

III.

There is no more jealousy fear or shyness
Our girlfriends are strong and healthy
They are beautiful and simple and tall
And they all know how to dress
They are not intelligent women but they are very shrewd
They have no fear of loving
They are not afraid of taking
They also know how to give
Each of them has had to fight against family social position other
    people or something else
Now
They have simplified their lives and are filled with childishness
No more furniture no more trinkets they love animals big cars and their
    own smiles
They travel
They hate music but every one of them brings a record player

IV.

There are three of them I like especially
The first
An old woman sensitive beautiful and kind
Lovably chatty and of a sovereign elegance
A socialite but so gluttonous that she liberated herself from social rules
The second is the wild child of the Hotel Meurice
All day she combs her long hair and nibbles at her Guerlain lipstick
Banana trees black wet nurse hummingbirds
Her country is so far away you travel six weeks on a river covered with
    flowers with moss with mushrooms as big as ostrich eggs

She is so beautiful in the evening in the hotel lobby that the men are all
    crazy about her
Her sharpest smile is for me because I know how to laugh like the wild
    bees of her village
The last one is too rich to be happy
But she has already made great progress
It's not right away that you find your balance and the simplicity of life
    among all the complications of wealth
It takes stubbornness
She knows this well she who rides so divinely she who becomes a part
    of her big Argentine stallion
May your will be like your riding crop
But don't use it
Too
Often

V.

There is yet one more who is still like a very little girl
Despite her horrible husband this terrible divorce and confinement in a
    convent
She is as wild as day and night
She is more beautiful than an egg
More beautiful than a circle
But she is always too naked her beauty spills over she still doesn't know
    how to dress
Also she eats too much and her belly swells out as though she were two
    little months pregnant
She has such an appetite and such a taste for life
We are going to teach her all that and teach her how to dress
And tell her the best places to go

VI.

One
There is still one more
One I love more than anything in the world
I give my whole self to her like a pepsin because she needs a tonic
Because she is too soft
Because she is still a little fearful
Because happiness is a very heavy thing to bear
Because beauty needs a nice quarter-hour's exercise every morning

VII.

We don't want to be sad
It's too easy
It's too stupid
It's too convenient
It comes up all the time
It isn't smart
Everyone is sad
We don't want to be sad anymore

1924

Various Poems

One of Modigliani's two frontispiece portraits of Cendrars for
the first edition of *Nineteen Elastic Poems*.

Shrapnels

I.

In the fog the rifle fire crackles and the cannon's voice comes right
    up to us
The American bison is not more terrible
Nor more beautiful
Gun mounting
Like the swan of Cameroon

II.

I have clipped your wings, O my explosive forehead
And you don't want a kepi
On the national highway 400 thousand feet pound out sparks to the
    clanking of mess kits
I think
I pass by
Brazen and stupid
Stinking ram

III.

All my men are bedded down under the acacias the shells rip through
O blue sky of the Marne
Woman
With the smile of an airplane
We are forgotten

October 1914

Homage to Guillaume Apollinaire

The bread is rising
France
Paris
An entire generation
I address the poets who were there
Friends
Apollinaire is not dead
You followed an empty hearse
Apollinaire is a magus
He's the one who was smiling in the silk of the flags at the windows
He enjoyed throwing you flowers and wreaths
While you walked behind his hearse
Then he bought a little three-colored cockade
I saw him that same night demonstrating on the boulevards
He was astride the hood of an American truck and waving an enormous
    international flag spread out like an airplane
LONG LIVE FRANCE

The times change
The years roll by like clouds
The soldiers have gone back home
To the houses
Where they live
And look a new generation is rising
The dream of the BREASTS is coming true!
Little French children, half English, half black, half Russian, a bit
    Belgian, Italian, Annamite, Czech
One with a Canadian accent, another with Hindu eyes
Teeth face bones joints lines smile bearing
They all have something foreign about them and are still part of us

Among them, Apollinaire, like that statue of the Nile, the father of the
  waters, stretched out with kids that flow all over him
Between his feet, under his arms, in his beard
They look like their father and go their own way
And they all speak the language of Apollinaire

Paris, November 1918

Dictated over the Telephone

IN THE FOREST OF BROCELIANDE (FAIRY OPERA)

Quite the opposite of Caruso
Opposite prompter, prompt side
When Cycca, the road tenor, sings
Only the hens don't hear him

KLAXON

Jazz has the jitters
And is jazzing the jitterbugs
What do I care about etymology
If this little Klaxon amuses me

LEAVING PARIS

Baby Cadum wishes you a safe and pleasant journey
Thanks, Michelin, for when I get back
Like the African fetishes in the bush
The gas pumps are naked

AMERICAN-STYLE PROVERB

Time is money
Yes, but Bugatti is twice as fast

Current Events

Plato does not grant city rights to the poet
Friends, close friends
You don't have customs anymore and no new habits yet
We must be free of the tyranny of newspapers
Literature
Poor life
Misplaced pride
Woman, the dance Nietzsche wanted to teach us to dance
Woman
But irony?

Continual coming and going
Procuring in the street
All men, all countries
And so you are no longer a burden
Can no longer be felt
Etc.

To the Heart
of the World

(Fragments)

Portrait of Cendrars by Modigliani, 1919.

This Paris sky is purer than a winter sky crisp with cold.
I've never seen nights as starry and leafy as this spring's
Where the trees along the boulevards are like shadows from the sky,
Foliage in the rivers mixed with elephant ears,
Leaves of sycamores, heavy chestnuts.

A water lily on the Seine, it's the flowing moon.
The Milky Way is swooning in the sky over Paris and embracing it
Wild and naked and lying back, its mouth is sucking Notre-Dame.
The Great Bear and the Little Bear are growling around Saint-Merry.
My amputated hand is shining in the constellation Orion.

In this cold, hard light, trembling and more than unreal,
Paris is like the cooled image of a plant
That reappears in its ashes. Sad simulacrum.
As straight as an arrow, the ageless houses and streets are just
Stone and iron heaped up in an unlikely desert.

Babylon and Thebaid are not deader, tonight, than the dead city of
    Paris,
Blue and green, ink and tar, its edges white with starlight.
Not a sound. No one. It's the heavy silence of war.
My eye goes from the pissoirs to the violet eye of the streetlamp.
It's the only bright spot I can drag my worries to.

And so I walk all the way across Paris every night
From Batignolles to the Latin Quarter, the way I would cross the Andes
Beneath the light of new stars, bigger and more alarming,
The Southern Cross more prodigious with every step you take toward it
    as you emerge from the Old World
On its new continent.

I'm the man who doesn't have a past. —Only my stump hurts.—
I've rented a hotel room to be completely alone with myself.

I have a brand-new wicker basket where my manuscripts are piling up.
I have no books or paintings, no aesthetic trinkets.

A newspaper is strewn across my table.
I work in my empty room, behind a cloudy mirror,
Bare feet on the red tiles, and play with balloons and a little toy
    trumpet:
I'm working on THE END OF THE WORLD.

Hôtel Notre-Dame

I went back to the Quarter
As I did when I was young
I think it's a waste of time
Because nothing in me recognizes
My dreams or my despair
What I did eighteen years old

Blocks of houses are torn down
The names of the streets are changed
Saint-Séverin is stripped bare
The place Maubert is now larger
And the rue Saint-Jacques has been widened
I think it all looks much better
New and older at the same time

And so by whisking my beard
Off and with very short hair
I bear the face of today
And my grandfather's skull

That's why I have no regrets
And I call to the wrecking crew
Knock my fucking childhood to the ground
My family and my habits
Put a train station in its place
Or leave an empty lot
Which will release my origin

I am not my father's son
And I love only my great-grandfather

I made a new name for myself
Visible as a blue and red
Billboard upon a scaffolding
Behind which new futures
Are being built

Suddenly the sirens wail and I run to my window.
Already the cannons are thundering over toward Aubervilliers.
The sky is starred with Jerry planes, shells, crisscrosses, rockets,
Cries, whistles, and melismas that melt and moan beneath the bridges.

The Seine is darker than an abyss, with its heavy barges that are
Long like the coffins of the tall Merovingian kings
Bedizened with stars that drown—in the depths—in the depths.
I turn and blow out the lamp and light a big cigar.

The people running for it in the street, thundering, still half-asleep,
Will take refuge in the basement of police headquarters that smells like
    powder and saltpeter.
The police commissioner's purple car meets the firechief's red car,
Magical and supple, wild and caressing, tigresses like shooting stars.

The sirens miaow and fall silent. The shindig is going full blast. Up
    there. It's insane.
At bay. Cracking and heavy silence. Then a shrill falling and dull
    vehemence of the bombs.
The crashing down of millions of tons. Flashes. Fire. Smoke. Flame.
Accordion of the 75s. Fits. Cries. Fall. Stridencies. Coughing.
    Collapses and cave-ins.

The sky is jumping with imperceptible winking
Pupils, multicolored streaks, that cut, that divide, that revive the
    melodious propellers.
A searchlight suddenly hits the billboard of Baby Cadum
Then leaps into the sky and bores a milky hole in it like a baby bottle.

I get my hat and now I go down into the dark streets.
Here are the portly old houses that lean against each other like old men.
The chimneys and weathervanes all point to the sky with their fingers.
I walk up the rue Saint-Jacques, shoulders jammed into my pockets.

Here's the Sorbonne and its tower, the church, the Lycée Louis-le-
    Grand.
A little further up I go in and ask a butcher for a light.
I light up a new cigar and we exchange a smile.
He has a nice tattoo, a name, a rose, and a heart with a dagger through it.

It's a name I know well: it's my mother's.
I rush out into the street. I'm facing the building.
Stabbed heart—first point of impact—
And more beautiful than your naked torso, handsome butcher—
The building where I was born.

My Mother's Belly

It's my first residence
It was all round
Often I imagine
What I was like . . .

My feet on your heart mama
My knees against your liver
My hand clutching at the canal
That ended at your womb

My back twisted in a spiral
My ears full my eyes empty
Everything shriveled tight
My head almost outside your body

My skull at your orifice
I enjoyed your health
The warmth of your blood
Daddy's embraces

Often a hybrid fire
Electrified my darkness
A thump on my skull relaxed me
And I kicked against your heart

The big muscle of your vagina
Then squeezed tight again
I gave in sorrowfully
And you flooded me with your blood

My forehead is still bumpy
From these my father's thumps

Why must we always give in
Half strangled like that?

If I could have opened my mouth
I would have bitten you
If I'd been able to talk
I would have said:
Shit, I don't want to live!

I stand on the sidewalk across the street and look at the building for a
   long time.
It's the building where the *Romance of the Rose* was written.
216 rue Saint-Jacques, Hôtel des Etrangers.
At 218 is the sign of a first-class midwife.

Since she was full she sent my mother to the hotel next door to get
   some sleep and to have me.
Five days later I was taking the packet-boat at Brindisi. My mother
   going to rejoin my father in Egypt.
(The packet-boat—the packet, the courier, the mail-boat; they still say
   "the Indian mail" and they still use the term "long courier" for the
   three-masters that go around Cape Horn.)

Am I pelagic like my Egyptian nanny or Swiss like my father
Or Italian, French, Scottish, and Flemish like my grandfather or
   whichever of my great-grandfathers was an organ-maker in the
   Rhineland and in Burgundy, or that other one
The best biographer of Rubens?
And there was yet another one who used to sing at the Chat Noir, Erik
   Satie told me.
However, I'm the first one with my name since I'm the one who made
   it up.

I have Lavater's blood in my veins and the blood of Euler,
That famous mathematician called to the Russian court by Catherine II
   and who, gone blind at 86, dictated to his grandson Hans, age 12,
A treatise on algebra that reads like a novel
To prove to himself that if he had lost his sight, he had lost neither his
   lucidity
Nor his logic.

I stand on the sidewalk across the street and I look at the tall, narrow
   building facing me

Which is reflected deep down inside me, like blood. Smoke rises from
   the chimneys.
It's dark. Never have I seen such a starry night. The bombs are bursting.
   The bursts rain down.
The gutted pavement exposes the Etruscan graveyard laid out over the
   mammoths' graveyard exposed
On the construction site where they're building the Prince of Monaco's
   Oceanographic Institute
Against whose fence I step back and stagger and glue myself
A new poster on the old defaced ones.

O rue Saint-Jacques! Old slit of Paris, shaped like a vagina and whose
   life I'd like to have made a movie of, shown on the silver screen its
   formation, the grouping, the radiating out from around its hub,
Notre-Dame,
Deep old slit, long walk
From the Porte des Flandres to Montrouge,
O rue Saint-Jacques! Yes, I stagger, but I'm not mortally wounded, not
   even touched.

If I stagger it's because that building scares me and I enter
—Second point of impact—this Hôtel des Etrangers, where many times
   I've rented a room for the day
Or the night, mama,
With a woman of color, with a painted girl, from the d'Harcourt or the
   Boul' Mich'

And where I stayed for a month with that American girl who was
   supposed to go back to her family in New York
And who let boat after boat sail away
Because she was naked in my room and dancing in front of the fire
   burning
In my fireplace and we had fun making love every time the corner
   florist brought us a basket of Parma violets
And we read together, going all the way, *The Physiology of Love* or *The
   Mystic Latin* by Remy de Gourmont.

But tonight, mama, I go in alone.

Hôtel des Etrangers

What Love is my love's name?
One enters One finds a washstand a hair-
Pin forgotten on the corner
Or on the marble
Mantle or fallen
Into a groove in the floor
Behind the chest of drawers
But the name Love what is my love's name
In the mirror?

.   .   .   .

Paris, 1917

POÉSIES COMPLÈTES

Les Pâques à New-York

A *Agnès*

Flecte ramos, arbor alta, tensa laxa viscera
Et rigor lentescat ille quem dedit nativitas
Ut superni membra Regis miti tendas stipite . . .

        FORTUNAT.—*Pange lingua.*

Fléchis tes branches, arbre géant, relâche un peu la tension des viscères,
Et que ta rigueur naturelle s'alentisse,
N'écartèle pas si rudement les membres du Roi supérieur . . .

        REMY DE GOURMONT.—*Le Latin Mystique.*

Seigneur, c'est aujourd'hui le jour de votre Nom,
J'ai lu dans un vieux livre la geste de votre Passion,

Et votre angoisse et vos efforts et vos bonnes paroles
Qui pleurent dans le livre, doucement monotones.

Un moine d'un vieux temps me parle de votre mort.
Il traçait votre histoire avec des lettres d'or

Dans un missel, posé sur ses genoux.
Il travaillait pieusement en s'inspirant de Vous.

A l'abri de l'autel, assis dans sa robe blanche,
Il travaillait lentement du lundi au dimanche.

Les heures s'arrêtaient au seuil de son retrait.
Lui, s'oubliait, penché sur votre portrait.

A vêpres, quand les cloches psalmodiaient dans la tour,
Le bon frère ne savait si c'était son amour

Ou si c'était le Vôtre, Seigneur, ou votre Père
Qui battait à grands coups les portes du monastère.

Je suis comme ce bon moine, ce soir, je suis inquiet.
Dans la chambre à côté, un être triste et muet

Attend derrière la porte, attend que je l'appelle!
C'est Vous, c'est Dieu, c'est moi,—c'est l'Éternel.

Je ne Vous ai pas connu alors—ni maintenant.
Je n'ai jamais prié quand j'étais un petit enfant.

Ce soir pourtant je pense à Vous avec effroi.
Mon âme est une veuve en deuil au pied de votre Croix;

Mon âme est une veuve en noir,—c'est votre Mère
Sans larme et sans espoir, comme l'a peinte Carrière.

Je connais tous les Christs qui pendent dans les musées;
Mais Vous marchez, Seigneur, ce soir à mes côtés.

Je descends à grands pas vers le bas de la ville,
Le dos voûté, le cœur ridé, l'esprit fébrile.

Votre flanc grand-ouvert est comme un grand soleil
Et vos mains tout autour palpitent d'étincelles.

Les vitres des maisons sont toutes pleines de sang
Et les femmes, derrière, sont comme des fleurs de sang,

D'étranges mauvaises fleurs flétries, des orchidées,
Calices renversés ouverts sous vos trois plaies.

Votre sang recueilli, elles ne l'ont jamais bu.
Elles ont du rouge aux lèvres et des dentelles au cul.

Les fleurs de la Passion sont blanches, comme des cierges,
Ce sont les plus douces fleurs au Jardin de la Bonne Vierge.

C'est à cette heure-ci, c'est vers la neuvième heure,
Que votre Tête, Seigneur, tomba sur votre Cœur.

Je suis assis au bord de l'océan
Et je me remémore un cantique allemand,

Où il est dit, avec des mots très doux, très simples, très purs,
La beauté de votre Face dans la torture.

Dans une église, à Sienne, dans un caveau,
J'ai vu la même Face, au mur, sous un rideau.

Et dans un ermitage, à Bourrié-Wladislasz,
Elle est bossuée d'or dans une châsse.

De troubles cabochons sont à la place des yeux
Et des paysans baisent à genoux Vos yeux.

Sur le mouchoir de Véronique Elle est empreinte
Et c'est pourquoi Sainte Véronique est votre sainte.

C'est la meilleure relique promenée par les champs,
Elle guérit tous les malades, tous les méchants.

Elle fait encore mille et mille autres miracles,
Mais je n'ai jamais assisté à ce spectacle.

Peut-être que la foi me manque, Seigneur, et la bonté
Pour voir ce rayonnement de votre Beauté.

Pourtant, Seigneur, j'ai fait un périlleux voyage
Pour contempler dans un béryl l'intaille de votre image.

Faites, Seigneur, que mon visage appuyé dans les mains
Y laisse tomber le masque d'angoisse qui m'étreint.

Faites, Seigneur, que mes deux mains appuyées sur ma bouche
N'y lèchent pas l'écume d'un désespoir farouche.

Je suis triste et malade. Peut-être à cause de Vous,
Peut-être à cause d'un autre, peut-être à cause de Vous.

Seigneur, la foule des pauvres pour qui vous fîtes le Sacrifice
Est ici, parquée, tassée, comme du bétail, dans les hospices.

D'immenses bateaux noirs viennent des horizons
Et les débarquent, pêle-mêle, sur les pontons.

Il y a des Italiens, des Grecs, des Espagnols,
Des Russes, des Bulgares, des Persans, des Mongols.

Ce sont des bêtes de cirque qui sautent les méridiens.
On leur jette un morceau de viande noire, comme à des chiens.

C'est leur bonheur à eux que cette sale pitance.
Seigneur, ayez pitié des peuples en souffrance.

Seigneur dans les ghettos grouille la tourbe des Juifs.
Ils viennent de Pologne et sont tous fugitifs.

Je le sais bien, ils t'ont fait ton Procès;
Mais je t'assure, ils ne sont pas tout à fait mauvais.

Ils sont dans des boutiques sous des lampes de cuivre,
Vendent des vieux habits, des armes et des livres.

Rembrandt aimait beaucoup les peindre dans leurs défroques.
Moi, j'ai, cé soir, marchandé un microscope.

Hélas! Seigneur, Vous ne serez plus là, après Pâques!
Seigneur, ayez pitié des Juifs dans les baraques.

Seigneur, les humbles femmes qui vous accompagnèrent à Golgotha,
Se cachent. Au fond des bouges, sur d'immondes sophas,

Elles sont polluées par la misère des hommes.
Des chiens leur ont rongé les os, et dans le rhum

Elles cachent leur vice endurci qui s'écaille.
Seigneur, quand une de ces femme me parle, je défaille.

Je voudrais être Vous pour aimer les prostituées.
Seigneur, ayez pitié des prostituées.

Seigneur, je suis dans le quartier des bons voleurs,
Des vagabonds, des va-nu-pied, des receleurs.

Je pense aux deux larrons qui étaient avec vous à la Potence,
Je sais que vous daignez sourire à leur malchance.

Seigneur, l'un voudrait une corde avec un nœud au bout,
Mais ça n'est pas gratis, la corde, ça coûte vingt sous.

Il raisonnait comme un philosophe, ce vieux bandit.
Je lui ai donné de l'opium pour qu'il aille plus vite en paradis.

Je pense aussi aux musiciens des rues,
Au violoniste aveugle, au manchot qui tourne l'orgue de Barbarie,

A la chanteuse au chapeau de paille avec des roses de papier;
Je sais que ce sont eux qui chantent durant l'éternité.

Seigneur, faites-leur l'aumône, autre que de la lueur des becs de gaz,
Seigneur, faites-leur l'aumône de gros sous ici-bas.

Seigneur, quand vous mourûtes, le rideau se fendit,
Ce que l'on vit derrière, personne ne l'a dit.

La rue est dans la nuit comme une déchirure,
Pleine d'or et de sang, de feu et d'épluchures.

Ceux que vous aviez chassé du temple avec votre fouet,
Flagellent les passants d'une poignée de méfaits.

L'Etoile qui disparut alors du tabernacle,
Brûle sur les murs dans la lumière crue des spectacles.

Seigneur, la Banque illuminée est comme un coffre-fort,
Où s'est coagulé le Sang de votre mort.

Les rues se font désertes et deviennent plus noires.
Je chancelle comme un homme ivre sur les trottoirs.

J'ai peur des grands pans d'ombre que les maisons projettent.
J'ai peur. Quelqu'un me suit. Je n'ose tourner la tête.

Un pas clopin-clopant saute de plus en plus près.
J'ai peur. J'ai le vertige. Et je m'arrête exprès.

Un effroyable drôle m'a jeté un regard
Aigu, puis a passé, mauvais, comme un poignard.

Seigneur, rien n'a changé depuis que vous n'êtes plus Roi.
Le Mal s'est fait une béquille de votre Croix.

Je descends les mauvaises marches d'un café
Et me voici, assis, devant un verre de thé.

Je suis chez des Chinois, qui comme avec le dos
Sourient, se penchent et sont polis comme des magots.

La boutique est petite, badigeonnée de rouge
Et de curieux chromos sont encadrés dans du bambou.

Ho-Kousaï a peint les cent aspects d'une montagne.
Que serait votre Face peinte par un Chinois? . . .

Cette dernière idée, Seigneur, m'a d'abord fait sourire.
Je vous voyais en raccourci dans votre martyre.

Mais le peintre, pourtant, aurait peint votre tourment
Avec plus de cruauté que nos peintres d'Occident.

Des lames contournées auraient scié vos chairs,
Des pinces et des peignes auraient strié vos nerfs,

On vous aurait passé le col dans un carcan,
On vous aurait arraché les ongles et les dents,

D'immenses dragons noirs se seraient jetés sur Vous,
Et vous auraient soufflé des flammes dans le cou,

On vous aurait arraché la langue et les yeux,
On vous aurait empalé sur un pieu.

Ainsi, Seigneur, vous auriez souffert toute l'infamie,
Car il n'y a pas de plus cruelle posture.

Ensuite, on vous aurait forjeté aux pourceaux
Qui vous auraient rongé le ventre et les boyaux.

Je suis seul à présent, les autres sont sortis,
Je me suis étendu sur un banc contre le mur.

J'aurais voulu entrer, Seigneur, dans une église;
Mais il n'y a pas de cloches, Seigneur, dans cette ville.

Je pense aux cloches tues:—où sont les cloches anciennes?
Où sont les litanies et les douces antiennes?

Où sont les longs offices et où les beaux cantiques?
Où sont les liturgies et les musiques?

Où sont tes fiers prélats, Seigneur, où tes nonnains?
Où l'aube blanche, l'amict des Saintes et des Saints?

La joie du Paradis se noie dans la poussière,
Les feux mystiques ne rutilent plus dans les verrières.

L'aube tarde à venir, et dans le bouge étroit
Des ombres crucifiées agonisent aux parois.

C'est comme un Golgotha de nuit dans un miroir
Que l'on voit trembloter en rouge sur du noir.

La fumée, sous la lampe, est comme un linge déteint
Qui tourne, entortillé, tout autour de vos reins.

Par au-dessus, la lampe pâle est suspendue,
Comme votre Tête, triste et morte et exsangue.

Des reflets insolites palpitent sur les vitres . . .
J'ai peur,—et je suis triste, Seigneur, d'être si triste.

«*Dic nobis, Maria, quid vidisti in via?*»
—La lumière frissonner, humble dans le matin.

«*Dic nobis, Maria, quid vidisti in via?*»
—Des blancheurs éperdues palpiter comme des mains.

«*Dic nobis, Maria, quid vidisti in via?*»
—L'augure du printemps tressaillir dans mon sein.

Seigneur, l'aube a glissé froide comme un suaire
Et a mis tout à nu les gratte-ciel dans les airs.

Déjà un bruit immense retentit sur la ville.
Déjà les trains bondissent, grondent et défilent.

Les métropolitains roulent et tonnent sous terre.
Les ponts sont secoués par les chemins de fer.

La cité tremble. Des cris, du feu et des fumées,
Des sirènes à vapeur rauquent comme des huées.

Une foule enfiévrée par les sueurs de l'or
Se bouscule et s'engouffre dans de longs corridors.

Trouble, dans le fouillis empanaché des toits,
Le soleil, c'est votre Face souillée par les crachats.

Seigneur, je rentre fatigué, seul et très morne . . .
Ma chambre est nue comme un tombeau . . .

Seigneur, je suis tout seul et j'ai la fièvre . . .
Mon lit est froid comme un cercueil . . .

Seigneur, je ferme les yeux et je claque des dents . . .
Je suis trop seul. J'ai froid. Je vous appelle . . .

Cent mille toupies tournoient devant mes yeux . . .
Non, cent mille femmes . . . Non, cent mille violoncelles . . .

Je pense, Seigneur, à mes heures malheureuses . . .
Je pense, Seigneur, à mes heures en allées . . .

Je ne pense plus à Vous. Je ne pense plus à Vous.

New-York, Avril 1912

Prose du Transsibérien
et de la Petite Jeanne de France

Dédiée aux musiciens

En ce temps-là j'étais en mon adolescence
J'avais à peine seize ans et je ne me souvenais déjà plus de mon enfance
J'étais à 16.000 lieues du lieu de ma naissance
J'étais à Moscou, dans la ville des mille et trois clochers et des sept gares
Et je n'avais pas assez des sept gares et des mille et trois tours
Car mon adolescence était alors si ardente et si folle
Que mon cœur, tour à tour, brûlait comme le temple d'Ephèse ou comme la Place
    Rouge de Moscou
Quand le soleil se couche.
Et mes yeux éclairaient des voies anciennes.
Et j'étais déjà si mauvais poète
Que je ne savais pas aller jusqu'au bout.

Le Kremlin était comme un immense gâteau tartare
Croustillé d'or
Avec les grandes amandes des cathédrales toutes blanches
Et l'or mielleux des cloches . . .
Un vieux moine me lisait la légende de Novgorode
J'avais soif
Et je déchiffrais des caractères cunéiformes
Puis, tout à coup, les pigeons du Saint-Esprit s'envolaient sur la place
Et mes mains s'envolaient aussi avec des bruissements d'albatros
Et ceci, c'était les dernières réminiscences du dernier jour
Du tout dernier voyage
Et de la mer.

Pourtant, j'étais fort mauvais poète.
Je ne savais pas aller jusqu'au bout.
J'avais faim
Et tous les jours et toutes les femmes dans les cafés et tous les verres
J'aurais voulu les boire et les casser
Et toutes les vitrines et toutes les rues
Et toutes les maisons et toutes les vies
Et toutes les roues des fiacres qui tournaient en tourbillon sur les mauvais pavés
J'aurais voulu les plonger dans une fournaise de glaives
Et j'aurais voulu broyer tous les os
Et arracher toutes les langues
Et liquéfier tous ces grands corps étranges et nus sous les vêtements qui m'affolent . . .
Je pressentais la venue du grand Christ rouge de la révolution russe . . .

Et le soleil était une mauvaise plaie
Qui s'ouvrait comme un brasier.

En ce temps-là j'étais en mon adolescence
J'avais à peine seize ans et je ne me souvenais déjà plus de ma naissance
J'étais à Moscou, où je voulais me nourrir de flammes
Et je n'avais pas assez des tours et des gares que constellaient mes yeux
En Sibérie tonnait le canon, c'était la guerre
La faim le froid la peste le choléra
Et les eaux limoneuses de l'Amour charriaient des millions de charognes
Dans toutes les gares je voyais partir tous les derniers trains
Personne ne pouvait plus partir car on ne délivrait plus de billets
Et les soldats qui s'en allaient auraient bien voulu rester . . .
Un vieux moine me chantait la légende de Novgorode.

Moi, le mauvais poète qui ne voulais aller nulle part, je pouvais aller partout
Et aussi les marchands avaient encore assez d'argent
Pour aller tenter faire fortune.
Leur train partait tous les vendredis matin.
On disait qu'il y avait beaucoup de morts.
L'un emportait cent caisses de réveils et de coucous de la Forêt-Noire
Un autre, des boîtes à chapeaux, des cylindres et un assortiment de tire-bouchon de
        Sheffield
Un autre, des cercueils de Malmoë remplis de boîtes de conserve et de sardines à l'huile
Puis il y avait beaucoup de femmes
Des femmes des entre-jambes à louer qui pouvaient aussi servir
Des cercueils
Elles étaient toutes patentées
On disait qu'il y avait beaucoup de morts là-bas
Elles voyageaient à prix réduits
Et avaient toutes un compte-courant à la banque.

Or, un vendredi matin, ce fut aussi mon tour
On était en décembre
Et je partis moi aussi pour accompagner le voyageur en bijouterie qui se rendait à
        Kharbine
Nous avions deux coupés dans l'express et 34 coffres de joaillerie de Pforzheim
De la camelote allemande «*Made in Germany*»
Il m'avait habillé de neuf, et en montant dans le train, j'avais perdu un bouton
—Je m'en souviens, je m'en souviens, j'y ai souvent pensé depuis—
Je couchais sur les coffres et j'étais tout heureux de pouvoir jouer avec le browning
        nickelé qu'il m'avait aussi donné

J'étais très heureux insouciant
Je croyais jouer aux brigands
Nous avions volé le trésor de Golconde
Et nous allions, grâce au transsibérien, le cacher de l'autre côté du monde
Je devais le défendre contre les voleurs de l'Oural qui avaient attaqué les saltimbanques
        de Jules Verne
Contre les Khoungouzes, les boxers de la Chine

Et les enragés petits mongols du Grand-Lama
Alibaba et les quarante voleurs
Et les fidèles du terrible Vieux de la montagne
Et surtout, contre les plus modernes
Les rats d'hôtel
Et les spécialistes des express internationaux.

Et pourtant, et pourtant
J'étais triste comme un enfant
Les rythmes du train
La *« moëlle chemin-de-fer »* des psychiatres américains
Le bruit des portes des voix des essieux grinçant sur les rails congelés
Le ferlin d'or de mon avenir
Mon browning le piano et les jurons des joueurs de cartes dans le compartiment
    d'à côté
L'épatante présence de Jeanne
L'homme aux lunettes bleues qui se promenait nerveusement dans le couloir et qui me
    regardait en passant
Froissis de femmes
Et le sifflement de la vapeur
Et le bruit éternel des roues en folie dans les ornières du ciel
Les vitres sont givrées
Pas de nature!
Et derrière, les plaines sibériennes le ciel bas et les grandes ombres des Taciturnes qui
    montent et qui descendent
Je suis couché dans un plaid
Bariolé
Comme ma vie
Et ma vie ne me tient pas plus chaud que ce châle
Ecossais
Et l'Europe tout entière aperçue au coupe-vent d'un express à toute vapeur
N'est pas plus riche que ma vie
Ma pauvre vie
Ce châle
Effiloché sur des coffres remplis d'or
Avec lesquels je roule
Que je rêve
Que je fume
Et la seule flamme de l'univers
Est une pauvre pensée . . .

Du fond de mon cœur des larmes me viennent
Si je pense, Amour, à ma maîtresse;
Elle n'est qu'une enfant, que je trouvai ainsi
Pâle, immaculée, au fond d'un bordel.

Ce n'est qu'une enfant, blonde, rieuse et triste,
Elle ne sourit pas et ne pleure jamais;
Mais au fond de ses yeux, quand elle vous y laisse boire,
Tremble un doux lys d'argent, la fleur du poète.

Elle est douce et muette, sans aucun reproche,
Avec un long tressaillement à votre approche;
Mais quand moi je lui viens, de-ci, de-là, de fête,
Elle fait un pas, puis ferme les yeux—et fait un pas.

Car elle est mon amour, et les autres femmes
N'ont que des robes d'or sur de grands corps de flammes,
Ma pauvre amie est si esseulée,
Elle est toute nue, n'a pas de corps—elle est trop pauvre.

Elle n'est qu'une fleur candide, fluette,
La fleur du poète, un pauvre lys d'argent,
Tout froid, tout seul, et déjà si fané
Que les larmes me viennent si je pense à son cœur.

Et cette nuit est pareille à cent mille autres quand un train file dans la nuit
—Les comètes tombent—
Et que l'homme et la femme, même jeunes, s'amusent à faire l'amour.

Le ciel est comme la tente déchirée d'un cirque pauvre dans un petit village de pêcheurs
En Flandres
Le soleil est un fumeux quinquet
Et tout au haut d'un trapèze une femme fait la lune.
La clarinette le piston une flûte aigre et un mauvais tambour
Et voici mon berceau
Mon berceau
Il était toujours près du piano quand ma mère comme Madame Bovary jouait les
        sonates de Beethoven
J'ai passé mon enfance dans les jardins suspendus de Babylone
Et l'école buissonnière, dans les gares devant les trains en partance
Maintenant, j'ai fait courir tous les trains derrière moi
Bâle-Tombouctou
J'ai aussi joué aux courses à Auteuil et à Longchamp
Paris-New-York
Maintenant, j'ai fait courir tous les trains tout le long de ma vie
Madrid-Stockholm
Et j'ai perdu tous mes paris
Il n'y a plus que la Patagonie, la Patagonie, qui convienne à mon immense tristesse, la
        Patagonie et un voyage dans les mers du Sud
Je suis en route
J'ai toujours été en route
Je suis en route avec la petite Jehanne de France
Le train fait un saut périlleux et retombe sur toutes ses roues
Le train retombe sur ses roues
Le train retombe toujours sur toutes ses roues

«Blaise, dis, sommes-nous bien loin de Montmartre?»

Nous sommes loin, Jeanne, tu roules depuis sept jours
Tu es loin de Montmartre, de la Butte qui t'a nourrie du Sacré-Cœur contre lequel tu
        t'es blottie

Paris a disparu et son énorme flambée
Il n'y a plus que les cendres continues
La pluie qui tombe
La tourbe qui se gonfle
La Sibérie qui tourne
Les lourdes nappes de neige qui remontent
Et le grelot de la folie qui grelotte comme un dernier désir dans l'air bleu
Le train palpite au cœur des horizons plombés
Et ton chagrin ricane...

«Dis, Blaise, sommes-nous bien loin de Montmartre?»

Les inquiétudes
Oublie les inquiétudes
Toutes les gares lézardées obliques sur la route
Les fils téléphoniques auxquels elles pendent
Les poteaux grimaçants qui gesticulent et les étranglent
Le monde s'étire s'allonge et se retire comme un harmonica qu'une main sadique
        tourmente
Dans les déchirures du ciel, les locomotives en furie
S'enfuient
Et dans les trous,
Les roues vertigineuses les bouches les voix
Et les chiens du malheur qui aboient à nos trousses
Les démons sont déchaînés
Ferrailles
Tout est un faux accord
Le broun-roun-roun des roues
Chocs
Rebondissements
Nous sommes un orage sous le crâne d'un sourd...

«Dis, Blaise, sommes-nous bien loin de Montmartre?»

Mais oui, tu m'énerves, tu le sais bien, nous sommes bien loin
La folie surchauffée beugle dans la locomotive
La peste le choléra se lèvent comme des braises ardentes sur notre route
Nous disparaissons dans la guerre en plein dans un tunnel
La faim, la putain, se cramponne aux nuages en débandade et fiente des batailles en tas
        puants de morts
Fais comme elle, fais ton métier...

«Dis, Blaise, sommes-nous bien loin de Montmartre?»

Oui, nous le sommes, nous le sommes
Tous les boucs émissaires ont crevé dans ce désert
Entends les clochettes de ce troupeau galeux
Tomsk Tchéliabinsk Kainsk Obi Taïchet Verkné-Oudinsk Kourgane Samara Pensa-
        Touloune
La mort en Mandchourie
Est notre débarcadère est notre dernier repaire

Ce voyage est terrible
Hier matin
Ivan Oulitch avait les cheveux blancs
Et Kolia Nicolaï Ivanovitch se ronge les doigts depuis quinze jours . . .
Fais comme elles la Mort la Famine fais ton métier
Ça coûte cent sous, en transsibérien, ça coûte cent roubles
Enfièvre les banquettes et rougoie sous la table
Le diable est au piano
Ses doigts noueux excitent toutes les femmes
La Nature
Les Gouges
Fais ton métier
Jusqu'à Kharbine . . .

«Dis, Blaise, sommes-nous bien loin de Montmartre?»

Non mais . . . fiche-moi la paix . . . laisse-moi tranquille
Tu as les hanches angulaires
Ton ventre est aigre et tu as la chaude-pisse
C'est tout ce que Paris a mis dans ton giron
C'est aussi un peu d'âme . . . car tu es malheureuse
J'ai pitié j'ai pitié viens vers moi sur mon cœur
Les roues sont les moulins à vent du pays de Cocagne
Et les moulins à vent sont les béquilles qu'un mendiant fait tournoyer
Nous sommes les culs-de-jatte de l'espace
Nous roulons sur nos quatre plaies
On nous a rogné les ailes
Les ailes de nos sept péchés
Et tous les trains sont les bilboquets du diable
Basse-cour
Le monde moderne
La vitesse n'y peut mais
Le monde moderne
Les lointains sont par trop loin
Et au bout du voyage c'est terrible d'être un homme avec une femme . . .

«Blaise, dis, sommes-nous bien loin de Montmartre?»

J'ai pitié j'ai pitié viens vers moi je vais te conter une histoire
Viens dans mon lit
Viens sur mon cœur
Je vais te conter une histoire . . .

Oh viens! viens!

Aux Fidji règne l'éternel printemps
La paresse
L'amour pâme les couples dans l'herbe haute et la chaude syphilis rôde sous les
    bananiers
Viens dans les îles perdues du Pacifique!
Elles ont nom du Phénix, des Marquises

Bornéo et Java
Et Célèbes à la forme d'un chat.

Nous ne pouvons pas aller au Japon
Viens au Mexique!
Sur ses hauts plateaux les tulipiers fleurissent
Les lianes tentaculaires sont la chevelure du soleil
On dirait la palette et les pinceaux d'un peintre
Des couleurs étourdissantes comme des gongs,
Rousseau y a été
Il y a ébloui sa vie
C'est le pays des oiseaux
L'oiseau du paradis, l'oiseau-lyre
Le toucan l'oiseau moqueur
Et le colibri niche au cœur des lys noirs
Viens!
Nous nous aimerons dans les ruines majestueuses d'un temple aztèque
Tu seras mon idole
Une idole bariolée enfantine un peu laide et bizarrement étrange
Oh viens!

Si tu veux nous irons en aéroplane et nous survolerons le pays des mille lacs,
Les nuits y sont démesurément longues
L'ancêtre préhistorique aura peur de mon moteur
J'atterrirai
Et je construirai un hangar pour mon avion avec les os fossiles de mammouth
Le feu primitif réchauffera notre pauvre amour
Samowar
Et nous nous aimerons bien bourgeoisement près du pôle
Oh viens!

Jeanne Jeannette Ninette nini ninon nichon
Mimi mamour ma poupoule mon Pérou
Dodo dondon
Carotte ma crotte
Chouchou p'tit-cœur
Cocotte
Chérie p'tite chèvre
Mon p'tit-péché mignon
Concon
Coucou
Elle dort.

Elle dort
Et de toutes les heures du monde elle n'en a pas gobé une seule
Tous les visages entrevus dans les gares
Toutes les horloges
L'heure de Paris l'heure de Berlin l'heure de Saint-Pétersbourg et l'heure de toutes
    les gares
Et à Oufa, le visage ensanglanté du canonnier
Et le cadran bêtement lumineux de Grodno

Et l'avance perpétuelle du train
Tous les matins on met les montres à l'heure
Le train avance et le soleil retarde
Rien n'y fait, j'entends les cloches sonores
Le gros bourdon de Notre-Dame
La cloche aigrelette du Louvre qui sonna la Barthélemy
Les carillons rouillés de Bruges-la-Morte
Les sonneries électriques de la bibliothèque de New-York
Les campanes de Venise
Et les cloches de Moscou, l'horloge de la Porte-Rouge qui me comptait les heures
    quand j'étais dans un bureau
Et mes souvenirs
Le train tonne sur les plaques tournantes
Le train roule
Un gramophone grasseye une marche tzigane
Et le monde, comme l'horloge du quartier juif de Prague, tourne éperdument
    à rebours.

Effeuille la rose des vents
Voici que bruissent les orages déchaînés
Les trains roulent en tourbillon sur les réseaux enchevêtrés
Bilboquets diaboliques
Il y a des trains qui ne se rencontrent jamais
D'autres se perdent en route
Les chefs de gare jouent aux échecs
Tric-trac
Billard
Caramboles
Paraboles
La voie ferrée est une nouvelle géométrie
Syracuse
Archimède
Et les soldats qui l'égorgèrent
Et les galères
Et les vaisseaux
Et les engins prodigieux qu'il inventa
Et toutes les tueries
L'histoire antique
L'histoire moderne
Les tourbillons
Les naufrages
Même celui du Titanic que j'ai lu dans le journal
Autant d'images-associations que je ne peux pas développer dans mes vers
Car je suis encore fort mauvais poète
Car l'univers me déborde
Car j'ai négligé de m'assurer contre les accidents de chemin de fer
Car je ne sais pas aller jusqu'au bout
Et j'ai peur.

J'ai peur
Je ne sais pas aller jusqu'au bout

Comme mon ami Chagall je pourrais faire une série de tableaux déments
Mais je n'ai pas pris de notes en voyage
«Pardonnez-moi mon ignorance
«Pardonnez-moi de ne plus connaître l'ancien jeu des vers»
Comme dit Guillaume Apollinaire
Tout ce qui concerne la guerre on peut le lire dans les *Mémoires de Kouropatkine*
Ou dans les journaux japonais qui sont aussi cruellement illustrés
A quoi bon me documenter
Je m'abandonne
Aux sursauts de ma mémoire . . .

A partir d'Irkoutsk le voyage devint beaucoup trop lent
Beaucoup trop long
Nous étions dans le premier train qui contournait le lac Baïkal
On avait orné la locomotive de drapeaux et de lampions
Et nous avions quitté la gare aux accents tristes de l'hymne au Tsar.
Si j'étais peintre je déverserais beaucoup de rouge, beaucoup de jaune sur la fin de
    ce voyage
Car je crois bien que nous étions tous un peu fous
Et qu'un délire immense ensanglantait les faces énervées de mes compagnons de voyage
Comme nous approchions de la Mongolie
Qui ronflait comme un incendie.
Le train avait ralenti son allure
Et je percevais dans le grincement perpétuel des roues
Les accents fous et les sanglots
D'une éternelle liturgie

J'ai vu
J'ai vu les trains silencieux les trains noirs qui revenaient de l'Extrême-Orient et qui
    passaient en fantômes
Et mon œil, comme le fanal d'arrière, court encore derrière ces trains
A Talga 100.000 blessés agonisaient faute de soins
J'ai visité les hôpitaux de Krasnoïarsk
Et à Khilok nous avons croisé un long convoi de soldats fous
J'ai vu dans les lazarets des plaies béantes des blessures qui saignaient à pleines orgues
Et les membres amputés dansaient autour ou s'envolaient dans l'air rauque
L'incendie était sur toutes les faces dans tous les cœurs
Des doigts idiots tambourinaient sur toutes les vitres
Et sous la pression de la peur les regards crevaient comme des abcès
Dans toutes les gares on brûlait tous les wagons
Et j'ai vu
J'ai vu des trains de 60 locomotives qui s'enfuyaient à toute vapeur pourchassées par les
    horizons en rut et des bandes de corbeaux qui s'envolaient désespérément après
Disparaître
Dans la direction de Port-Arthur.

A Tchita nous eûmes quelques jours de répit
Arrêt de cinq jours vu l'encombrement de la voie
Nous les passâmes chez Monsieur Iankéléwitch qui voulait me donner sa fille unique
    en mariage
Puis le train repartit.

Maintenant c'était moi qui avais pris place au piano et j'avais mal aux dents
Je revois quand je veux cet intérieur si calme le magasin et les yeux de la fille qui venait
   le soir dans mon lit
Moussorgsky
Et les lieder de Hugo Wolf
Et les sables du Gobi
Et à Khaïlar une caravane de chameaux blancs
Je crois bien que j'étais ivre durant plus de 500 kilomètres
Moi j'étais au piano et c'est tout ce que je vis
Quand on voyage on devrait fermer les yeux
Dormir
J'aurais tant voulu dormir
Je reconnais tous les pays les yeux fermés à leur odeur
Et je reconnais tous les trains au bruit qu'ils font
Les trains d'Europe sont à quatre temps tandis que ceux d'Asie sont à cinq ou sept temps
D'autres vont en sourdine sont des berceuses
Et il y en a qui dans le bruit monotone des roues me rappellent la prose lourde de
   Maeterlinck
J'ai déchiffré tous les textes confus des roues et j'ai rassemblé les éléments épars d'une
   violente beauté
Que je possède
Et qui me force

Tsitsikar et Kharbine
Je ne vais pas plus loin
C'est la dernière station
Je débarquai à Kharbine comme on venait de mettre le feu aux bureaux de la
   Croix-Rouge.

O Paris
Grand foyer chaleureux avec les tisons entre-croisés de tes rues et tes vieilles maisons
   qui se penchent au-dessus et se réchauffent
Comme des aïeules
Et voici des affiches, du rouge du vert multicolores comme mon passé bref du jaune
Jaune la fière couleur des romans de la France à l'étranger.
J'aime me frotter dans les grandes villes aux autobus en marche
Ceux de la ligne Saint-Germain-Montmartre m'emportent à l'assaut de la Butte
Les moteurs beuglent comme les taureaux d'or
Les vaches du crépuscule broutent le Sacré-Cœur
O Paris
Gare centrale débarcadère des volontés carrefour des inquiétudes
Seuls les marchands de couleur ont encore un peu de lumière sur leur porte
La Compagnie Internationale des Wagons-Lits et des Grands Express Européens m'a
   envoyé son prospectus
C'est la plus belle église du monde
J'ai des amis qui m'entourent comme des garde-fous
Ils ont peur quand je pars que je ne revienne plus
Toutes les femmes que j'ai rencontrées se dressent aux horizons
Avec les gestes piteux et les regards tristes des sémaphores sous la pluie
Bella, Agnès, Catherine et la mère de mon fils en Italie
Et celle, la mère de mon amour en Amérique

Il y a des cris de sirène qui me déchirent l'âme
Là-bas en Mandchourie un ventre tressaille encore comme dans un accouchement
Je voudrais
Je voudrais n'avoir jamais fait mes voyages
Ce soir un grand amour me tourmente
Et malgré moi je pense à la petite Jehanne de France.
C'est par un soir de tristesse que j'ai écrit ce poème en son honneur
Jeanne
La petite prostituée
Je suis triste je suis triste
J'irai au *Lapin agile* me ressouvenir de ma jeunesse perdue
Et boire des petits verres
Puis je rentrerai seul

Paris

Ville de la Tour unique du grand Gibet et de la Roue

Paris, 1913

Le Panama ou Les Aventures de Mes Sept Oncles

A *Edmond Bertrand, barman au Matachine*

Des livres
Il y a des livres qui parlent du Canal de Panama
Je ne sais pas ce que disent les catalogues des bibliothèques
Et je n'écoute pas les journaux financiers
Quoique les bulletins de la Bourse soient notre prière quotidienne

Le Canal de Panama est intimement lié à mon enfance . . .
Je jouais sous la table
Je disséquais les mouches
Ma mère me racontait les aventures de ses sept frères
De mes sept oncles
Et quand elle recevait des lettres
Eblouissement!
Ces lettres avec les beaux timbres exotiques qui portent les vers de Rimbaud en exergue
Elle ne me racontait rien ce jour-là
Et je restais triste sous ma table

C'est aussi vers cette époque que j'ai lu l'histoire du tremblement de terre de Lisbonne
Mais je crois bien
Que le crach du Panama est d'une importance plus universelle
Car il a bouleversé mon enfance.

J'avais un beau livre d'images
Et je voyais pour la première fois
La baleine
Le gros nuage
Le morse
Le soleil
Le grand morse
L'ours le lion le chimpanzé le serpent à sonnette et la mouche
La mouche
La terrible mouche
—Maman, les mouches! les mouches! et les troncs d'arbres!
—Dors, dors, mon enfant.
Ahasvérus est idiot

J'avais un beau livre d'images
Un grand lévrier qui s'appelait Dourak
Une bonne anglaise
Banquier
Mon père perdit les trois-quarts de sa fortune
Comme nombre d'honnêtes gens qui perdirent leur argent dans ce crach,
Mon père
Moins bête
Perdait celui des autres,
Coups de revolver.
Ma mère pleurait.
Et ce soir-là on m'envoya coucher avec la bonne anglaise

Puis au bout d'un nombre de jours bien long...
Nous avions dû déménager
Et les quelques chambres de notre petit appartement étaient bourrées de meubles
Nous n'étions plus dans notre villa de la côte
J'étais seul des jours entiers
Parmi les meubles entassés
Je pouvais même casser de la vaisselle
Fendre les fauteuils
Démolir le piano...
Puis au bout d'un nombre de jours bien long
Vint une lettre d'un de mes oncles

C'est le crach du Panama qui fit de moi un poète!
C'est épatant
Tous ceux de ma génération sont ainsi
Jeunes gens
Qui ont subi des ricochets étranges
On ne joue plus avec des meubles
On ne joue plus avec des vieilleries

On casse toujours et partout la vaisselle
On s'embarque
On chasse les baleines
On tue les morses
On a toujours peur de la mouche tsé-tsé
Car nous n'aimons pas dormir

L'ours le lion le chimpanzé le serpent à sonnette m'avaient appris à lire . . .
Oh cette première lettre que je déchiffrai seul et plus grouillante que toute la création
Mon oncle disait:
Je suis boucher à Galveston
Les abattoirs sont à 6 lieues de la ville
C'est moi qui ramène les bêtes saignantes, le soir, tout le long de la mer
Et quand je passe les pieuvres se dressent en l'air
Soleil couchant . . .
Et il y avait encore quelque chose
La tristesse
Et le mal du pays.

Mon oncle, tu as disparu durant le cyclone de 1895
J'ai vu depuis la ville reconstruite et je me suis promené au bord de la mer où tu menais
    les bêtes saignantes
Il y avait une fanfare salutiste qui jouait dans un kiosque en treillage
On m'a offert une tasse de thé
On n'a jamais retrouvé ton cadavre
Et à ma vingtième année j'ai hérité de tes 400 dollars d'économie
Je possède aussi la boîte à biscuits qui te servait de reliquaire
Elle est en fer-blanc
Toute ta pauvre religion
Un bouton d'uniforme
Une pipe kabyle
Des graines de cacao
Une dizaine d'aquarelles de ta main
Et les photos des bêtes à prime, les taureaux géants que tu tiens en laisse
Tu es en bras de chemise avec un tablier blanc

Moi aussi j'aime les animaux
Sous la table
Seul
Je joue déjà avec les chaises
Armoires portes
Fenêtres
Mobilier modern-style
Animaux préconçus
Qui trônent dans les maisons
Comme les reconstitutions des bêtes antédiluviennes dans les musées
Le premier escabeau est un aurochs!
J'enfonce les vitrines
Et j'ai jeté tout cela
La ville, en pâture à mon chien
Les images

Les livres
La bonne
Les visites
Quels rires!

Comment voulez-vous que je prépare des examens?
Vous m'avez envoyé dans tous les pensionnats d'Europe
Lycées
Gymnases
Université
Comment voulez-vous que je prépare des examens
Quand une lettre est sous la porte
J'ai vu
La belle pédagogie!
J'ai vu au cinéma le voyage qu'elle a fait
Elle a mis soixante-huit jours pour venir jusqu'à moi
Chargée de fautes d'orthographe
Mon deuxième oncle:
J'ai marié la femme qui fait le meilleur pain du district
J'habite à trois journées de mon plus proche voisin
Je suis maintenant chercheur d'or à Alaska
Je n'ai jamais trouvé plus de 500 francs d'or dans ma pelle
La vie non plus ne se paye pas à sa valeur!
J'ai eu trois doigts gelés
Il fait froid . . .
Et il y avait encore quelque chose
La tristesse
Et le mal du pays.

Oh mon oncle, ma mère m'a tout dit
Tu as volé des chevaux pour t'enfuir avec tes frères
Tu t'es fait mousse à bord d'un cargo-boat
Tu t'es cassé la jambe en sautant d'un train en marche
Et après l'hôpital, tu as été en prison pour avoir arrêté une diligence
Et tu faisais des poésies inspirées de Musset
San-Francisco
C'est là que tu lisais l'histoire du général Suter qui a conquis la Californie aux
    États-Unis
Et qui, milliardaire, a été ruiné par la découverte des mines d'or sur ses terres
Tu as longtemps chassé dans la vallée du Sacramento où j'ai travaillé au défrichement
    du sol
Mais qu'est-il arrivé
Je comprends ton orgueil
Manger le meilleur pain du district et la rivalité des voisins
12 femmes par 1.000 kilomètres carrés
On t'a trouvé
La tête trouée d'un coup de carabine
Ta femme n'était pas là
Ta femme s'est remariée depuis avec un riche fabricant de confitures

J'ai soif
Nom de Dieu

De nom de dieu
De nom de dieu
Je voudrais lire la *Feuille d'Avis de Neuchâtel* ou *le Courrier de Pampelune*
Au milieu de l'Atlantique on n'est pas plus à l'aise que dans une salle de rédaction
Je tourne dans la cage des méridiens comme un écureuil dans la sienne
Tiens voilà un Russe qui a une tête sympathique
Où aller
Lui non plus ne sait où déposer son bagage
A Léopoldville ou à la Sedjérah près Nazareth, chez Mr Junod ou chez mon vieil
    ami Perl
Au Congo en Bessarabie à Samoa
Je connais tous les horaires
Tous les trains et leurs correspondances
L'heure d'arrivée l'heure du départ
Tous les paquebots tous les tarifs et toutes les taxes
Ça m'est égal
J'ai des adresses
Vivre de la tape
Je reviens d'Amérique à bord du *Volturno*, pour 35 francs de New-York à Rotterdam

C'est le baptême de la ligne
Les machines continues s'appliquent de bonnes claques
Boys
Platch
Les baquets d'eau
Un Américain les doigts tachés d'encre bat la mesure
La télégraphie sans fil
On danse avec les genoux dans les pelures d'orange et les boîtes de conserve vides
Une délégation est chez le capitaine
Le Russe révolutionnaire expériences érotiques
Gaoupa
Le plus gros mot hongrois
J'accompagne une marquise napolitaine enceinte de 8 mois
C'est moi qui mène les émigrants de Kichinef à Hambourg
C'est en 1901 que j'ai vu la première automobile,
En panne,
Au coin d'une rue
Ce petit train que les Soleurois appellent un fer à repasser
Je téléphonerai à mon consul
Délivrez-moi immédiatement un billet de 3ᵉ classe
The Uranium Steamship Cᵒ
J'en veux pour mon argent
Le navire est à quai
Débraillé
Les sabords grand ouverts
Je quitte le bord comme on quitte une sale putain

En route
Je n'ai pas de papier pour me torcher
Et je sors
Comme le dieu Tangaloa qui en pêchant à la ligne tira le monde hors des eaux

La dernière lettre de mon troisième oncle:
Papeete, le 1ᵉʳ septembre 1887.
Ma sœur, ma très chère sœur
Je suis bouddhiste membre d'une secte politique
Je suis ici pour faire des achats de dynamite
On en vend chez les épiciers comme chez vous la chicorée
Par petis paquets
Puis je retournerai à Bombay faire sauter les Anglais
Ça chauffe
Je ne te reverrai jamais plus . . .
Et il y avait encore quelque chose
La tristesse
Et le mal du pays.

Vagabondage
J'ai fait de la prison à Marseille et l'on me ramène de force à l'école
Toutes les voix crient ensemble
Les animaux et les pierres
C'est le muet qui a la plus belle parole
J'ai été libertin et je me suis permis toutes les privautés avec le monde
Vous qui aviez la foi pourquoi n'êtes-vous pas arrivé à temps
A votre âge
Mon oncle
Tu étais joli garçon et tu jouais très bien du cornet à pistons
C'est ça qui t'a perdu comme on dit vulgairement
Tu aimais tant la musique que tu préféras le ronflement des bombes aux symphonies des
    habits noirs
Tu as travaillé avec de joyeux Italiens à la construction d'une voie ferrée dans les
    environs de Baghavapour
Boute en train
Tu étais le chef de file de tes compagnons
Ta belle humeur et ton joli talent d'orphéoniste
Tu es la coqueluche des femmes du baraquement
Comme Moïse tu as assommé ton chef d'équipe
Tu t'es enfui
On est resté douze ans sans aucune nouvelle de toi
Et comme Luther un coup de foudre t'a fait croire à Dieu
Dans ta solitude
Tu apprends le bengali et l'urlu pour apprendre à fabriquer les bombes
Tu as été en relation avec les comités secrets de Londres
C'est à White-Chapel que j'ai retrouvé ta trace
Tu es convict
Ta vie circoncise
Telle que
J'ai envie d'assassiner quelqu'un au boudin ou à la gaufre pour avoir l'occasion de
    te voir
Car je ne t'ai jamais vu
Tu dois avoir une longue cicatrice au front

Quant à mon quatrième oncle il était le valet de chambre du général Robertson qui a
    fait la guerre aux Boërs

Il écrivait rarement des lettres ainsi conçues
Son Excellence a daigné m'augmenter de 50 £
Ou
Son Excellence emporte 48 paires de chaussures à la guerre
Ou
Je fais les ongles de Son Excellence tous les matins . . .
Mais je sais
Qu'il y avait encore quelque chose
La tristesse
Et le mal du pays.

Mon oncle Jean, tu es le seul de mes sept oncles que j'aie jamais vu
Tu étais rentré au pays car tu te sentais malade
Tu avais un grand coffre en cuir d'hippopotame qui était toujours bouclé
Tu t'enfermais dans ta chambre pour te soigner
Quand je t'ai vu pour la première fois, tu dormais
Ton visage était terriblement souffrant
Une longue barbe
Tu dormais depuis quinze jours
Et comme je me penchais sur toi
Tu t'es réveillé
Tu étais fou
Tu as voulu tuer grand'mère
On t'a enfermé à l'hospice
Et c'est là que je t'ai vu pour la deuxième fois
Sanglé
Dans la camisole de force
On t'a empêché de débarquer
Tu faisais de pauvres mouvements avec tes mains
Comme si tu allais ramer
Transvaal
Vous étiez en quarantaine et les horse-guards avaient braqué un canon sur votre navire
Prétoria
Un Chinois faillit t'étrangler
Le Tougéla
Lord Robertson est mort
Retour à Londres
La garde-robe de Son Excellence tombe à l'eau ce qui te va droit au cœur
Tu es mort en Suisse à l'asile d'aliénés de Saint-Aubain
Ton entendement
Ton enterrement
Et c'est là que je t'ai vu pour la troisième fois
Il neigeait
Moi, derrière ton corbillard, je me disputais avec les croque-morts à propos de leur
    pourboire
Tu n'as aimé que deux choses au monde
Un cacatoès
Et les ongles roses de Son Excellence

Il n'y a pas d'espérance
Et il faut travailler

Les vies encloses sont les plus denses
Tissus stéganiques
Remy de Gourmont habite au 71 de la rue des Saints-Pères
Filagore ou seizaine
«Séparés un homme rencontre un homme mais une montagne ne rencontre jamais une
    autre montagne»
Dit un proverbe hébreu
Les précipices se croisent
J'étais à Naples
1896
Quand j'ai reçu le *Petit Journal Illustré*
Le capitaine Dreyfus dégradé devant l'armée
Mon cinquième oncle:
Je suis chef au Club-Hôtel de Chicago
J'ai 400 gâte-sauces sous mes ordres
Mais je n'aime pas la cuisine des Yankees
Prenez bonne note de ma nouvelle adresse
Tunis etc.
Amitiés de la tante Adèle
Prenez bonne note de ma nouvelle adresse
Biarritz etc.

Oh mon oncle, toi seul tu n'as jamais eu le mal du pays
Nice Londres Buda-Pest Bermudes Saint-Pétersbourg Tokio Memphis
Tous les grands hôtels se disputent tes services
Tu es le maître
Tu as inventé nombre de plats doux qui portent ton nom
Ton art
Tu te donnes tu te vends on te mange
On ne sait jamais où tu es
Tu n'aimes pas rester en place
Il paraît que tu possèdes une *Histoire de la Cuisine à travers tous les âges et chez tous les
    peuples*
En 12 vol. in-8°
Avec les portraits des plus fameux cuisiniers de l'histoire
Tu connais tous les évènements
Tu as toujours été partout où il se passait quelque chose
Tu es peut-être à Paris.
Tes menus
Sont la poésie nouvelle

J'ai quitté tout cela
J'attends
La guillotine est le chef-d'œuvre de l'art plastique
Son déclic
Mouvement perpétuel
Le sang des bandits
Les chants de la lumière ébranlent les tours
Les couleurs croulent sur la ville
Affiche plus grande que toi et moi
Bouche ouverte et qui crie

Denver, the Residence City and Commercial Center

DENVER is the capital of Colorado and the commercial metropolis of the Rocky Mountain Region. The city is in its fifty-fifth year and has a population of approximately 225.000 as indicated by the U. S. Census of 1910. Many people who have not visited Colorado, believe Denver is situated in the mountains. This city is located 12 miles east of the foothills of the Rocky Mountains, near the north central part of the state, at the junction of the Platte River and Cherry Creek. The land is rolling, giving the city perfect drainage. Altitude one mile above sea level. Area 60 square miles.

Ideal Climate, Superior Educational Advantages Unequalled Park System

DENVER has the lowest death rate of the cities of the United States.

DENVER has 61 grade schools, 4 high schools, 1 manual training school, 1 trade and 1 technical school.

DENVER has 209 churches of every denomination.

DENVER has 29 parks; total area 1,238 acres.

DENVER has 11 playgrounds — 8 in parks, 3 in individual tracts.

DENVER has 56 miles of drives in its parks.

Commercial and Manufacturing City

Annual Bank C l e a r i n g s , $ 487,848,305.95.

Per capita clearings, $ 180.00.

Annual manufacturing output, $ 57,711,000 (1912).
Eighteen trunk lines entering Denver, tapping the richest agricultural sections of the United States.

DENVER has 810 factories, in which 16,251 wage earners were employed during 1911. The output of factories in DENVER in 1911 was valued at $ 52,000,000. The payroll for the year was $ 12,066,000 — OVER A MILLION DOLLARS A MONTH !

DENVER, COLORADO, BERLIN, GERMANY and MANCHESTER, ENGLAND, are cited by Economists as examples of inland cities which have become great because they are located at a sort of natural cross-roads.

For detailed information, apply to the *Denver Chamber of Commerce.*   *Prospectus free.*

Dans laquelle nous brûlons
Les trois jeunes gens ardents
Hananie Mizaël Azarie
Adam's Express Co
Derrière l'Opéra
Il faut jouer à saute-mouton
A la brebis qui broute
Femme-tremplin
Le beau joujou de la réclame
En route!
Siméon, Siméon
Paris-adieux

C'est rigolo
Il y a des heures qui sonnent
Quai-d'Orsay-Saint-Nazaire!
On passe sous la Tour Eiffel—boucler la boucle—pour retomber de l'autre côté
    du monde

Puis on continue

Les catapultes du soleil assiègent les tropiques irascibles
Riche Péruvien propriétaire de l'exploitation du guano d'Angamos
On lance l'Acaraguan Bananan
A l'ombre
Les mulâtres hospitaliers
J'ai passé plus d'un hiver dans ces îles fortunées
L'oiseau-secrétaire est un éblouissement
Belles dames plantureuses
On boit des boissons glacées sur la terrasse
Un torpilleur brûle comme un cigare
Une partie de polo dans le champ d'ananas
Et les palétuviers éventent les jeunes filles studieuses
My gun
Coup de feu
Un observatoire au flanc du volcan
De gros serpents dans la rivière desséchée
Haie de cactus
Un âne clics la queue en l'air
La petite Indienne qui louche veut se vendre à Buenos-Ayres
Le musicien allemand m'emprunte ma cravache à pommeau d'argent et une paire de
    gants de Suède
Ce gros Hollandais est géographe
On joue aux cartes en attendant le train
C'est l'anniversaire de la Malaise
Je reçois un paquet à mon nom, 200.000 pésétas et une lettre de mon sixième oncle:
Attends-moi à la factorerie jusqu'au printemps prochain
Amuse-toi bien bois sec et n'épargne pas les femmes
Le meilleur électuaire
Mon neveu . . .

Et il y avait encore quelque chose
La tristesse
Et le mal du pays.

Oh mon oncle, je t'ai attendu un an et tu n'es pas venu
Tu étais parti avec une compagnie d'astronomes qui allait inspecter le ciel sur la côte
    occidentale de la Patagonie
Tu leur servais d'interprète et de guide
Tes conseils
Ton expérience
Il n'y en avait pas deux comme toi pour viser l'horizon au sextant
Les instruments en équilibre
Electro-magnétiques
Dans les fjords de la Terre de Feu
Aux confins du monde
Vous pêchiez des mousses protozoaires en dérive entre deux eaux à la lueur des poissons
    électriques
Vous collectionniez des aérolithes de peroxyde de fer
Un dimanche matin:
Tu vis un évêque mitré sortir des eaux
Il avait une queue de poisson et t'aspergeait de signes de croix
Tu t'es enfui dans la montagne en hurlant comme un vari blessé
La nuit même
Un ouragan détruisit le campement
Tes compagnons durent renoncer à l'espoir de te retrouver vivant
Ils emportèrent soigneusement les documents scientifiques
Et au bout de trois mois,
Les pauvres intellectuels,
Ils arrivèrent un soir à un feu de gauchos où l'on causait justement de toi
J'étais venu à ta rencontre
Tupa
La belle nature
Les étalons s'enculent
200 taureaux noirs mugissent
Tango-argentin

Bien quoi
Il n'y a donc plus de belles histoires
La Vie des Saints
Das Nachtbuechlein von Schuman
Cymballum mundi
La Tariffa delle Puttane di Venegia
Navigation de Jean Struys, Amsterdam, 1528
Shalom Aleïchem
Le crocodile de Saint-Martin
Strindberg a démontré que la terre n'est pas ronde
Déjà Gavarni avait aboli la géométrie
Pampas
Disque
Les iroquoises du vent
Saupiquets

L'hélice des gemmes
Maggi
Byrrh
Daily Chronicle
La vague est une carrière où l'orage en sculpteur abat de blocs de taille
Quadriges d'écume qui prennent le mors aux dents
Éternellement
Depuis le commencement du monde
Je siffle
Un frissoulis de bris

Mon septième oncle
On n'a jamais su ce qu'il est devenu
On dit que je te ressemble

Je vous dédie ce poème
Monsieur Bertrand
Vous m'avez offert des liqueurs fortes pour me prémunir contre les fièvres du canal
Vous vous êtes abonné à l'Argus de la Presse pour recevoir toutes les coupures qui me
    concernent.
Dernier Français de Panama (il n'y en a pas 20)
Je vous dédie ce poème
Barman du Matachine
Des milliers de Chinois sont morts où se dresse maintenant le Bar flamboyant
Vous distillez
Vous vous êtes enrichi en enterrant les cholériques
Envoyez-moi la photographie de la forêt de chênes-liège qui pousse sur les
    400 locomotives abandonnées par l'entreprise française
Cadavres-vivants
Le palmier greffé dans la banne d'une grue chargée d'orchidées
Les canons d'Aspinwall rongés par les toucans
La drague aux tortues
Les pumas qui nichent dans le gazomètre défoncé
Les écluses perforées par les poissons-scie
La tuyauterie des pompes bouchée par une colonie d'iguanes
Les trains arrêtés par l'invasion des chenilles
Et l'ancre gigantesque aux armoiries de Louis XV dont vous n'avez su m'expliquer la
    présence dans la forêt
Tous les ans vous changez les portes de votre établissement incrustées de signatures
Tous ceux qui passèrent chez vous
Ces 32 portes quel témoignage
Langues vivantes de ce sacré canal que vous chérissez tant

Ce matin est le premier jour du monde
Isthme
D'où l'on voit simultanément tous les astres du ciel et toutes les formes de la végétation
Préexcellence des montagnes équatoriales
Zone unique
Il y a encore le vapeur de l'Amidon Paterson
Les initiales en couleurs de l'Atlantic-Pacific Tea-Trust

Le Los Angeles limited qui part à 10 h. 02 pour arriver le troisième jour et qui est le
    seul train au monde avec wagon-coiffeur
Le Trunk les éclipses et les petites voitures d'enfants
Pour vous apprendre à épeler l'A B C de la vie sous la férule des sirènes en partance
Toyo Kisen Kaïsha
J'ai du pain et du fromage
Un col propre
La poésie date d'aujourd'hui

La voie lactée autour du cou
Les deux hémisphères sur les yeux
A toute vitesse
Il n'y a plus de pannes
Si j'avais le temps de faire quelques économies je prendrais part au rallye aérien
J'ai réservé ma place dans le premier train qui passera le tunnel sous la Manche
Je suis le premier aviateur qui traverse l'Atlantique en monocoque
900 millions

Terre Terre Eaux Océans Ciels
J'ai le mal du pays
Je suis tous les visages et j'ai peur des boîtes aux lettres
Les villes sont des ventres
Je ne suis plus les voies
Lignes
Câbles
Canaux
Ni les ponts suspendus!

Soleils lunes étoiles
Mondes apocalyptiques
Vous avez encore tous un beau rôle à jouer
Un siphon éternue
Les cancans littéraires vont leur train
Tout bas
A la Rotonde
Comme tout au fond d'un verre

J'attends

Je voudrais être la cinquième roue du char
Orage
Midi à quatorze heures
Rien et partout

PARIS ET SA BANLIEUE.
    Saint-Cloud, Sèvres, Montmorency, Courbevoie, Bougival, Rueil, Montrouge, Saint-
Denis, Vincennes, Étampes, Melun, Saint-Martin, Méréville, Barbizon, Forges-en-Bière.

Juin 1913–Juin 1914

Dix-Neuf Poèmes Élastiques

I. Journal

Christ
Voici plus d'un an que je n'ai plus pensé à Vous
Depuis que j'ai écrit mon avant-dernier poème Pâques
Ma vie a bien changé depuis
Mais je suis toujours le même
J'ai même voulu devenir peintre
Voici les tableaux que j'ai faits et qui ce soir pendent aux murs
Ils m'ouvrent d'étranges vues sur moi-même qui me font penser à Vous.

Christ
La vie
Voilà ce que j'ai fouillé

Mes peintures me font mal
Je suis trop passionné
Tout est orangé.

J'ai passé une triste journée à penser à mes amis
Et à lire le journal
Christ
Vie crucifiée dans le journal grand ouvert que je tiens les bras tendus
Envergures
Fusées
Ebullition
Cris.
On dirait un aéroplane qui tombe.
C'est moi.

Passion
Feu
Roman-feuilleton
Journal
On a beau ne pas vouloir parler de soi-même
Il faut parfois crier

Je suis l'autre
Trop sensible

Août 1913

2. Tour

1910
Castellamare
Je dînais d'une orange à l'ombre d'un oranger
Quand, tout à coup...
Ce n'était pas l'éruption du Vésuve
Ce n'était pas le nuage de sauterelles, une des dix plaies d'Egypte
Ni Pompéi
Ce n'était pas les cris ressuscités des mastodontes géants
Ce n'était pas la Trompette annoncée
Ni la grenouille de Pierre Brisset
Quand, tout à coup,
Feux
Chocs
Rebondissements
Etincelle des horizons simultanés
Mon sexe

      O Tour Eiffel!
Je ne t'ai pas chaussée d'or
Je ne t'ai pas fait danser sur les dalles de cristal
Je ne t'ai pas vouée au Python comme une vierge de
     Carthage
Je ne t'ai pas revêtue du péplum de la Grèce
Je ne t'ai jamais fait divaguer dans l'enceinte des menhirs
Je ne t'ai pas nommée Tige de David ni Bois de la Croix
Lignum Crucis
      O Tour Eiffel
Feu d'artifice géant de l'Exposition Universelle!
Sur le Gange
A Bénarès
Parmi les toupies onanistes des temples hindous
Et les cris colorés des multitudes de l'Orient
Tu te penches, gracieux Palmier!
C'est toi qui à l'époque légendaire du peuple hébreu
Confondis la langue des hommes
O Babel!
Et quelques mille ans plus tard, c'est toi qui retombais en langues de feu sur les Apôtres
    rassemblés dans ton église
En pleine mer tu es un mât
Et au Pôle-Nord
Tu resplendis avec toute la magnificence de l'aurore boréale de ta télégraphie sans fil
Les lianes s'enchevêtrent aux eucalyptus
Et tu flottes, vieux tronc, sur le Mississipi
Quand
Ta gueule s'ouvre
Et un caïman saisit la cuisse d'un nègre
En Europe tu es comme un gibet
(Je voudrais être la tour, pendre à la Tour Eiffel!)

Et quand le soleil se couche derrière toi
La tête de Bonnot roule sous la guillotine
Au cœur de l'Afrique c'est toi qui cours
Girafe
Autruche
Boa
Équateur
Moussons
En Australie tu as toujours été tabou
Tu es la gaffe que le capitaine Cook employait pour diriger son bateau d'aventuriers
O sonde céleste!
Pour le Simultané Delaunay, à qui je dédie ce poème,
Tu es le pinceau qu'il trempe dans la lumière

Gong tam-tam zanzibar bête de la jungle rayons-X express bistouri symphonie
Tu es tout
Tour
Dieu antique
Bête moderne
Spectre solaire
Sujet de mon poème
Tour
Tour du monde
Tour en mouvement

Août 1913

3. Contrastes

Les fenêtres de ma poésie sont grand'ouvertes sur les Boulevards et dans ses vitrines
Brillent
Les pierreries de la lumière
Ecoute les violons des limousines et les xylophones des linotypes
Le pocheur se lave dans l'essuie-main du ciel
Tout est taches de couleur
Et les chapeaux des femmes qui passent sont des comètes dans l'incendie du soir

L'unité
Il n'y a plus d'unité
Toutes les horloges marquent maintenant 24 heures après avoir été retardées
    de dix minutes
Il n'y a plus de temps.
Il n'y a plus d'argent.
A la Chambre
On gâche les éléments merveilleux de la matière première

Chez le bistro
Les ouvriers en blouse bleue boivent du vin rouge
Tous les samedis poule au gibier
On joue
On parie
De temps en temps un bandit passe en automobile
Ou un enfant joue avec l'Arc de Triomphe . . .
Je conseille à M. Cochon de loger ses protégés à la Tour Eiffel.

Aujourd'hui
Changement de propriétaire
Le Saint-Esprit se détaille chez les plus petits boutiquiers
Je lis avec ravissement les bandes de calicot
De coquelicot
Il n'y a que les pierres ponces de la Sorbonne qui ne sont jamais fleuries
L'enseigne de la Samaritaine laboure par contre la Seine
Et du côté de Saint-Séverin
J'entends
Les sonnettes acharnées des tramways

Il pleut les globes électriques
Montrouge Gare de l'Est Métro Nord-Sud bâteaux-mouches monde
Tout est halo
Profondeur
Rue de Buci on crie *L'Intransigeant* et *Paris-Sports*
L'aérodrome du ciel est maintenant, embrasé, un tableau de Cimabue
Quand par devant
Les hommes sont
Longs
Noirs
Tristes
Et fument, cheminées d'usine

Octobre 1913

4

I. PORTRAIT

Il dort
Il est éveillé
Tout à coup, il peint
Il prend une église et peint avec une église
Il prend une vache et peint avec une vache
Avec une sardine
Avec des têtes, des mains, des couteaux
Il peint avec un nerf de bœuf
Il peint avec toutes les sales passions d'une petite ville juive
Avec toute la sexualité exacerbée de la province russe
Pour la France

Sans sensualité
Il peint avec ses cuisses
Il a les yeux au cul
Et c'est tout à coup votre portrait
C'est toi lecteur
C'est moi
C'est lui
C'est sa fiancée
C'est l'épicier du coin
La vachère
La sage-femme
Il y a des baquets de sang
On y lave les nouveau-nés
Des ciels de folie
Bouches de modernité
La Tour en tire-bouchon
Des mains
Le Christ
Le Christ c'est lui
Il a passé son enfance sur la Croix
Il se suicide tous les jours
Tout à coup, il ne peint plus
Il était éveillé
Il dort maintenant
Il s'étrangle avec sa cravate
Chagall est étonné de vivre encore

II. ATELIER

La Ruche
Escaliers, portes, escaliers
Et sa porte s'ouvre comme un journal
Couverte de cartes de visite
Puis elle se ferme.
Désordre, on est en plein désordre
Des photographies de Léger, des photographies de Tobeen, qu'on ne voit pas
Et au dos
Au dos
Des œuvres frénétiques
Esquisses, dessins, des œuvres frénétiques
Et des tableaux . . .
Bouteilles vides
«*Nous garantissons la pureté absolue de notre sauce tomate*»
Dit une étiquette
La fenêtre est un almanach
Quand les grues gigantesques des éclairs vident les péniches du ciel à grand fracas et
      déversent des bannes de tonnerre
Il en tombe

Pêle-mêle

Des cosaques le Christ un soleil en décomposition
Des toits
Des somnambules des chèvres
Un lycanthrope
Pétrus Borel
La folie l'hiver
Un génie fendu comme une pêche
Lautréamont
Chagall
Pauvre gosse auprès de ma femme
Délectation morose
Les souliers sont éculés
Une vieille marmite pleine de chocolat
Une lampe qui se dédouble
Et mon ivresse quand je lui rends visite
Des bouteilles vides
Des bouteilles
Zina
(Nous avons beaucoup parlé d'elle)
Chagall
Chagall
Dans les échelles de la lumière

Octobre 1913

5. Ma Danse

Platon n'accorde pas droit de cité au poète
Juif errant
Don Juan métaphysique
Les amis, les proches
Tu n'as plus de coutumes et pas encore d'habitudes
Il faut échapper à la tyrannie des revues
Littérature
Vie pauvre
Orgueil déplacé
Masque
La femme, la danse que Nietzsche a voulu nous apprendre à danser
La femme
Mais l'ironie?

Va-et-vient continuel
Vagabondage spécial
Tous les hommes, tous les pays
C'est ainsi que tu n'es plus à charge
Tu ne te fais plus sentir . . .

Je suis un monsieur qui en des express fabuleux traverse les toujours mêmes Europes
    et regarde découragé par la portière
Le paysage ne m'intéresse plus

Mais la danse du paysage
La danse du paysage
Danse-paysage
Paritatitata
Je tout-tourne

Février 1914

6. Sur la Robe Elle A un Corps

Le corps de la femme est aussi bosselé que mon crâne
Glorieuse
Si tu t'incarnes avec esprit
Les couturiers font un sot métier
Autant que la phrénologie
Mes yeux sont des kilos qui pèsent la sensualité des femmes

Tout ce qui fuit, saille avance dans la profondeur
Les étoiles creusent le ciel
Les couleurs déshabillent
«Sur la robe elle a un corps»
Sous les bras des bruyères mains lunules et pistils quand les eaux se déversent
    dans le dos avec les omoplates glauques
Le ventre un disque qui bouge
La double coque des seins passe sous le pont des arcs-en-ciel
Ventre
Disque
Soleil
Les cris perpendiculaires des couleurs tombent sur les cuisses
ÉPÉE DE SAINT MICHEL

Il y a des mains qui se tendent
Il y a dans la traîne la bête tous les yeux toutes les fanfares tous les habitués
    du bal Bullier
Et sur la hanche
La signature du poete

Février 1914

7. Hamac

Onoto-visage
Cadran compliqué de la Gare Saint-Lazare
Apollinaire
Avance, retarde, s'arrête parfois.
Européen
Voyageur occidental
Pourquoi ne m'accompagnes-tu pas en Amérique?
J'ai pleuré au débarcadère
New-York

Les vaisseaux secouent la vaisselle
Rome Prague Londres Nice Paris
Oxo-Liebig fait frise dans ta chambre
Les livres en estacade

Les tromblons tirent à noix de coco
«*Julie ou j'ai perdu ma rose*»

Futuriste

Tu as longtemps écrit à l'ombre d'un tableau
A l'Arabesque tu songeais
O toi le plus heureux de nous tous
Car Rousseau a fait ton portrait
Aux étoiles
Les œillets du poète *Sweet Williams*

Apollinaire
1900—1911
Durant 12 ans seul poète de France

                                    Décembre 1913

8. Mardi-Gras

Les gratte-ciel s'écartèlent
J'ai trouvé tout au fond Canudo non rogné
Pour cinq sous
Chez un bouquiniste de la 14ᵉ rue
Religieusement
Ton improvisation sur la IXᵉ Symphonie de Beethoven
On voit New-York comme la Venise mercantile de l'océan occidental

La Croix s'ouvre
Danse
Il n'y a pas de commune
Il n'y a pas d'aéropage
Il n'y a pas de pyramide spirituelle
Je ne comprends pas très bien le mot «Impérialisme»
Mais dans ton grenier
Parmi les ouistitis les Indiens les belles dames
Le poète est venu
Verbe coloré

Il y a des heures qui sonnent
Montjoie!
L'olifant de Roland
Mon taudis de New-York
Les livres

Les messages télégraphiques
Et le soleil t'apporte le beau corps d'aujourd'hui dans les coupures des journaux
Ces langes

Février 1914

9. Crépitements

Les arcencielesques dissonnances de la Tour dans sa télégraphie sans fil
Midi
Minuit
On se dit merde de tous les coins de l'univers

Étincelles
Jaune de chrome
On est en contact
De tous les côtés les transatlantiques s'approchent
S'éloignent
Toutes les montres sont mises à l'heure
Et les cloches sonnent
Paris-Midi annonce qu'un professeur allemand a été mangé par les cannibales
    au Congo
C'est bien fait
L'Intransigeant ce soir publie des vers pour cartes postales
C'est idiot quand tous les astrologues cambriolent les étoiles
On n'y voit plus
J'interroge le ciel
L'Institut Météorologique annonce du mauvais temps
Il n'y a pas de futurisme
Il n'y a pas de simultanéité
Bodin a brûlé toutes les sorcières
Il n'y a rien
Il n'y a plus d'horoscopes et il faut travailler
Je suis inquiet
L'Esprit
Je vais partir en voyage
Et j'envoie ce poème dépouillé à mon ami R . . .

Septembre 1913

10. Dernière Heure

Oklahoma, *20 janvier 1914*
Trois forçats se procurent des revolvers
Ils tuent leur geôlier et s'emparent des clefs de la prison
Ils se précipitent hors de leurs cellules et tuent quatre gardiens dans la cour
Puis ils s'emparent de la jeune sténo-dactylographe de la prison
Et montent dans une voiture qui les attendait à la porte

Ils partent à toute vitesse
Pendant que les gardiens déchargent leurs revolvers dans la direction des fugitifs

Quelques gardiens sautent à cheval et se lancent à la poursuite des forçats
Des deux côtés des coups de feu sont échangés
La jeune fille est blessée d'un coup de feu tiré par un des gardiens

Une balle frappe à mort le cheval qui emportait la voiture
Les gardiens peuvent approcher
Ils trouvent les forçats morts le corps criblé de balles
Mr. Thomas, ancien membre du Congrès qui visitait la prison
Félicite la jeune fille

Télégramme-poème copié dans *Paris-Midi*

Janvier 1914

11. Bombay-Express

La vie que j'ai menée
M'empêche de me suicider
Tout bondit
Les femmes roulent sous les roues
Avec de grands cris
Les tape-cul en éventail sont à la porte des gares.
J'ai de la musique sous les ongles.

Je n'ai jamais aimé Mascagni
Ni l'Art ni les Artistes
Ni les barrières ni les ponts
Ni les trombones ni les pistons
Je ne sais plus rien
Je ne comprends plus . . .
Cette caresse
Que la carte géographique en frissonne

Cette année ou l'année prochaine
La critique d'art est aussi imbécile que l'espéranto
Brindisi
Au revoir au revoir

Je suis né dans cette ville
Et mon fils également
Lui dont le front est comme le vagin de sa mère
Il y a des pensées qui font sursauter les autobus
Je ne lis plus les livres qui ne se trouvent que dans les bibliothèques
Bel A B C du monde

Bon voyage!

Que je t'emporte
Toi qui ris du vermillon

Avril 1914

12. F.I.A.T.

J'ai l'ouïe déchiré

J'envie ton repos
Grand paquebot des usines
A l'ancre
Dans la banlieue des villes

Je voudrais m'être vidé
Comme toi
Après ton accouchement
Les pneumatiques vessent dans mon dos
J'ai des pommettes électriques au bout des nerfs

Ta chambre blanche moderne nickelée
Le berceau
Les rares bruits de l'Hôpital
Sainte Clothilde
Je suis toujours en fièvre
Paris-Adresses

Etre à ta place
Tournant brusque!
C'est la première fois que j'envie une femme
Que je voudrais être femme
Etre femme
Dans l'univers
Dans la vie
Etre
Et s'ouvrir à l'avenir enfantin
Moi qui suis ébloui

Phares Blériot
Mise en marche automatique
Vois

Mon stylo caracole

Caltez!

Avril 1914

13. Aux 5 Coins

Oser et faire du bruit
Tout est couleur mouvement explosion lumière
La vie fleurit aux fenêtres du soleil
Qui se fond dans ma bouche
Je suis mûr
Et je tombe translucide dans la rue

Tu parles, mon vieux

Je ne sais pas ouvrir les yeux?
Bouche d'or
La poésie est en jeu

Février 1914

14. Natures Mortes

pour Roger de la Fresnaye

Vert
Le gros trot des artilleurs passe sur la géométrie
Je me dépouille
Je ne serais bientôt qu'en acier
Sans l'équerre de la lumière
Jaune
Clairon de modernité
Le classeur américain
Est aussi sec et
Frais
Que vertes les campagnes premières
Normandie
Et la table de l'architecte
Est ainsi strictement belle
Noir
Avec une bouteille d'encre de Chine
Et des chemises bleues
Bleu
Rouge
Puis il y a aussi un litre, un litre de sensualité
Et cette haute nouveauté
Blanc
Des feuilles de papier blanc

Avril 1914

15. Fantômas

Tu as étudié le grand-siècle dans l'*Histoire de la Marine Française* par Eugène
Sue
Paris, au Dépôt de la Librairie, 1835,
4 vol. in-16 jésus
Fine fleur des pois du catholicisme pur
Moraliste
Plutarque
Le simultanéisme est passéiste

Tu m'as mené au Cap chez le père Moche au Mexique
Et tu m'as ramené à Saint-Pétersbourg où j'avais déjà été
C'est bien par là
On tourne à droite pour aller prendre le tramway
Ton argot est vivant ainsi que la niaiserie sentimentale de ton cœur qui beugle
Alma mater Humanité Vache
Mais tout ce qui est machinerie mise en scène changement de décors etc. etc.
Est directement plagié de Homère, ce Châtelet

Il y a aussi une jolie page
«. . . vous vous imaginiez monsieur Barzum, que j'allais tranquillement vous permettre
«de ruiner mes projets, de livrer ma fille à la justice, vous aviez pensé cela? . . . allons!
«sous votre apparence d'homme intelligent, vous n'étiez qu'un imbécile . . .»
Et ce n'est pas mon moindre mérite que de citer le roi des Voleurs
Vol. 21, le Train perdu, p. 367.

Nous avons encore beaucoup de traits communs
J'ai été en prison
J'ai dépensé des fortunes mal acquises
Je connais plus de 120.000 timbres-poste tous différents et plus joyeux que les Nᵒ Nᵒ
    du Louvre
Et
Comme toi
Héraldiste industriel
J'ai étudié les marques de fabrique enregistrées à l'Office international des Patentes
    internationales

Il y a encore de jolis coups à faire
Tous les matins de 9 à 11

Mars 1914

16. Titres

Formes sueurs chevelures
Le bond d'être
Dépouillé
Premier poème sans métaphores
Sans images
Nouvelles
L'esprit nouveau
Les accidents des féeries
400 fenêtres ouvertes
L'hélice des gemmes des foires des menstrues
Le cône rabougri
Les déménagements à genoux
Dans les dragues
A travers l'accordéon du ciel et des voix télescopées
Quand le journal fermente comme un éclair claquemuré
Manchette

Juillet 1914

17. Mee Too Buggi

Comme chez les Grecs on croit que tout homme bien élevé doit savoir pincer la lyre
Donne-moi le fango-fango
Que je l'applique à mon nez
Un son doux et grave
De la narine droite
Il y a la description des paysages
Le récit des événements passés
Une relation des contrées lointaines
Bolotoo
Papalangi
Le poète entre autres choses fait la description des animaux
Les maisons sont renversées par d'énormes oiseaux
Les femmes sont trop habillées
Rimes et mesures dépourvues
Si l'on fait grâce à un peu d'exagération
L'homme qui se coupa lui-même la jambe réussissait dans le genre simple et gai
Mee low folla
Mariwagi bat le tambour à l'entrée de sa maison

Juillet 1914

18. La Tête

La guillotine est le chef-d'œuvre de l'art plastique
Son déclic
Crée le mouvement perpétuel
Tout le monde connaît l'œuf de Christophe Colomb
Qui était un œuf plat, un œuf fixe, l'œuf d'un inventeur
La sculpture d'Archipenko est le premier œuf ovoïdal
Maintenu en équilibre intense
Comme une toupie immobile
Sur sa pointe animée
Vitesse
Il se dépouille
Des ondes multicolores
Des zones de couleur
Et tourne dans la profondeur
Nu.
Neuf.
Total.

Juillet 1914

19. Construction

De la couleur, de la couleur et des couleurs . . .
Voici Léger qui grandit comme le soleil de l'époque tertiaire
Et qui durcit
Et qui fixe
La nature morte
La croûte terrestre
Le liquide
Le brumeux
Tout ce qui se ternit
La géométrie nuageuse
Le fil à plomb qui se résorbe
Ossification.
Locomotion.
Tout grouille
L'esprit s'anime soudain et s'habille à son tour comme les animaux et les plantes
Prodigieusement
Et voici
La peinture devient cette chose énorme qui bouge
La roue
La vie
La machine
L'âme humaine
Une culasse de 75
Mon portrait

Février 1919

La Guerre au Luxembourg

CES ENFANTINES
sont dédiées
à mes camarades
de la Légion Étrangère
Mieczyslaw KOHN, Polonais
tué à Frise;
Victor CHAPMAN, Américain
tué à Verdun;
Xavier de CARVALHO, Portugais
tué à la ferme de Navarin;
Engagés Volontaires

MORTS
POUR LA FRANCE

BLAISE CENDRARS
MCMXVI

«Une deux, une deux
Et tout ira bien . . .»
Ils chantaient
Un blessé battait la mesure avec sa béquille
Sous le bandeau son œil
Le sourire du Luxembourg
Et les fumées des usines de munitions
Au-dessus des frondaisons d'or
Pâle automne fin d'été
On ne peut rien oublier
Il n'y a que les petits enfants qui jouent à la guerre
La Somme Verdun
Mon grand frère est aux Dardanelles
Comme c'est beau
Un fusil   MOI!
Cris voix flûtées
Cris   MOI!
Les mains se tendent
Je ressemble à papa
On a aussi des canons
Une fillette fait le cycliste   MOI!
Un dada caracole
Dans le bassin les flottilles s'entre-croisent
Le méridien de Paris est dans le jet d'eau

On part à l'assaut du garde qui seul a un sabre authentique
Et on le tue à force de rire
Sur les palmiers encaissés le soleil pend
Médaille Militaire
On applaudit le dirigeable qui passe du côté de la Tour Eiffel
Puis on relève les morts
Tout le monde veut en être
Ou tout au moins blessé   ROUGE
Coupe coupe
Coupe le bras coupe la tête   BLANC
On donne tout
Croix-Rouge   BLEU
Les infirmières ont 6 ans
Leur cœur est plein d'émotion
On enlève les yeux aux poupées pour réparer les aveugles
J'y vois! j'y vois!
Ceux qui faisaient les Turcs sont maintenant brancardiers
Et ceux qui faisaient les morts ressuscitent pour assister à la merveilleuse opération
A présent on consulte les journaux illustrés
Les photographies
On se souvient de ce que l'on a vu au cinéma
Ça devient plus sérieux
On crie et l'on cogne mieux que Guignol
Et au plus fort de la mêlée
Chaud chaudes
Tout le monde se sauve pour aller manger les gaufres
Elles sont prêtes.   R
Il est cinq heures.   Ê
Les grilles se ferment.   V
On rentre.   E
Il fait soir.   U
On attend le zeppelin qui ne vient pas   R
Las   S
Les yeux aux fusées des étoiles
Tandis que les bonnes vous tirent par la main
Et que les mamans trébuchent sur les grandes automobiles d'ombre

Le lendemain ou un autre jour
Il y a une tranchée dans le tas de sable
Il y a un petit bois dans le tas de sable
Des villes
Une maison
Tout le pays   La Mer
Et peut-être bien la mer
L'artillerie improvisée tourne autour des barbelés imaginaires
Un cerf-volant rapide comme un avion de chasse
Les arbres se dégonflent et les feuilles tombent par-dessus bord et tournent en parachute
Las 3 veines du drapeau se gonflent à chaque coup de l'obusier du vent
Tu ne seras pas emportée petite arche de sable

Enfants prodiges, plus que les ingénieurs
On joue en riant au tank aux gaz-asphyxiants au sous-marin-devant-new-york-qui-ne-
    peut-pas-passer
Je suis Australien, tu es nègre, il se lave pour faire la-vie-des-soldats-anglais-en-Belgique
Casquette russe
1 Légion d'honneur en chocolat vaut 3 boutons d'uniforme
Voilà le général qui passe
Une petite fille dit
J'aime beaucoup ma nouvelle maman américaine
Et un petit garçon:—Non pas Jules Verne mais achète encore le beau communiqué
    du dimanche

A PARIS
Le jour de la Victoire quand les soldats reviendront . . .
Tout le monde voudra LES voir
Le soleil ouvrira de bonne heure comme un marchand de nougat un jour de fête
Il fera printemps au Bois de Boulogne ou du côté de Meudon
Toutes les automobiles seront parfumées et les pauvres chevaux mangeront des fleurs
Aux fenêtres les petites orphelines de la guerre auront toutes de belles robes patriotiques
Sur les marronniers des boulevards les photographes à califourchon braqueront leur œil
    à déclic
On fera cercle autour de l'opérateur du cinéma qui mieux qu'un mangeur de serpents
    engloutira le cortège historique
Dans l'après-midi
Les blessés accrocheront leurs Médailles à l'Arc-de-Triomphe et rentreront à la maison
    sans boiter
Puis
Le soir
La place de l'Étoile montera au ciel
Le Dôme des Invalides chantera sur Paris comme une immense cloche d'or
Et les mille voix des journaux acclameront la Marseillaise
Femme de France

Paris, octobre 1916

Sonnets Dénaturés

OpOetic

à Jean COctO

quels crimes ne
cOmmet-On pas
en tOn nOm!

Il y avait une fOis des pOètes qui parlaient la bOuche en rOnd
ROnds de saucissOn ses beaux yeux et fum*ée*
Les cheveux d'Ophélie Ou celle parfum*ée*
D'Orph*ée*
Tu rOtes des rOnds de chapeau pOur trOuver une rime en *ée*-aiguë cOmme des dents
    qui grignOtteraient tes vers
BOuche b*ée*
Puisque tu fumes pOurquOi ne répètes-tu fum*ée*
C'est trOp facile Ou c'est trOp difficile
Les 7 PiOns et les Dames sont là pour les virgules
Oh POE sie
Ah! Oh!
CacaO
Puisque tu prends le tram pourquoi n'écris-tu pas tramw*ée*
VOis la grimace écrite de ce mOt bien franç*ée*
Le clOwn anglais la fait avec ses jambes
COmme l'AmOur l'Arétin
L'Esprit jalOuse l'affiche du cirque et les pOstures alphabétiques de l'hOmme-serpent
Où sOnt les pOètes qui parlent la bOuche en rOnd?

Il faut leur assOuplir les  enfant

POESIE

Nov. 16

Académie Médrano

A Conrad Moricand.

Danse avec ta langue, Poète, fais un entrechat
Un tour de piste
                sur un tout petit basset
                        noir ou haquenée
Mesure les beaux vers mesurés et fixe les formes fixes
Que sont *L E S B E L L E S L E T T R E S* apprises
Regarde:
         Les Affiches se fichent de toi te mordent
                  avec leurs dents en couleur
                  entre les doigts de pied
La fille du directeur a des lumières électriques
Les jongleurs sont aussi les trapézistes
                xuellirép tuaS
        teuof ed puoC
aç-emirpxE
Le clown est dans le tonneau malaxé
            passe à la caisse
Il faut que ta langue   les soirs où
           fasse l'orchestre
Les **Billets de faveur** sont supprimés

                        Novembre 1916

Le Musickissme

A Erik Satie.

Que nous chaut Venizelos
Seul Raymond ■ mettons Duncan trousse encore la défroque grecque
Musique aux oreilles végétales
Autant qu'éléphantiaques
Les poissons crient dans le gulf-stream
Bidon juteux plus que figue
Et la voix basque du microphone marin
Duo de music-hall
Sur accompagnement d'auto
Gong
Le phoque musicien
50 mesures de do-ré do-ré do-ré do-ré do-ré
do-ré do-ré do-ré do-ré do-ré do-ré do-ré do-ré
Ça y est!
Et un accord diminué en la bémol mineur
                        ETC.!

Quand c'est beau un beau joujou bruiteur danse la sonnette
Entr'acte
A la rentrée
Thème: CHARLOT chef d'orchestre bat la mesure
Devant
L'européen chapeauté et sa femme en corset
Contrepoint: Danse
Devant l'européen ahuri et sa femme
Aussi
Coda: Chante
Ce qu'il fallait démontrer

Nov. 1916

Poèmes Nègres

Continent Noir

Afrique
Strabon la jugeait si peu considérable
Grigris d'un usage général
C'est par les femmes que se compte la descendance mâle et que se fait tout le travail
Un père un jour imagina de vendre son fils; celui-ci le prévint en le vendant lui-même.
Ce peuple est adonné au vol
Tout ce qui frappe ses yeux excite sa cupidité
Ils saisissent tout avec le gros orteil et pliant les genoux enfouissent tout sous leur pagne
Ils étaient soumis à des chefs qui avaient l'autorité et qui comptaient parmi leurs droits
    celui d'avoir la première nuit de noces de toutes les vierges qui se marient
Ils ne s'embarrassaient pas de celle des veuves,
Ajoute le vieil auteur.
L'île merveilleuse de Saint-Borandion où le hasard a conduit quelques voyageurs
On dit qu'elle paraît et disparaît de temps en temps.
Les Forêts de Madère brûlent sept ans.
Mumbo-Jumbo idole des Madingos
Côte-d'Or
Le Gouverneur de Guina a une dispute avec les nègres
Manquant de boulets il charge ses canons avec de l'or
Toto Papo
Ce n'est que l'intérêt qui leur fait souffrir l'étranger
Le commerce des Européens sur cette côte et leur libertinage ont fait une nouvelle race
    d'hommes qui est peut-être la plus méchante de toutes
Et ils sont de neuf espèces
Le sacata, le griffe, le marabout, le mulâtre, le quarteron, le métis, le mamelone,
    le quarteronné, le sang-mêlé
Heureuse la Bossum consacrée à l'idole domestique

1916

Les Grands Fétiches

I

Une gangue de bois dur
Deux bras d'embryon
L'homme déchire son ventre
Et adore son membre dressé

II

Qui menaces-tu
Toi qui t'en vas
Poings sur les hanches
A peine d'aplomb
Juste hors de grossir?

III

Nœud de bois
Tête en forme de gland
Dur et réfractaire
Visage dépouillé
Jeune dieu insexué et cyniquement hilare

IV

L'envie t'a rongé le menton
La convoitise te pipe
Tu te dresses
Ce qui te manque du visage
Te rend géométrique
Arborescent
Adolescent

V

Voici l'homme et la femme
Également laids, également nus
Lui moins gras qu'elle mais plus fort
Les mains sur le ventre et la bouche en tire-lire

VI

Elle
Le pain de son sexe qu'elle fait cuire trois fois par jour
Et la pleine outre du ventre
Tirent
Sur le cou et les épaules

VII

Je suis laid!
Dans ma solitude à force de renifler l'odeur des filles
Ma tête enfle et mon nez va bientôt tomber

VIII

J'ai voulu fuir les femmes du chef
J'ai eu la tête fracassée par la pierre du soleil
Dans le sable
Il ne reste plus que ma bouche
Ouverte comme le vagin de ma mère
Et qui crie

IX

Lui
Chauve
N'a qu'une bouche
Un membre qui descend aux genoux
Et les pieds coupés

X

Voici la femme que j'aime le plus
Deux rides aigues autour d'une bouche en entonnoir
Un front bleu
Du blanc sur les tempes
Et le regard astiqué comme un cuivre

British Museum
Londres, février 1916

Documentaires

WEST

I. Roof-Garden

Pendant des semaines les ascenseurs ont hissé hissé des caisses des caisses de terre
    végétale
Enfin
A force d'argent et de patience
Des bosquets s'épanouissent
Des pelouses d'un vert tendre
Une source vive jaillit entre les rhododendrons et les camélias
Au sommet de l'édifice l'édifice de briques et d'acier
Le soir
Les waiters graves comme des diplomates vêtus de blanc se penchent sur le gouffre
    de la ville
Et les massifs s'éclairent d'un million de petites lampes versicolores
Je crois Madame murmura le jeune homme d'une voix vibrante de passion contenue
Je crois que nous serons admirablement ici
Et d'un large geste il montrait la large mer
Le va-et-vient
Les fanaux des navires géants
La géante statue de la Liberté
Et l'énorme panorama de la ville coupée de ténèbres perpendiculaires et de lumières
    crues
Le vieux savant et les deux milliardaires sont seuls sur la terrasse
Magnifique jardin
Massifs de fleurs
Ciel étoilé
Les trois vieillards demeurent silencieux prêtent l'oreille au bruit des rires et des voix
    joyeuses qui montent des fenêtres illuminées
Et à la chanson murmurée de la mer qui s'enchaîne au gramophone

II. Sur l'Hudson

Le canot électrique glisse sans bruit entre les nombreux navires ancrés dans l'immense
    estuaire et qui battent pavillon de toutes les nations du monde
Les grands clippers chargés de bois et venus du Canada ferlaient leurs voiles géantes
Les paquebots de fer lançaient des torrents de fumée noire
Un peuple de dockers appartenant à toutes les races du globe s'affairait dans le tapage
    des sirènes à vapeur et les sifflets des usines et des trains

L'élégante embarcation est entièrement en bois de teck
Au centre se dresse une sorte de cabine assez semblable à celle des gondoles vénitiennes

III. Amphitryon

Après le dîner servi dans les jardins d'hiver au milieu des massifs de citronniers de
    jasmins d'orchidées
Il y a bal sur la pelouse du parc illuminé
Mais la principale attraction sont les cadeaux envoyés à Miss Isadora
On remarque surtout un rubis «sang de pigeon» dont la grosseur et l'éclat sont
    incomparables
Aucune des jeunes filles présentes n'en possède un qui puisse lui être comparé
Élégamment vêtus
D'habiles détectives mêlés à la foule des invités veillent sur cette gemme et la protègent

IV. Office

Radiateurs et ventilateurs à air liquide
Douze téléphones et cinq postes de T. S. F.
D'admirables classeurs électriques contiennent les myriades de dossiers industriels et
    scientifiques sur les affaires les plus variées
Le milliardaire ne se sent vraiment chez lui que dans ce cabinet de travail
Les larges verrières donnent sur le parc et la ville
Le soir les lampes à vapeur de mercure y répandent une douce lueur azurée
C'est de là que partent les ordres de vente et d'achat qui culbutent parfois les cours de
    Bourse dans le monde entier

V. Jeune Fille

Légère robe en crêpe de Chine
La jeune fille
Élégance et richesse
Cheveux d'un blond fauve où brille un rang de perles
Physionomie régulière et calme qui reflète la franchise et la bonté
Ses grands yeux d'un bleu de mer presque vert sont clairs et hardis
Elle a ce teint frais et velouté d'une roseur spéciale qui semble l'apanage des jeunes filles
    américaines

VI. Jeune Homme

C'est le Brummel de la Fifth Avenue
Cravate en toile d'or semée de fleurettes de diamants
Complet en étoffe métallique rose et violet
Bottine en véritable peau de requin et dont chaque bouton est une petite perle noire
Il exhibe un pyjama en flanelle d'amiante un autre complet en étoffe de verre un gilet
    en peau de crocodile

Son valet de chambre savonne ses pièces d'or
Il n'a jamais en portefeuille que des banknotes neuves et parfumées

VII. Travail

Des malfaiteurs viennent de faire sauter le pont de l'estacade
Les wagons ont pris feu au fond de la vallée
Des blessés nagent dans l'eau bouillante que lâche la locomotive éventrée
Des torches vivantes courent parmi les décombres et les jets de vapeur
D'autres wagons sont restés suspendus à 60 mètres de hauteur
Des hommes armés de torches électriques et à l'acétylène descendent le sentier
    de la vallée
Et les secours s'organisent avec une silencieuse rapidité
Sous le couvert des joncs des roseaux des saules les oiseaux aquatiques font un joli
    remue-ménage
L'aube tarde à venir
Que déjà une équipe de cent charpentiers appelés par télégraphe et venus par train
    spécial s'occupent à reconstruire le pont
Pan pan-pan
Passe-moi les clous

VIII. Trestle-Work

Recontre-t-on un cours d'eau ou une vallée profonde
On la passe sur un pont de bois en attendant que les recettes de la compagnie
    permettent d'en construire un en pierre ou en fer
Les charpentiers américains n'ont pas de rivaux dans l'art de construire ces ponts
On commence par poser un lit de pierres dures
Puis on dresse un premier chevalet
Lequel en supporte un second puis un troisième puis un quatrième
Autant qu'il en faut pour atteindre le niveau de la rive
Sur le dernier chevalet deux poutres
Sur les deux poutres deux rails
Ces constructions audacieuses ne sont renforcées ni par des croix de St. André ni par
    des fers en T
Elles ne tiennent que par quelques poutrelles et quelques chevilles qui maintiennent
    l'écartement des chevalets
Et c'est tout
C'est un pont
Un beau pont

IX. Les Mille Iles

En cet endroit le paysage est un des plus beaux qui se trouvent en Amérique du Nord
La nappe immense du lac est d'un bleu presque blanc
Des centaines et des centaines de petites îles verdoyantes flottent sur la calme surface
    des eaux limpides

Les délicieux cottages construits en briques de couleurs vives donnent à ce paysage
    l'aspect d'un royaume enchanté
Des luxueux canots d'érable d'acajou élégamment pavoisés et couverts de tentes
    multicolores vont et viennent d'une île à l'autre
Toute idée de fatigue de labeur de misère est absente de ce décor gracieux pour
    milliardaires

Le soleil disparaît à l'horizon du lac Ontario
Les nuages baignent leurs plis dans des cuves de pourpre violette d'écarlate et d'orangé
Quel beau soir murmurent Andrée et Frédérique assises sur la terrasse d'un château du
    moyen âge
Et les dix mille canots moteurs répondent à leur extase

X. Laboratoire

Visite des serres
Le thermo siphon y maintient une température constante
La terre est saturée d'acide formique de manganèse et d'autres substances qui impriment
    à la végétation une puissance formidable
D'un jour à l'autre les feuilles poussent les fleurs éclosent les fruits mûrissent
Les racines grâce à un dispositif ingénieux baignent dans un courant électrique qui
    assure cette croissance monstrueuse
Les canons paragrêle détruisent nimbus et cumulus
Nous rentrons en ville en traversant les landes
La matinée est radieuse
Les bruyères d'une sombre couleur de pourpre et les genêts d'or ne sont pas encore
    défleuris
Les goélands et les mauves tracent de grands cercles dans le bleu léger du ciel

FAR-WEST

I. Cucumingo

L'hacienda de San-Bernardino
Elle est bâtie au centre d'une verdoyante vallée arrosée par une multitude de petits
    ruisseaux venus des montagnes circonvoisines
Les toits sont de tuiles rouges sous les ombrages des sycomores et des lauriers

Les truites pullulent dans les ruisseaux
D'innombrables troupeaux paissent en liberté dans les grasses prairies
Les vergers regorgent de fruits poires pommes raisins ananas figues oranges
Et dans les potagers
Les légumes du vieux monde poussent à côté de ceux des contrées tropicales

Le gibier abonde dans le canton
Le colin de Californie

Le lapin à queue de coton *cottontrail*
Le lièvre aux longues oreilles *jackass*
La caille la tourterelle la perdrix
Le canard et l'oie sauvages
L'antilope
Il est vrai qu'on y rencontre encore le chat sauvage et le serpent à sonnette *rattlesnake*
Mais il n'y a plus de puma aujourd'hui

II. Dorypha

Les jours de fête
Quand les indiens et les vaqueros s'enivrent de whisky et de pulque
Dorypha danse
Au son de la guitare mexicaine
Habaneras si entraînantes
Qu'on vient de plusieurs lieues pour l'admirer

Aucune femme ne sait aussi bien qu'elle
Draper la mantille de soie
Et parer sa chevelure blonde
D'un ruban
D'un peigne
D'une fleur

III. L'Oiseau-Moqueur

La chaleur est accablante
Balcon ombragé de jasmin de Virginie et de chèvrefeuille pourpré
Dans le grand silence de la campagne sommeillante
On discerne
Le glou-glou des petits torrents
Le mugissement lointain des grands troupeaux de bœufs dans les pâturages
Le chant du rossignol
Le sifflement cristallin des crapauds géants
Le hululement des rapaces nocturnes
Et le cri de l'oiseau-moqueur dans les cactus

IV. Ville-Champignon

Vers la fin de l'année 1911 un groupe de financiers yankees décide la fondation d'une
    ville en plein Far-West au pied des Montagnes Rocheuses
Un mois ne s'est pas écoulé que la nouvelle cité encore sans aucune maison est déjà
    reliée par trois lignes au réseau ferré de l'Union
Les travailleurs accourent de toutes parts
Dès le deuxième mois trois églises sont édifiées et cinq théâtres en pleine exploitation
Autour d'une place où subsistent quelques beaux arbres une forêt de poutres métalliques
    bruit nuit et jour de la cadence des marteaux
Treuils

Halètement des machines
Les carcasses d'acier des maisons de trente étages commencent à s'aligner
Des parois de briques souvent de simples plaques d'aluminium bouchent les interstices
    de la charpente de fer
On coule en quelques heures des édifices en béton armé selon le procédé Edison
Par une sorte de superstition on ne sait comment baptiser la ville et un concours est
    ouvert avec une tombola et des prix par le plus grand journal de la ville qui cherche
    également un nom

V. Club

La rue bien qu'indiquée sur le plan officiel de la ville n'est encore constituée que par
    des clôtures de planches et des monceaux de gravats
On ne la franchit qu'en sautant au petit bonheur les flaques d'eau et les fondrières
Au bout du boulevard inachevé qu'éclairent de puissantes lampes à arc est le club des
    Haricots Noirs qui est aussi une agence matrimoniale
Coiffés d'un feutre de cow-boy ou d'une casquette à oreillettes
Le visage dur
Des hommes descendent de leur 60 chevaux qu'ils étrennent s'inscrivent consultent
    l'album des photographies
Choisissent leur fiancée qui sur un câble s'embarquera à Cherbourg sur le *Kaiser
    Wilhelm* et arrivera à toute vapeur
Ce sont surtout des Allemandes
Un lad vêtu de noir chaussé de molleton d'une correction glaciale ouvre la porte et toise
    le nouveau venu d'un air soupçonneux
Je bois un cocktail au whisky puis un deuxième puis un troisième
Puis un mint-julep un milk-mother un prairy-oyster un night-cape

VI. Squaw-Wigwam

Quand on a franchi la porte vermoulue faite de planches arrachées à des caisses
    d'emballage et à laquelle des morceaux de cuir servent de gonds
On se trouve dans une salle basse
Enfumée
Odeur de poisson pourri
Relents de graisse rance avec affectation

Panoplies barbares
Couronnes de plumes d'aigle colliers de dents de puma ou de griffes d'ours
Arcs flèches tomahawks
Mocassins
Bracelets de graines et de verroteries
On voit encore
Des couteaux à scalper une ou deux carabines d'ancien modèle un pistolet à pierre
    des bois d'élan et de renne et toute une collection de petits sacs brodés pour mettre
    le tabac
Plus trois calumets très anciens formés d'une pierre tendre emmanchée d'un roseau

Éternellement penchée sur le foyer
La centenaire propriétaire de cet établissement se conserve comme un jambon et
  s'enfume et se couenne et se boucane comme sa pipe centenaire et le noir de sa
  bouche et le trou noir de son œil

VII. Ville-de-Frisco

C'est une antique carcasse dévorée par la rouille
Vingt fois réparée la machine ne donne pas plus de 7 à 8 nœuds à l'heure
D'ailleurs par économie on ne brûle que des escarbilles et des déchets de charbon
On hisse des voiles de fortune chaque fois que le vent est favorable
Avec sa face écarlate ses sourcils touffus son nez bourgeonnant master Hopkins est un
  véritable marin
Des petits anneaux d'argent percent ses oreilles
Ce navire est exclusivement chargé de cercueils de Chinois décédés en Amérique et qui
  ont désiré se faire enterrer dans la terre natale
Caisses oblongues coloriées de rouge ou de bleu clair ou couvertes d'inscriptions dorées
C'est là un genre de marchandise qu'il est interdit de transporter

VIII. Vancouver

Dix heures du soir viennent de sonner à peine distinctes dans l'épais brouillard qui
  ouate les docks et les navires du port
Les quais sont déserts et la ville livrée au sommeil
On longe une côte basse et sablonneuse où souffle un vent glacial et où viennent
  déferler les longues lames du Pacifique
Cette tache blafarde dans les ténèbres humides c'est la gare du Canadian du Grand
  Tronc
Et ces halos bleuâtres dans le vent sont les paquebots en partance pour le Klondyke le
  Japon et les grandes Indes
Il fait si noir que je puis à peine déchiffrer les inscriptions des rues où je cherche avec
  une lourde valise un hôtel bon marché

Tout le monde est embarqué
Les rameurs se courbent sur leurs avirons et la lourde embarcation chargée jusqu'au
  bordage pousse entre les hautes vagues
Un petit bossu corrige de temps en temps la direction d'un coup de barre
Se guidant dans le brouillard sur les appels d'une sirène
On se cogne contre la masse sombre du navire et par la hanche tribord grimpent des
  chiens samoyèdes
Filasses dans le gris-blanc-jaune
Comme si l'on chargeait du brouillard

TERRES ALÉOUTIENNES

I

Hautes falaises contre les vents glacés du pôle
Au centre de fertiles prairies
Rennes élans bœufs musqués
Les renards bleus les castors
Ruisseaux poissonneux
Une plage basse a été aménagée pour l'élevage des phoques à fourrure
Sur le sommet de la falaise on recueille les nids de l'eider dont les plumes constituent
    une véritable richesse

II

Vastes et solides bâtiments qui abritent un nombre assez considérable de trafiquants
Tout autour d'un petit jardin où l'on a réuni tous les végétaux capables de résister aux
    rigueurs du climat
Sorbiers pins saules arctiques
Plates-bandes de bruyères et de plantes alpestres

III

Baie parsemée d'îlots rocheux
Par groupes de cinq ou six les phoques se chauffent au soleil
Ou étendus sur le sable
Ils jouent entre eux avec cette espèce de cri guttural qui ressemble à un aboiement
A côté de la hutte des Esquimaux il y a un hangar pour la préparation des peaux

FLEUVE

Mississippi

A cet endroit le fleuve est presque aussi large qu'un lac
Il roule des eaux jaunâtres et boueuses entre deux berges marécageuses
Plantes aquatiques que continuent les acréages des cotonniers
Çà et là apparaissent les villes et les villages tapis au fond de quelque petite baie avec
    leurs usines avec leurs hautes cheminées noires avec leurs longues estacades qui
    s'avancent leurs longues estacades sur pilotis qui s'avancent bien avant dans l'eau

Chaleur accablante
La cloche du bord sonne pour le lunch
Les passagers arborent des complets à carreaux des cravates hurlantes des gilets rutilants
    comme les cocktails incendiaires et les sauces corrosives

On aperçoit beaucoup de crocodiles
Les jeunes alertes et frétillants
Le gros le dos recouvert d'une mousse verdâtre se laissent aller à la dérive

La végétation luxuriante annonce l'approche de la zone tropicale
Bambous géants palmiers tulipiers lauriers cèdres
Le fleuve lui-même a doublé de largeur
Il est tout parsemé d'îlots flottants d'où l'approche du bateau fait s'élever des nuées
    d'oiseaux aquatiques
Steam-boats voiliers chalands embarcations de toutes sortes et d'immenses trains de bois
Une vapeur jaune monte des eaux surchauffées du fleuve

C'est par centaines maintenant que les crocos s'ébattent autour de nous
On entend le claquement sec de leurs mâchoires et l'on distingue très bien leur petit œil
    féroce
Les passagers s'amusent à leur tirer dessus avec des carabines de précision
Quand un tireur émérite réussit ce tour de force de tuer ou de blesser une bête à mort
Ses congénères se précipitent sur elle la déchirent
Férocement
Avec des petits cris assez semblables au vagissement d'un nouveau-né

LE SUD

I. Tampa

Le train vient de faire halte
Deux voyageurs seulement descendent par cette matinée brûlante de fin d'été
Tous deux sont vêtus de complets couleur kaki et coiffés de casques de liège
Tous deux sont suivis d'un domestique noir chargé de porter leurs valises
Tous deux jettent le même regard distrait sur les maisons trop blanches de la ville sur le
    ciel trop bleu
On voit le vent soulever des tourbillons de poussière et les mouches tourmenter les deux
    mulets de l'unique fiacre
Le cocher dort la bouche ouverte

II. Bungalow

L'habitation est petite mais très confortable
La varangue est soutenue par des colonnes de bambou
Des pieds de vanille grimpante s'enroule tout autour
Des pois d'Angole

Des jasmins
Au-dessus éclatent les magnolias et les corolles des flamboyants

La salle à manger est aménagée avec le luxe particulier aux créoles de la Caroline
D'énormes blocs de glace dans des vases de marbre jaune y maintiennent une fraîcheur
    délicieuse
La vaisselle plate et les cristaux étincellent
Et derrière chaque convive se tient un serviteur noir

Les invités s'attardent longtemps
Étendus dans des rocking-chairs ils s'abandonnent à ce climat amollissant
Sur un signe de son maître le vieux Jupiter sort d'un petit meuble laqué
Une bouteille de Xérès
Un seau à glace
Des citrons
Et une boîte de cigares de La Havane

Personne ne parlait plus
La sueur ruisselait sur tous les visages
Il n'y avait plus un souffle dans l'air
On entendait dans le lointain le rire énorme de la grenouille-taureau qui abonde dans
    ces parages

III. Vomito Negro

Le paysage n'est plus égayé par des jardins ou des forêts
C'est la plaine nue et morne où s'élève à peine de loin en loin
Une touffe de bambous
Un saule rabougri
Un eucalyptus tordu par les vents
Puis c'est le marais
Vous voyez ces fumées jaunâtres
Ce brouillard gris au ras du sol agité d'un tressaillement perpétuel
Ce sont des millions de moustiques et les exhalaisons jaune de la pourriture
Il y a là des endroits où les noirs eux-mêmes ne sauraient vivre

De ce côté le rivage est bordé de grands palétuviers
Leurs racines enchevêtrées qui plongent dans la vase sont recouvertes de grappes
    d'huîtres empoisonnées

Les moustiques et les insectes venimeux forment un nuage épais au-dessus des eaux
    croupissantes
A côté des inoffensives grenouilles-taureaux on aperçoit des crapauds d'une prodigieuse
    grosseur
Et ce fameux serpent-cercueil qui donne la chasse à ses victimes en gambadant comme
    un chien
Il y a des mares où pullulent les sangsues couleur ardoise
Les hideux crabes écarlates s'ébattent autour des caïmans endormis
Dans les passages où le sol est le plus ferme on rencontre des fourmis géantes
Innombrables et voraces

Sur ces eaux pourries dans ces fanges vénéneuses
S'épanouissent des fleurs d'un parfum étourdissant et d'une senteur capiteuse et têtue
Éclatent des floraisons d'azur de pourpre
Des feuillages chromés
Partout
L'eau noire se couvre d'un tapis de fleurs que troue la tête plate des serpents

J'ai traversé un buisson de grands mimosas
Ils s'écartaient de moi sur mon passage
Ils écartaient leurs branches avec un petit sifflement
Car ce sont des arbres de sensibilité et presque de nervosité
Au milieu des lianes de jalap pleines de corolles parlantes
Les grands échassiers gris et roses se régalent de lézards croustillants et s'envolent avec
    un grand bruit d'ailes à notre approche
Puis ce sont d'immenses papillons aux couleurs de soufre de gentiane d'huile lourde
Et des chenilles de taille

IV. Ruine Espagnole

La nef est construite dans le style espagnol du XVIIIᵉ siècle
Elle est lézardée en de nombreux endroits
La voûte humide est blanche de salpêtre et porte encore des traces de dorures
Les rayons de la lanterne montrent dans un coin un tableau moisi
C'est une Vierge Noire
De longues mousses et des champignons vénéneusement zébrés pointillés perlés
    couvrent le pavé du sanctuaire
Il y a aussi une cloche avec des inscriptions latines

V. Golden-Gate

C'est le vieux grillage qui a donné son nom à la maison
Barres de fer grosses comme le poignet qui séparent la salle des buveurs du comptoir où
    sont alignés les liqueurs et les alcools de toutes provenances
Au temps où sévissait la fièvre de l'or
Où les femmes amenées par les traitants du Chili ou du Mexique se vendaient
    couramment aux enchères
Tous les bars étaient pourvus de grillages semblables
Alors les barmen ne servaient leurs clients que le revolver au poing
Il n'était pas rare qu'un homme fût assassiné pour un gobelet
Il est vrai qu'aujourd'hui le grillage n'est plus là que pour le pittoresque
Tout de même des Chinois sont là et boivent
Des Allemands des Mexicains
Et aussi quelques Canaques venus avec les petits vapeurs chargés de nacre de copra
    d'écaille de tortue
Chanteuses
Maquillage atroce employés de banque bandits matelots aux mains énormes

VI. Oyster-Bay

Tente de coutil et sièges de bambou
De loin en loin sur ces plages désertes on aperçoit une hutte couverte de feuilles de
    palmier ou l'embarcation d'un nègre pêcheur de perles

Maintenant le paysage a changé du tout au tout
A perte de vue
Les plages sont recouvertes d'un sable brillant
Deux ou trois requins s'ébattent dans le sillage du yacht
La Floride disparaît à l'horizon

On prend dans le meuble d'ébène un régalia couleur d'or
On le fait craquer d'un coup d'ongle
On l'allume voluptueusement
Fumez fumeur fumez fumée fait l'hélice

LE NORD

I. Printemps

Le printemps canadien a une vigueur et une puissance que l'on ne trouve dans aucun
    autre pays du monde
Sous la couche épaisse des neiges et des glaces
Soudainement
La généreuse nature
Touffes de violettes blanches bleues et roses
Orchidées tournesols lis tigrés
Dans les vénérables avenues d'érables de frênes noirs et de bouleaux
Les oiseaux volent et chantent
Dans les taillis recouverts de bourgeons et de pousses neuves et tendres
Le gai soleil est couleur réglisse

En bordure de la route s'étendent sur une longueur de plus de cinq milles les bois
    et les cultures
C'est un des plus vastes domaines du district de Winnipeg
Au milieu s'élève une ferme solidement construite en pierres de taille et qui a des
    allures de gentilhommière
C'est là que vit mon bon ami Coulon
Levé avant le jour il chevauche de ferme en ferme monté sur une haute jument isabelle
Les pattes de son bonnet de peau de lièvre flottent sur ses épaules
Œil noir et sourcils broussailleux
Tout guilleret
La pipe sur le menton

La nuit est brumeuse et froide
Un furieux vent d'ouest fait gémir les sapins élastiques et les mélèzes
Une petite lueur va s'élargissant
Un brasier crépite
L'incendie qui couvait dévore les buissons et les brindilles
Le vent tumultueux apporte des bouquets d'arbres résineux
Coup sur coup d'immenses torches flambent
L'incendie tourne l'horizon avec une imposante lenteur
Troncs blancs et troncs noirs s'ensanglantent
Dôme de fumée chocolat d'où un million d'étincelles de flammèches jaillissent en
    tournoyant très haut et très bas
Derrière ce rideau de flammes on aperçoit des grandes ombres qui se tordent et
    s'abattent
Des coups de cognée retentissent
Un âcre brouillard s'étend sur la forêt incandescente que l'équipe des bûcherons
    circonscrit

II. Campagne

Paysage magnifique
Verdoyantes forêts de sapins de hêtres de châtaigniers coupées de florissantes cultures
    de blé d'avoine de sarrasin de chanvre
Tout respire l'abondance
Le pays d'ailleurs est absolument désert
A peine rencontre-t-on par-ci par-là un paysan conduisant une charrette de fourrage
Dans le lointain les bouleaux sont comme des colonnes d'argent

III. Pêche et Chasse

Canards sauvages pilets sarcelles oies vanneaux outardes
Coqs de bruyère grives
Lièvre arctique perdrix de neige ptamigans
Saumons truites arc-en-ciel anguilles
Gigantesques brochets et écrevisses d'une saveur particulièrement exquise

La carabine en bandoulière
Le bowie-knife à la ceinture
Le chasseur et le peau-rouge plient sous le poids du gibier
Chapelets de ramiers de perdrix rouges
Paons sauvages
Dindons des prairies
Et même un grand aigle blanc et roux descendu des nuages

IV. Moisson

Une six-cylindres et deux Fords au milieu des champs
De tous les côtés et jusqu'à l'horizon les javelles légèrement inclinées tracent un damier
    de losanges hésitants

Pas un arbre
Du nord descend le tintamarre de la batteuse et de la fourragère automobiles
Et du sud montent les douze trains vides qui viennent charger le blé

ILES

I. Victuailles

Le petit port est très animé ce matin
Des coolies—tagals chinois malais—déchargent activement une grande jonque à poupe
    dorée et aux voiles en bambou tressé
La cargaison se compose de porcelaines venues de la grande île de Nippon
De nids d'hirondelles récoltés dans les cavernes de Sumatra
D'holothuries
De confitures de gingembre
De pousses de bambou confites dans du vinaigre
Tous les commerçants sont en émoi
Mr. Noghi prétentieusement vêtu d'un complet à carreaux de fabrication américaine
    parle très couramment l'anglais
C'est en cette langue que s'engage la discussion entre ces messieurs
Japonais Canaques Taïtiens Papous Maoris et Fidjiens

II. Prospectus

Visitez notre île
C'est l'île la plus au sud des possessions japonaises
Notre pays est certainement trop peu connu en Europe
Il mérite d'attirer l'attention
La faune et la flore sont très variées et n'ont guère été étudiées jusqu'ici
Enfin vous trouverez partout de pittoresques points de vue
Et dans l'intérieur
Des ruines de temples bouddhiques qui sont dans leur genre de pures merveilles

III. La Vipère a Crête Rouge

A l'aide de la seringue Pravaz il pratique plusieurs injections de sérum du docteur Yersin
Puis il agrandit la blessure du bras en pratiquant au scalpel une incision cruciale
Il fait saigner la plaie
Puis la cautérise avec quelques gouttes d'hypochlorite de chaux

IV. Maison Japonaise

Tiges de bambou
Légères planches
Papier tendu sur des châssis
Il n'existe aucun moyen de chauffage sérieux

V. Petit Jardin

Lis chrysanthèmes
Cycas et bananiers
Cerisiers en fleurs
Palmiers orangers et superbes cocotiers chargés de fruits

VI. Rocailles

Dans un bassin rempli de dorades de Chine et de poissons aux gueules monstrueuses
Quelques-uns portent des petits anneaux d'argent passés dans les ouïes

VII. Léger et Subtil

L'air est embaumé
Musc ambre et fleur de citronnier
Le seul fait d'exister est un véritable bonheur

VIII. Keepsake

Le ciel et la mer
Les vagues viennent caresser les racines des cocotiers et des grands tamarins au feuillage
    métallique

IX. Anse Poissonneuse

L'eau est si transparente et si calme
On aperçoit dans les profondeurs les broussailles blanches des coraux
Le balancement prismatique des méduses suspendues
Les envols des poissons jaunes roses lilas
Et au pied des algues onduleuses les holothuries azurées et les oursins verts et violets

X. Hatouara

Elle ne connaît pas les modes européennes
Crépus et d'un noir bleuâtre ses cheveux sont relevés à la japonaise et retenus par des
    épingles en corail
Elle est nue sous son kimono de soie
Nue jusqu'aux coudes

Lèvres fortes
Yeux langoureux
Nez droit

Teint couleur de cuivre clair
Seins menus
Hanches opulentes

Il y a en elle une vivacité une franchise des mouvements et des gestes
Un jeune regard d'animal charmant

Sa science: la grammaire de la démarche

Elle nage comme on écrit un roman de 400 pages
Infatigable
Hautaine
Aisée
Belle prose soutenue
Elle capture de tout petits poissons qu'elle met dans le creux de sa bouche
Puis elle plonge hardiment
Elle file entre les coraux et les varechs polycolores
Pour reparaître bientôt à la surface
Souriante
Tenant à la main deux grosses dorades au ventre d'argent

Toute fière d'une robe de soie bleue toute neuve de ses babouches brodées d'or d'un joli
    collier de corail qu'on vient de lui donner le matin même
Elle m'apporte un panier de crabes épineux et fantasques et de ces grosses crevettes des
    mers tropicales que l'on appelle des «caraques» et qui sont longues comme la main

XI. Amolli

Jardin touffu comme une clairière
Sur le rivage paresse l'éternelle chanson bruissante du vent dans les feuillages des filaos
Coiffé d'un léger chapeau de rotin armé d'un grand parasol de papier
Je contemple les jeux des mouettes et des cormorans
Ou j'examine une fleur
Ou quelque pierre
A chaque geste j'épouvante les écureuils et les rats palmistes

Par la fenêtre ouverte je vois la coque allongée d'un steamer de moyen tonnage
Ancré à environ deux kilomètres de la côte et qu'entourent déjà les jonques les sampans
    et les barques chargés de fruits et de marchandises locales
Enfin le soleil se couche

L'air est d'une pureté cristalline
Les mêmes rossignols s'égosillent
Et les grandes chauves-souris vampires passent silencieusement devant la lune sur leurs
    ailes de velours

Passe une jeune fille complètement nue
La tête couverte d'un de ces anciens casques qui font aujourd'hui la joie des
    collectionneurs

Elle tient à la main un gros bouquet de fleurs pâles et d'une pénétrante odeur qui
    rappelle à la fois la tubéreuse et le narcisse
Elle s'arrête court devant la porte du jardin
Des mouches phosphorescentes sont venues se poser sur la corne qui somme son casque
    et ajoutent encore au fantastique de l'apparition

Rumeurs nocturnes
Branches mortes qui se cassent
Soupirs des bêtes en rut
Rampements
Bruissements d'insectes
Oiseaux au nid
Voix chuchotées

Les platanes géants sont gris pâle sous la lune
Du sommet de leur voûte retombent des lianes légères qu'une bouche invisible balance
    dans la brise

Les étoiles fondent comme du sucre

FLEUVE

Le Bahr-el-Zeraf

Il n'y a pas de hautes herbes le long des rives
De grandes étendues de terres basses se perdent au loin
Des îles affleurent la surface de l'eau
De grands crocos se chauffent au soleil
Des milliers de grands oiseaux couvrent les bancs de sable ou de boue

Le pays se modifie
Il y a maintenant une brousse assez claire parsemée d'arbres rachitiques
Il y a des petits oiseaux ravissants de couleur et des bandes de pintades
Le soir à plusieurs reprises on entend rugir un lion dont on aperçoit la silhouette sur
    la rive ouest
J'ai tué ce matin un grand varan d'un mètre et demi

Toujours le même paysage de plaines inondées
Le pilote arabe a aperçu des éléphants
L'intérêt est grand
Tout le monde monte sur le pont supérieur
Pour chacun de nous c'est la première fois que va se montrer l'empereur des animaux
Les éléphants sont à trois cents mètres environ on en voit deux gros un moyen trois ou
    quatre petits
Pendant le déjeuner on signale dix grosses têtes d'hippos qui nagent devant nous

Le thermomètre ne varie guère
Vers 14 heures il y a régulièrement de 33 à 38°

Le vêtement est costume kaki bonnes chaussures guêtres et pas de chemise
On fait honneur à la bonne cuisine du bord et aux bouteilles de Turin brun
Le soir on ajoute seulement au costume de table un veston blanc
Milans et vautours passent en nous frôlant de l'aile

Après le dîner le bateau va se placer au milieu du fleuve pour éviter autant que possible
  les moustiques
Les rives se déroulent couvertes de papyrus et d'euphorbes géants
Le voyage est lent en suivant les méandres du fleuve
On voit beaucoup d'antilopes et de gazelles peu sauvages
Puis un vieux buffle et pas de rhinocéros

CHASSE A L'ÉLÉPHANT

I

Terrain infernal
Haute futaie sur marais avec un enchevêtrement de lianes et un sous-étage de palmiers
  bas d'un énorme diamètre de feuillage
Piquants droits
Vers midi et demi nous entendons une bande des grands animaux que nous cherchons
On perd l'équilibre à chaque instant
L'approche est lente
A peine ai-je aperçu les éléphants qu'ils prennent la fuite

II

La nuit
Il y a des éléphants dans les plantations
Au bruit strident des branches cassées arrachées succède le bruit plus sourd des gros
  bananiers renversés d'une poussée lente
Nous allons directement sur eux
En montant sur un petit tertre je vois l'avant de la bête la plus rapprochée
La lune perpendiculaire l'éclaire favorablement c'est un bel éléphant
La trompe en l'air l'extrémité tournée vers moi
Il m'a senti il ne faut pas perdre une demi-seconde
Le coup part
A l'instant une nouvelle balle passe dans le canon de la Winchester
Puis je fume ma pipe
L'énorme bête semble dormir dans la clairière bleue

III

Nous arrivons sur un terrain d'argile
Après avoir pris leur bain de boue les bêtes ont traversé des fourrés particulièrement
  épais

A quinze mètres on ne distingue encore que des masses informes sans qu'il soit possible de se rendre compte ni de la taille ni des défenses
J'ai rarement aussi bien entendu les bruits intestinaux des éléphants leurs ronflements le bruit des branches cassées
Tout cela succédant à de longs silences pendant lesquels on a peine à croire leur présence si rapprochée

IV

Du campement nous entendons des éléphants dans la forêt
Je garde un homme avec moi pour porter le grand kodak
A douze mètres je distingue mal une grande bête
A côté d'elle il me semble voir un petit
Ils sont dans l'eau marécageuse
Littéralement je les entends se gargariser
Le soleil éclaire en plein la tête et le poitrail de la grande femelle maintenant irritée
Quelle photo intéressante a pu prendre l'homme de sangfroid qui se tenait à côté de moi

V

Le terrain est impossible
Praticable seulement en suivant les sentiers tracés par les éléphants eux-mêmes
Sentiers encombrés d'obstacles de troncs renversés
De lianes que ces puissants animaux enjambent ou bien écartent avec leur trompe
Sans jamais les briser ou les supprimer pour ne plus les rencontrer sur leur chemin
En cela ils sont comme les indigènes qui n'enlèvent pas non plus les obstacles même dans leurs sentiers les plus battus

VI

Nous recoupons la piste d'un grand mâle
La bête nous mène droit vers l'ouest tout au travers de la grande plaine
Parcourt cinq cents mètres en forêt
Circule quelque temps dans un espace découvert encore inconnu de nous
Puis rentre en forêt
Maintenant la bête est parfaitement immobile un ronflement trahit seulement sa présence de temps en temps
A dix mètres j'aperçois vaguement quelque chose
Est-ce bien la bête?
Oui voilà bien une énorme dent très blanche
A ce moment une pluie torrentielle se met à tomber et une obscurité noire
Le film est raté

VII

Quelquefois les sentiers d'éléphants serpentent se croisent
Enserrés entre des murailles d'arbustes de ronces

Cette végétation est impénétrable même pour les yeux
Elle atteint de trois à six mètres d'élévation
Dans les sentiers les lianes descendent jusqu'à un deux trois pieds du sol
Puis remontent affectant les formes les plus bizarres
Les arbres sont tous énormes le collet de leurs racines aériennes est à quatre ou cinq
    mètres au-dessus du terrain

VIII

Nous entendons un troupeau
Il est dans une clairière
Les herbes et les broussailles y atteignent cinq à six mètres de haut
Il s'y trouve aussi des espaces restreints dénudés
Je fais rester mes trois hommes sur place chacun braquant son Bell-Howel
Et je m'avance seul avec mon petit kodak sur un terrain où je puis marcher sans bruit
Il n'y a rien d'aussi drôle que de voir s'élever s'abaisser se relever encore
Se contourner en tous sens
Les trompes des éléphants
Dont la tête et tout le corps immense demeurent cachés

IX

J'approche en demi-cercle
Soulevant son énorme tête ornée de grosses défenses
Brassant l'air de ses larges oreilles
La trompe tournée vers moi
Il prend le vent
Une photo et le coup part
L'éléphant reçoit le choc sans broncher
Je répète à toute vitesse
Piquant de la tête il roule à terre avec un râle formidable
Je lui tire ensuite une balle vers le cœur puis deux coups dans la tête
Le râle est toujours puissant enfin la vie l'abandonne
J'ai noté la position du cœur et ses dimensions qui sont de 55 centimètres de diamètre
    sur 40

X

Je n'aperçois le bel animal qu'un instant
Maintenant je l'entends patauger pesamment régulièrement
Il froisse les branches sur son passage
C'est une musique grandiose
Il est contre moi et je ne vois rien absolument rien
Tout à coup son énorme tête se dégage des broussailles
Plein de face
A six mètres
Me dominant
L'éléphant exécute une marche à reculons avec rapidité
A ce moment la pluie se met à tomber avec un fracas qui étouffe le bruit des pas

XI

Dans une grande plaine au nord
A la lisière de la forêt une grande femelle un petit mâle et trois jeunes éléphants
    de taille différente
La hauteur des herbes m'empêche de les photographier
Du haut d'une termitière je les observe longtemps avec ma jumelle Zeiss
Les éléphants semblent prendre leur dessert avec une délicatesse du toucher amusante
Quand les bêtes nous sentent elles détalent
La brousse s'entr'ouvre pour leur livrer passage et se referme comme un rideau sur leurs
    grosses masses

MENUS

I

Foie de tortue verte truffé
Langouste à la mexicaine
Faisan de la Floride
Iguane sauce caraïbe
Gombos et choux palmistes

II

Saumon du Rio Rouge
Jambon d'ours canadien
Roast-beef des prairies du Minnesota
Anguilles fumées
Tomates de San-Francisco
Pale-ale et vins de Californie

III

Saumon de Winnipeg
Jambon de mouton à l'Ecossaise
Pommes Royal-Canada
Vieux vins de France

IV

Kankal-Oysters
Salade de homard cœurs de céleris
Escargots de France vanillés au sucre

Poulet de Kentucky
Desserts café whisky canadian-club

V

Ailerons de requin confits dans la saumure
Jeunes chiens mort-nés préparés au miel
Vin de riz aux violettes
Crème au cocon de ver à soie
Vers de terre salés et alcool de Kawa
Confiture d'algues marines

VI

Conserves de bœuf de Chicago et salaisons allemandes
Langouste
Ananas goyaves nèfles du Japon noix de coco mangues pomme-crème
Fruits de l'arbre à pain cuits au four

VII

Soupe à la tortue
Huîtres frites
Patte d'ours truffée
Langouste à la Javanaise

VIII

Ragoût de crabes de rivière au piment
Cochon de lait entouré de bananes frites
Hérisson au ravensara
Fruits

En voyage 1887–1923

Feuilles de Route

I. LE FORMOSE

Ce cahier est dédié
à
mes bons amis de São-Paulo

PAUL PRADO
MARIO ANDRADE, SERGE MILLIET, TASTO DI
ALMEIDA, COUTO DE BARROS, RUBENS DE
MORAES, LUIZ ARANHA, OSWALD DE ANDRADE,
YAN

et
aux amis de Rio-de-Janeiro

GRAÇA ARANHA
SERGIO BUARQUE DE HOLLANDA, PRUDENTE
DE MORAES, GUILERMO DE ALMEIDA, RONALD
DE CARVALHO, AMERICO FACO

sans oublier
l'inimitable et cher

LEOPOLD DE FREITAS
du Rio-Grande-do-Sul

Dans le Rapide de 19 h. 40

Voici des années que je n'ai plus pris le train
J'ai fait des randonnées en auto
En avion
Un voyage en mer et j'en refais un autre un plus long

Ce soir me voici tout à coup dans ce bruit de chemin de fer qui m'était si familier
    autrefois
Et il me semble que je le comprends mieux qu'alors

Wagon-restaurant
On ne distingue rien dehors
Il fait nuit noire
Le quart de lune ne bouge pas quand on le regarde
Mais il est tantôt à gauche, tantôt à droite du train

Le rapide fait du 110 à l'heure
Je ne vois rien
Cette sourde stridence qui me fait bourdonner les tympans—le gauche en est
    endolori—c'est le passage d'une tranchée maçonnée
Puis c'est la cataracte d'un pont métallique
La harpe martellée des aiguilles la gifle d'une gare le double crochet à la mâchoire d'un
    tunnel furibond
Quand le train ralentit à cause des inondations on entend un bruit de water-chute
    et les pistons échauffés de la cent tonnes au milieu des bruits de vaisselle et de frein

Le Hâvre autobus ascenseur
J'ouvre les persiennes de la chambre d'hôtel
Je me penche sur les bassins du port et la grande lueur froide d'une nuit étoilée
Une femme chatouillée glousse sur le quai
Une chaîne sans fin tousse geint travaille

Je m'endors la fenêtre ouverte sur ce bruit de basse-cour
Comme à la campagne

Réveil

Je dors toujours les fenêtres ouvertes
J'ai dormi comme un homme seul
Les sirènes à vapeur et à air comprimé ne m'ont pas trop réveillé

Ce matin je me penche par la fenêtre
Je vois
Le ciel
La mer
La gare maritime par laquelle j'arrivais de New-York en 1911
La baraque du pilotage
Et
A gauche
Des fumées des cheminées des grues des lampes à arc à contre-jour

Le premier tram grelotte dans l'aube glaciale
Moi j'ai trop chaud
Adieu Paris
Bonjour soleil

Tu Es Plus Belle Que le Ciel et la Mer

Quand tu aimes il faut partir
Quitte ta femme quitte ton enfant
Quitte ton ami quitte ton amie
Quitte ton amante quitte ton amant
Quand tu aimes il faut partir

Le monde est plein de nègres et de négresses
Des femmes des hommes des hommes des femmes
Regarde les beaux magasins
Ce fiacre cet homme cette femme ce fiacre
Et toutes les belles marchandises

Il y a l'air il y a le vent
Les montagnes l'eau le ciel la terre
Les enfants les animaux
Les plantes et le charbon de terre

Apprends à vendre à acheter à revendre
Donne prends donne prends
Quand tu aimes il faut savoir
Chanter courir manger boire
Siffler
Et apprendre à travailler

Quand tu aimes il faut partir
Ne larmoie pas en souriant
Ne te niche pas entre deux seins
Respire marche pars va-t-en

Je prends mon bain et je regarde
Je vois la bouche que je connais
La main la jambe Le l'œil
Je prends mon bain et je regarde

Le monde entier est toujours là
La vie pleine de choses surprenantes
Je sors de la pharmacie
Je descends juste de la bascule
Je pèse mes 80 kilos
Je t'aime

Lettre

Tu m'as dit si tu m'écris
Ne tape pas tout à la machine
Ajoute une ligne de ta main
Un mot un rien oh pas grand'chose
Oui oui oui oui oui oui oui oui

Ma Remington est belle pourtant
Je l'aime beaucoup et travaille bien
Mon écriture est nette et claire
On voit très bien que c'est moi qui l'ai tapée

Il y a des blancs que je suis seul à savoir faire
Vois donc l'œil qu'a ma page
Pourtant pour te faire plaisir j'ajoute à l'encre
Deux trois mots
Et une grosse tache d'encre
Pour que tu ne puisses pas les lire

Claire de Lune

On tangue on tangue sur le bateau
La lune la lune fait des cercles dans l'eau
Dans le ciel c'est le mât qui fait des cercles
Et désigne toutes les étoiles du doigt

Une jeune Argentine accoudée au bastingage
Rêve à Paris en contemplant les phares qui dessinent la côte de France
Rêve à Paris qu'elle ne connaît qu'à peine et qu'elle regrette déjà
Ces feux tournants fixes doubles colorés à éclipses lui rappellent ceux qu'elle voyait de
     sa fenêtre d'hôtel sur les Boulevards et lui promettent un prompt retour
Elle rêve de revenir bientôt en France et d'habiter Paris
Le bruit de ma machine à écrire l'empêche de mener ce rêve jusqu'au bout
Ma belle machine à écrire qui sonne au bout de chaque ligne et qui est aussi rapide
     qu'un jazz
Ma belle machine à écrire qui m'empêche de rêver à babord comme à tribord
Et qui me fait suivre jusqu'au bout une idée
Mon idée

La Pallice

La Pallice et l'Ile de Ré sont posées sur l'eau et peintes
Minutieusement
Comme ces stores des petits bistros bretons des environs de la gare Montparnasse
Ou ces aquarelles infâmes que vend boulevard de la Madeleine un rapin hirsute habillé
     de velours qui a les deux mains nouées depuis sa naissance qui peint avec les coudes
     et qui vous fait le boniment à travers son bec-de-lièvre
Les vérités de la Pallice

Bilbao

Nous arrivons bien avant l'aube dans la rade de Bilbao
Un cirque de montagnes basses et de collines à contre-jour noir velours piqué des
    lumières de la ville
Ce décor simple et bien composé me rappelle et au risque de passer pour un imbécile
    puisque je suis en Espagne je le répète me rappelle un décor de Picasso

Il y a des barquettes montées par deux hommes seulement et munies d'une toute petite
    voile triangulaire qui prennent déjà le large
Deux marsouins font la roue
Dès que le soleil se lève de derrière les montagnes
Ce décor si simple
Est envahi
Par un déluge de couleurs
Qui vont de l'indigo au pourpre
Et qui transforment Picasso en expressionniste allemand
Les extrêmes se touchent

La Corugna

Un phare attendri comme une madone géante
De l'extérieur c'est une jolie petite ville espagnole
A terre c'est un tas de fumier
Deux trois gratte-ciel y poussent

Villa Garcia

Trois croiseurs rapides un navire hôpital
Le pavillon anglais
Des signaux optiques lumineux
Deux carabinieros dorment sur les fauteuils du pont
Enfin nous partons
Dans les vents sucrés

Porto Leixoës

On arrive tard et c'est dimanche
Le port est un fleuve déchaîné
Les pauvres émigrants qui attendent que les autorités viennent à bord sont rudement
    secoués dans de pauvres petites barques qui montent les unes sur les autres
    sans couler
Le port a un œil malade l'autre crevé
Et une grue énorme s'incline comme un canon à longue portée

Sur les Côtes du Portugal

Du Hâvre nous n'avons fait que suivre les côtes comme les navigateurs anciens
Au large du Portugal la mer est couverte de barques et de chalutiers de pêche
Elle est d'un bleu constant et d'une transparence pélagique
Il fait beau et chaud
Le soleil tape en plein
D'innombrables algues vertes microscopiques flottent à la surface
Elles fabriquent des aliments qui leur permettent de se multiplier rapidement
Elles sont l'inépuisable provende vers laquelle accourt la légion des infusoires et des
    larves marines délicates
Animaux de toutes sortes
Vers étoiles de mer oursins
Crustacés menus
Petit monde grouillant près de la surface des eaux toute pénétrée de lumière
Gourmands et friands
Arrivent les harengs les sardines les maquereaux
Que poursuivent les germons les thons les bonites
Que poursuivent les marsouins les requins les dauphins
Le temps est clair la pêche est favorable
Quand le temps se voile les pêcheurs sont mécontents et font entendre leurs
    lamentations jusqu'à la tribune du parlement

En Route pour Dakar

L'air est froid
La mer est d'acier
Le ciel est froid
Mon corps est d'acier
Adieu Europe que je quitte pour la première fois depuis 1914
Rien ne m'intéresse plus à ton bord pas plus que les émigrants de l'entrepont juifs russes
    basques espagnols portugais et saltimbanques allemands qui regrettent Paris
Je veux tout oublier ne plus parler tes langues et coucher avec des nègres et des négresses
    des indiens et des indiennes des animaux des plantes
Et prendre un bain et vivre dans l'eau
Et prendre un bain et vivre dans le soleil en compagnie d'un gros bananier
Et aimer le gros bourgeon de cette plante
Me segmenter moi-même
Et devenir dur comme un caillou
Tomber à pic
Couler à fond

35° 57' Latitude Nord
15° 16' Longitude Ouest

C'est aujourd'hui que c'est arrivé
Je guettais l'événement depuis le début de la traversée
La mer était belle avec une grosse houle de fond qui nous faisait rouler
Le ciel était couvert depuis le matin
Il était 4 heures de l'après-midi
J'étais en train de jouer aux dominos
Tout à coup je poussai un cri et courus sur le pont
C'est ça c'est ça
Le bleu d'oultremer
Le bleu perroquet du ciel
Atmosphère chaude
On ne sait pas comment cela s'est passé et comment définir la chose
Mais tout monte d'un degré de tonalité
Le soir j'en avais la preuve par quatre
Le ciel était maintenant pur
Le soleil couchant comme une roue
La pleine lune comme une autre roue
Et les étoiles plus grandes plus grandes

Ce point se trouve entre Madère à tribord et Casablanca à babord
Déjà

En Vue de l'Ile de Fuerteventura

Tout a encore grandi depuis hier
L'eau le ciel la pureté de l'atmosphère
Les îles Canaries ont l'aspect des rives du Lac de Côme
Des traînées de nuages sont comme des glaciers
Il commence à faire chaud

A Bord du Formose

Le ciel est noir strié de bandes lépreuses
L'eau est noire
Les étoiles grandissent encore et fondent comme des cierges larmoyants
Voici ce qui se passe à bord

Sur le gaillard avant quatre Russes sont installés dans un paquet de cordages et jouent
    aux cartes à la lueur d'une lanterne vénitienne

Sur la plage avant les Juifs en minorité comme chez eux en Pologne se tassent et cèdent
    le pas aux Espagnols qui jouent de la mandoline chantent et dansent la jota

Sur le château les émigrants portugais font une ronde paysanne un homme noir frappe
    deux longues castagnettes en os et les couples rompent la ronde évoluent
    se retournent frappent du talon tandis qu'une voix criarde de femme monte

Les passagers des premières regardent presque tous et envient ces jeux populaires

Au salon une Allemande prétentieuse joue du violon avec beaucoup de chichi avec
    beaucoup de chichi une jeune Française prétentieuse l'accompagne au piano

Sur le pont-promenade va et vient un Russe mystérieux officier de la garde grand duc
    incognito personnage à la Dostoïewsky que j'ai baptisé Dobro-Vétcher c'est un petit
    bonhomme triste ce soir il est pris d'une certaine agitation nerveuse il a mis des
    escarpins vernis un habit à basques et un énorme melon comme mon père en portait
    en 1895

Au fumoir on joue aux dominos un jeune médecin qui ressemble à Jules Romains et
    qui se rend dans le haut Soudan un armurier belge qui descendra à Pernambuco
    un Hollandais le front coupé en deux hémisphères par une cicatrice profonde il est
    directeur du Mont-de-Piété de Santiago del Chili et une jeune théâtreuse de
    Ménilmontant peuple gavrocharde qui s'occupe d'un tas de combines dans les autos
    elle m'offre même une mine de plomb au Brésil et un puits de pétrole à Bakou

Sur le château-arrière les émigrants allemands bien propres et soigneusement peignés
    chantent avec leurs femmes et leurs enfants des cantiques durs et des chansons
    sentimentales

Sur le pont-arrière on discute très fort et se chamaille dans toutes les langues de l'est
    européen

Dans la cambuse les Bordelais font une manille et dans son poste l'opérateur de T. S. F.
    s'engueule avec Santander et Mogador

Lettre-Océan

La lettre-océan n'est pas un nouveau genre poétique
C'est un message pratique à tarif regressif et bien meilleur marché qu'un radio
On s'en sert beaucoup à bord pour liquider des affaires que l'on n'a pas eu le temps de
    régler avant son départ et pour donner des dernières instructions
C'est également un messager sentimental qui vient vous dire bonjour de ma part entre
    deux escales aussi éloignées que Leixoës et Dakar alors que me sachant en mer pour
    six jours on ne s'attend pas à recevoir de mes nouvelles
Je m'en servirai encore durant la traversée du sud-atlantique entre Dakar et Rio-de-
    Janeiro pour porter des messages en arrière car on ne peut s'en servir que dans ce
    sens-là
La lettre-océan n'a pas été inventée pour faire de la poésie
Mais quand on voyage quand on commerce quand on est à bord quand on envoie des
    lettres-océan
On fait de la poésie

A la Hauteur de Rio de l'Ouro

Les cormorans nous suivent
Ils ont un vol beaucoup plus sûr que les mouettes ce sont des oiseaux beaucoup plus
    gros ils ont un plus beau plumage blanc bordé de noir brun ou tout noir comme
    les corneilles de mer
Nous croisons six petits voiliers chargés de sel qui font le service entre Dakar et
    les Grandes Canaries

En Vue du Cap Blanc

L'atmosphère est chaude sans excès
La lumière du soleil filtre à travers un air humide et nuageux
La température uniforme est plutôt élevée
C'est la période que traverse sans doute actuellement la planète Vénus
Ce sont les meilleures conditions pour paresser

Dakar

Enfin nous longeons et tournons autour des Deux Mamelles qui émergeaient depuis ce
    matin et grandissaient sur l'horizon
Nous les contournons et entrons dans le port de Dakar
Quand on se retourne
On voit une digue rouge un ciel bleu et une plage blanche éblouissante

Gorée

Un château-fort méditerranéen
Et derrière une petite île plate ruines portugaises et bungalows d'un jaune moderne très
    salon d'automne

Dans cet ancien repaire de négriers n'habitent plus que les fonctionnaires coloniaux qui
    ne trouvent pas à se loger à Dakar où sévit également la crise des loyers
J'ai visité d'anciens cachots creusés dans la basaltine rouge on voit encore les chaînes et
    les colliers qui maintenaient les noirs
Des airs de gramophone descendaient jusque dans ces profondeurs

Oeufs Artificiels

En attendant de pouvoir débarquer nous buvons des cocktails au fumoir
Un banquier nous raconte l'installation et le fonctionnement d'une fabrique d'œufs
    artificiels établie dans la banlieue de Bordeaux
On fabrique le blanc d'œuf avec de l'hémoglobine de sang de cheval
Le jaune d'œuf est fabriqué avec de la farine de maïs très impalpable et des huiles fines
Ce mélange est répandu dans des moules ronds qui passent au frigorifique
Ainsi on obtient une boule jaune que l'on trempe dans du coliure pour qu'une légère
    pellicule se forme autour

On met autour de ce produit de l'hémoglobine fouettée comme de la crème et le tout
  retourne au frigo où le blanc d'œuf artificiel se saisit exposé à température très basse
Nouveau bain de coliure puis on obtient par un procédé très simple un précipité
  calcaire qui forme la coquille
Ceci me rappelle que j'ai vu avant la guerre à Dusseldorf des machines à polir culotter
  et nuancer les grains de café
Et donner ainsi à des cafés de mauvaise qualité l'aspect des grains des cafés d'origine
  Jamaïque Bourbon Bornéo Arabie etc.

Les Boubous

Oh ces négresses que l'on rencontre dans les environs du village nègre chez les
  trafiquants qui aunent la percale de traite
Aucune femme au monde ne possède cette distinction cette noblesse cette démarche
  cette allure ce port cette élégance cette nonchalance ce raffinement cette propreté
  cette hygiène cette santé cet optimisme cette inconscience cette jeunesse ce goût
Ni l'aristocrate anglaise le matin à Hydepark
Ni l'Espagnole qui se promène le dimanche soir
Ni la belle Romaine du Pincio
Ni les plus belles paysannes de Hongrie ou d'Arménie
Ni la princesse russe raffinée qui passait autrefois en traîneau sur les quais de la Néva
Ni la Chinoise d'un bateau de fleurs
Ni les belles dactylos de New-York
Ni même la plus parisienne des Parisiennes
Fasse Dieu que durant toute ma vie ces quelques formes entrevues se balladent dans
  mon cerveau

Chaque mèche de leurs cheveux est une petite tresse de la même longueur ointe peinte
  lustrée
Sur le sommet de la tête elles portent un petit ornement de cuir ou d'ivoire qui est
  maintenu par des fils de soie colorés ou des chaînettes de perles vives
Cette coiffure représente des mois de travail et toute leur vie se passe à la faire et
  à la refaire
Des rangs de piécettes d'or percent le cartillage des oreilles
Certaines ont des incisions colorées dans le visage sous les yeux et dans le cou et toutes
  se maquillent avec un art prodigieux
Leurs mains sont recouvertes de bagues et de bracelets et toutes ont les ongles peints
  ainsi que la paume de la main
De lourds bracelets d'argent sonnent à leurs chevilles et les doigts de pieds sont bagués
Le talon est peint en bleu
Elles s'habillent de boubous de différentes longueurs qu'elles portent les uns par dessus
  les autres ils sont tous d'impression de couleur et de broderie variées elles arrivent
  à composer un ensemble inouï d'un goût très sûr où l'orangé le bleu l'or ou le blanc
  domine
Elles portent aussi des ceintures et de lourds grigris
D'autres plusieurs turbans célestes
Leur bien le plus précieux est leur dentition impeccable et qu'elles astiquent comme on
  entretient les cuivres d'un yacht de luxe
Leur démarche tient également d'un fin voilier
Mais rien ne peut dire les proportions souples de leur corps ou exprimer la nonchalance
  réfléchie de leur allure

Bijou-Concert

Non
Jamais plus
Je ne foutrai les pieds dans un beuglant colonial
Je voudrais être ce pauvre nègre je voudrais être ce pauvre nègre qui reste à la porte
Car les belles négresses seraient mes sœurs
Et non pas
Et non pas
Ces sales vaches françaises espagnoles serbes allemandes qui meublent les loisirs des
    fonctionnaires cafardeux en mal d'un Paris de garnison et qui ne savent comment
    tuer le temps
Je voudrais être ce pauvre nègre et perdre mon temps

Les Charognards

Le village nègre est moins moche est moins sale que la zone de Saint-Ouen
Les charognards qui le survolent plongent parfois et le nettoient

Sous les Tropiques

Dans ces parages le courant des vagues couvre les rochers d'une abondante floraison
    animale
Des éponges de toutes sortes
Des polypes si semblables par leur forme à des plantes qu'on les appelle
Des «lys de mer» quand ils ont l'air de fleurs vivantes fixées au fond de la mer par leur
    pédoncule
Des «palmiers marins» quand ils étalent au sommet d'une tige qui peut atteindre
    17 mètres leur panache de bras semblables à des feuilles de dattiers
Les uns ont cinq bras d'autres en ont dix semblables à des plumes couleur de rose et
    nagent en les faisant onduler
Sur les récifs d'innombrables mollusques traînent leur coquille dont la variété est infinie
Aux formes surbaissées et à bouche arrondie sont venues s'ajouter les longues coquilles
    aux tours d'hélice nombreux
La coquille renflée et polie
Celle à longue ouverture évasée échancrée ou prolongée en canal
Et le mollusque qui vole dans l'eau à l'aide de deux larges ailes dépendantes de son pied
    qui vole dans la haute mer comme les papillons volent dans l'air

Ornithichnites

Les oiseaux qui nous suivaient continuellement depuis Le Havre disparaissent
    aujourd'hui
Par contre à l'avant s'envolent des bandes de poissons-volants que le vent projette sur le
    pont
Ce sont de tout petits êtres qui sentent terriblement mauvais
Leur membrane est gluante

Bleus

La mer est comme un ciel bleu bleu bleu
Par au-dessus le ciel est comme le Lac Léman
Bleu-tendre

Couchers de Soleil

Tout le monde parle des couchers de soleil
Tous les voyageurs sont d'accord pour parler des couchers de soleil dans ces parages
Il y a plein de bouquins où l'on ne décrit que les couchers de soleil
Les couchers de soleil des tropiques
Oui c'est vrai c'est splendide
Mais je préfère de beaucoup les levers de soleil
L'aube
Je n'en rate pas une
Je suis toujours sur le pont
A poils
Et je suis toujours seul à les admirer
Mais je ne vais pas les décrire les aubes
Je vais les garder pour moi seul

Nuits Étoilées

Je passe la plus grande partie de la nuit sur le pont
Les étoiles familières de nos latitudes penchent penchent sur le ciel
L'étoile Polaire descend de plus en plus sur l'horizon nord
Orion—ma constellation—est au zénith
La Voie Lactée comme une fente lumineuse s'élargit chaque nuit
Le Chariot est une petite brume
Le sud est de plus en plus noir devant nous
Et j'attends avec impatience l'apparition de la Croix du Sud à l'est
Pour me faire patienter Vénus a doublé de grandeur et quintuplé d'éclat comme la lune
    elle fait une traînée sur la mer
Cette nuit j'ai vu tomber un bolide

Complet Blanc

Je me promène sur le pont dans mon complet blanc acheté à Dakar
Aux pieds j'ai mes espadrilles achetées à Villa Garcia
Je tiens à la main mon bonnet basque rapporté de Biarritz
Mes poches sont pleines de Caporal Ordinaire
De temps en temps je flaire mon étui en bois de Russie
Je fais sonner des sous dans ma poche et une livre sterling en or
J'ai mon gros mouchoir calabrais et des allumettes de cire de ces grosses que l'on
    ne trouve qu'à Londres
Je suis propre lavé frotté plus que le pont
Heureux comme un roi
Riche comme un milliardaire
Libre comme un homme

La Cabine N° 6

Je l'occupe
Je devrais toujours vivre ici
Je n'ai aucun mérite à y rester enfermé et à travailler
D'ailleurs je ne travaille pas j'écris tout ce qui me passe par la tête
Non tout de même pas tout
Car des tas de choses me passent par la tête mais n'entrent pas dans ma cabine
Je vis dans un courant d'air le hublot grand ouvert et le ventilateur ronflant
Je ne lis rien

Bagage

Dire que des gens voyagent avec des tas de bagages
Moi je n'ai emporté que ma malle de cabine et déjà je trouve que c'est trop que
    j'ai trop de choses
Voici ce que ma malle contient
Le manuscrit de Moravagine que je dois terminer à bord et mettre à la poste à Santos
    pour l'expédier à Grasset
Le manuscrit du Plan de l'Aiguille que je dois terminer le plus tôt possible pour
    l'expédier au Sans Pareil
Le manuscrit d'un ballet pour la prochaine saison des Ballets Suédois et que j'ai fait à
    bord entre Le Hâvre et la Pallice d'où je l'ai envoyé à Satie
Le manuscrit du Cœur du Monde que j'enverrai au fur et à mesure à Raymone
Le manuscrit de l'Equatoria
Un gros paquet de contes nègres qui formera le deuxième volume de mon Anthologie
Plusieurs dossiers d'affaires
Les deux gros volumes du dictionnaire Darmesteter
Ma Remington portable dernier modèle
Un paquet contenant des petites choses que je dois remettre à une femme à Rio
Mes babouches de Tombouctou qui portent les marques de la grande caravane
Deux paires de godasses mirifiques
Une paire de vernis

Deux complets
Deux pardessus
Mon gros chandail du Mont-Blanc
De menus objets pour la toilette
Une cravate
Six douzaines de mouchoirs
Trois liquettes
Six pyjamas
Des kilos de papier blanc
Des kilos de papier blanc
Et un grigri
Ma malle pèse 57 kilos sans mon galurin gris

Orion

C'est mon étoile
Elle a la forme d'une main
C'est ma main montée au ciel
Durant toute la guerre je voyais Orion par un créneau
Quand les Zeppelins venaient bombarder Paris ils venaient toujours d'Orion
Aujourd'hui je l'ai au-dessus de ma tête
Le grand mât perce la paume de cette main qui doit souffrir
Comme ma main coupée me fait souffrir percée qu'elle est par un dard continuel

L'Équateur

L'océan est d'un bleu noir le ciel bleu est pâle à côté
La mer se renfle tout autour de l'horizon
On dirait que l'Atlantique va déborder sur le ciel
Tout autour du paquebot c'est une cuve d'outremer pur

Le Passage de la Ligne

Naturellement j'ai été baptisé
C'est mon onzième baptême sur la ligne
Je m'étais habillé en femme et l'on a bien rigolé
Puis on a bu

Je Nage

Jusqu'à la ligne c'était l'hiver
Maintenant c'est l'été
Le commandant a fait installer une piscine sur le pont supérieur
Je plonge je nage je fais la planche
Je n'écris plus
Il fait bon vivre

S. Fernando Noronha

J'envoie un radio à Santos pour annoncer mon arrivée
Puis je remonte me mettre dans la piscine
Comme j'étais en train de nager sur le dos et de faire la baleine M. Mouton l'officier
    radiotélégraphiste du bord m'annonce qu'il est en communication avec le Belle-Isle
    et me demande si je ne veux pas envoyer une lettre-océan (à Madame Raymone
    ajoute-t-il avec un beau sourire)
J'envoie une lettre-océan pour dire qu'il fait bon vivre
Et je me remets dans l'eau
L'eau est fraîche
L'eau est salée

Amaralina

Ce poste de T. S. F. me fait dire qu'on m'attendra à Santos avec une auto
Je suis désespéré d'être bientôt arrivé
Encore six jours de mer seulement
J'ai le cafard
Je ne voudrais jamais arriver et faire sauter la Western

Les Souffleurs

Nous sommes à la hauteur de Bahia
J'ai vu un premier oiseau
Un cargo anglais
Et trois souffleurs au large
J'ai aussi vu une grande dorade

Dimanche

Il fait dimanche sur l'eau
Il fait chaud
Je suis dans ma cabine enfermé comme dans du beurre fondant

Le Poteau Noir

Nous sommes depuis plusieurs jours déjà dans la région du poteau
Je sais bien que l'on écrit depuis toujours le pot au noir
Mais ici à bord on dit le poteau
Le poteau est un poteau noir au milieu de l'océan où tous les bateaux s'arrêtent histoire
    de mettre une lettre à la poste
Le poteau est un poteau noir enduit de goudron où l'on attachait autrefois les matelots
    punis de corde ou de schlague
Le poteau est un poteau noir contre lequel vient se frotter le chat à neuf queues

Assurément quand l'orage est sur vous on est comme dans un pot de noir
Mais quand l'orage se forme on voit une barre noir dans le ciel cette barre noircit
    s'avance menace et dame le matelot le matelot qui n'a pas la conscience tranquille
    pense au poteau noir
D'ailleurs même si j'ai tort j'écrirai le poteau noir et non le pot au noir car j'aime
    le parler populaire et rien ne me prouve que ce terme n'est pas en train de muer
Et tous les hommes du Formose me donnent raison

Pedro Alvarez Cabral

Le Portugais Pedro Alvarez Cabral s'était embarqué à Lisbonne
En l'année 1500
Pour se rendre dans les Indes Orientales
Des vents contraires le portèrent vers l'ouest et le Brésil fut découvert

Terres

Un cargo pointe vers Pernambuco
Dans la lorgnette du barman c'est un vapeur anglais tout recouvert de toiles blanches
A l'œil nu il paraît enfoncé dans l'eau et cassé par le milieu comme la série des cargos
    américains construits durant la guerre
On discute ferme à ce sujet quand j'aperçois la côte
C'est une terre arrondie entourée de vapeurs chromées et surmontée de trois panaches
    de nacre
Deux heures plus tard nous voyons des montagnes triangulaires
Bleues et noires

Oeufs

La côte du Brésil est semée d'îlots ronds nus au milieu desquels nous naviguons depuis
    deux jours
On dirait des œufs bigarrés qu'un gigantesque oiseau a laissé choir
Ou des fientes volcaniques
Ou des sphingtéas de vautour

Papillon

C'est curieux
Depuis deux jours que nous sommes en vue des terres aucun oiseau n'est venu à notre
    rencontre ou se mettre dans notre sillage
Par contre
Aujourd'hui
A l'aube
Comme nous pénétrions dans la baie de Rio
Un papillon grand comme la main est venu virevolter tout autour du paquebot
Il était noir et jaune avec de grandes stries d'un bleu déteint

Rio de Janeiro

Tout le monde est sur le pont
Nous sommes au milieu des montagnes
Un phare s'éteint
On cherche le Pain de Sucre partout et dix personnes le découvrent à la fois dans cent
    directions différentes tant ces montagnes se ressemblent dans leur piriformité
M. Lopart me montre une montagne qui se profile sur le ciel comme un cadavre
    étendu et dont la silhouette ressemble beaucoup à celle de Napoléon sur son lit de
    mort
Je trouve qu'elle ressemble plutôt à Wagner un Richard Wagner bouffi d'orgueil ou
    envahi par la graisse
Rio est maintenant tout près et l'on distingue les maisons sur la plage
Les officiers comparent ce panorama à celui de la Corne d'Or
D'autres racontent la révolte des forts
D'autres regrettent unanimement la construction d'un grand hôtel moderne haut et
    carré qui défigure la baie (il est très beau)
D'autres encore protestent véhémentement contre l'abrasage d'une montagne
Penché sur le bastingage tribord je contemple
La végétation tropicale d'un îlot abandonné
Le grand soleil qui creuse la grande végétation
Une petite barque montée par trois pêcheurs
Ces hommes aux mouvements lents et méthodiques
Qui travaillent
Qui pêchent
Qui attrapent du poisson
Qui ne nous regardent même pas
Tout à leur métier

Sur Rade

On a hissé les pavillons
La jaune pour demander la visite de la santé
La bleu pour demander la police
Le rouge et blanc pour demander la douane
Celui constellé des Chargeurs Réunis
Et le bleu blanc rouge
Et le brésilien
Il y en a encore deux que je ne connais pas
Les passagers admirent les constructions déconfites de l'Exposition
Des vedettes des ferrys vont viennent et des grandes voiles latines très lentes comme sur
    le lac de Genève
Le soleil tape
Un aigle tombe

La Coupée

On est enfin à quai un quai rectiligne moderne armé de grues de Duisburg
Des mouchoirs s'agitent
On se fait des signes
Blanc-boubou-boubou-blanc m'a déjà oublié
Elle découvre dans la foule un long zigoto cuivré très chic et indolent que je crois bien
    avoir déjà rencontré à Paris
Elle est émue c'est beau puis lui fait signe de retenir un porteur et lui fait comprendre
    par cris et par gestes qu'elle a cinq malles de cabine et beaucoup beaucoup d'autres
    bagages des grands et des petits
Moi je sais même tout ce qu'elle a dans ces malles car je les lui ai bouclées ce matin
    alors qu'elle avait presque une crise de nerfs
Au revoir gosselette gosseline elle passe maintenant la coupée au bras de son type fin
    comme un chevreuil inquiétant et attirant
Comme tout mélange princier de sang blanc et noir
Je songe au grand grigri créole qu'il porte dans sa culotte
Une voix monte du quai Est-ce que Monsieur Blaise Cendrars est à bord?
Présent!
Douze chapeaux s'agitent
Je débarque
Et l'on me photographie
«Monte là-dessus . . . Monte là-dessus . . .»

Banquet

Une heure de taxi le long de la plage
Vitesse klaxon présentations rires jeunes gens Paris Rio Brésil France interviews
    présentations rires
Nous allons jusqu'à la Grotte de la Presse
Puis nous rentrons déjeuner en ville
Les plats ne sont pas encore servis que déjà les journaux parlent de moi et publient
    la photo de tout à l'heure
Bonne cuisine du pays vins portugais et pinga
A quatorze heures tapantes je suis à bord
Un jeune poète sympathique dégobille sur le pont je le ramène à terre où son
    compagnon dégobille à son tour
Les autres n'ont pu suivre
Je monte me plonger dans la piscine tandis que le Formose appareille
Vive l'eau

Belle Soirée

Le soir tombe sur la côte américaine
Pas un poisson pas un oiseau

Une chaîne continue de montagnes uniformes toutes recouvertes d'une végétation
	luxuriante
La mer est unie
Le ciel aussi
Je pense aux deux amis que je me suis fait à bord et qui viennent de me quitter à Rio
M. Lopart agent de change à Bruxelles gentil charmant qui me tenait tête à table ou
	le soir au fumoir devant une bouteille de whisky
Et Boubou-blanc-blanc-boubou la meilleure des copines avec qui je nageais des heures
	dans la piscine matin et soir
A nous trois nous faisions un groupe très gai qui pleurait aux larmes à force de rire
Nous avons embêté tout le monde à bord scandalisé les fonctionnaires et militaires
	(supérieurs) en mission
Je n'ai jamais autant ri depuis dix ans et ri durant vingt jours j'étais malade de rire et ai
	augmenté de six kilos
Au revoir mes bons amis à bientôt nous nous retrouverons à bord en rentrant en France
	ou un autre jour à Paris ou à Bruxelles ou ailleurs dans un train qui franchira
	les Andes ou à bord de l'Emperess qui cinglera vers l'Australie nous aurons toujours
	le même barman car le monde est bien petit pour d'aussi gais compagnons
A bientôt à bientôt

Pleine Nuit en Mer

La côte montagneuse est éclairée à giorno par la pleine lune qui voyage avec nous
La Croix du Sud est à l'est et le sud reste tout noir
Il fait une chaleur étouffante
De gros morceaux de bois nagent dans l'eau opaque
Sur le pont les deux acrobates allemandes se promènent aux trois quarts nues
Elles cherchent de la fraîcheur
Le petit médecin portugais qui accompagne les émigrants de sa nation jusqu'à Buenos-
	Aires cligne de l'œil en passant devant moi
Je le vois s'engouffrer avec les deux allemandes dans une grande cabine inoccupée
Deux navires passent à tribord puis trois à babord
Tous les cinq sont éclairés comme pour une fête de nuit
On se croirait dans le port de Monte-Carlo et la forêt vierge pousse jusque dans la mer
En dressant l'oreille et en tendant toutes mes facultés d'attention j'entends comme
	le bruissement des feuilles
Ou peut-être mon chagrin de quitter le bord demain
Au bout d'un grand quart d'heure je perçois la mince chanson d'un émigrant sur
	le gaillard avant où du linge sèche à la lune et me fait des signes

Paris

Je suis resté toute la nuit sur le pont écoutant les messages qui arrivaient par T. S. F.
	en déchiffrant quelques bribes
Et les traduisant en clignant des yeux pour les étoiles
Un astre nouveau brillait à la hauteur de mon nez
La braise de mon cigare
Je songeais distraitement à Paris
Et chaque étoile du ciel était remplacée parfois par un visage connu

J'ai vu Jean comme une torche follette l'œil malicieux d'Erik le regard posé de Fernand
    et les yeux d'un tas de cafés autour de Sanders
Les bésicles rondes d'Eugénia celles de Marcel
Le regard en flèche de Mariette et les yeux dodelinant du Gascon
De temps en temps Francis et Germaine passaient en auto et Abel faisait de la mise en
    scène et était triste
Puis la T. S. F. reprenait et je reregardais les étoiles
Et l'astre nouveau s'allumait à nouveau au bout de mon nez
Il m'éclairait comme Raymone
Tout près tout près

Aube

A l'aube je suis descendu au fond des machines
J'ai écouté pour une dernière fois la respiration profonde des pistons
Appuyé à la fragile main-courante de nickel j'ai senti pour une dernière fois cette sourde
    vibration des arbres de couche pénétrer en moi avec le relent des huiles surchauffées
    et la tiédeur de la vapeur
Nous avons encore bu un verre le chef mécanicien cet homme tranquille et triste qui a
    un si beau sourire d'enfant et qui ne cause jamais et moi
Comme je sortais de chez lui le soleil sortait tout naturellement de la mer et chauffait
    déjà dur
Le ciel mauve n'avait pas un nuage
Et comme nous pointions sur Santos notre sillage décrivait un grand arc-de-cercle
    miroitant sur la mer immobile

Iles

Iles
Iles
Iles où l'on ne prendra jamais terre
Iles où l'on ne descendra jamais
Iles couvertes de végétations
Iles tapies comme des jaguars
Iles muettes
Iles immobiles
Iles inoubliables et sans nom
Je lance mes chaussures par-dessus bord car je voudrais bien aller jusqu'à vous

Arrivée à Santos

Nous pénétrons entre des montagnes qui se referment derrière nous
On ne sait plus où est le large
Voici le pilote qui grimpe l'échelle c'est un métis aux grands yeux
Nous entrons dans une baie intérieure qui s'achève par un goulet
A gauche il y a une plage éblouissante sur laquelle circulent des autos à droite
    la végétation tropicale muette dure tombe à la mer comme un niagara de
    chlorophyle

Quand on a passé un petit fort portugais riant comme une chapelle de la banlieue
      de Rome et dont les canons sont comme des fauteuils où l'on voudrait s'asseoir
      à l'ombre on serpente une heure dans le goulet plein d'eau terreuse
Les rives sont basses
Celle de gauche plantée de mangliers et de bambous géants autour des bicoques rouges
      et noires ou bleues et noires des nègres
Celle de droite désolée marécageuse pleine de palmiers épineux
Le soleil est étourdissant

A Babord

Le port
Pas un bruit de machine pas un sifflet pas une sirène
Rien ne bouge on ne voit pas un homme
Aucune fumée monte aucun panache de vapeur
Insolation de tout un port
Il n'y a que le soleil cruel et la chaleur qui tombe du ciel et qui monte de l'eau
      la chaleur éblouissante
Rien ne bouge
Pourtant il y a là une ville de l'activité une industrie
Vingt-cinq cargos appartenant à dix nations sont à quai et chargent du café
Deux cents grues travaillent silencieusement
(A la lorgnette on distingue les sacs de café qui voyagent sur les tapis-roulants
      et les monte-charge continus
La ville est cachée derrière les hangars plats et les grands dépôts rectilignes en tôle
      ondulée)
Rien ne bouge
Nous attendons des heures
Personne ne vient
Aucune barque ne se détache de la rive
Notre paquebot a l'air de se fondre minute par minute et de couler lentement dans la
      chaleur épaisse de se gondoler et de couler à pic

A Tribord

Une frégate est suspendue en l'air
C'est un oiseau d'une souveraine élégance aux ailes à incidence variable et profilées
      comme un planeur
Deux gros dos squameux émergent de l'eau bourbeuse et replongent dans la vase
Des régimes de bananes flottent à vau-l'eau
Depuis que nous sommes là trois nouveaux cargos ont surgi derrière nous silencieux
      et las
La chaleur les écrase

Vie

Le Formose évite sur son ancre et nous virons imperceptiblement de bord
Une embarcation se détache de la rive

C'est une pirogue taillée dans un tronc d'arbre
Elle est montée par deux petits moricauds
L'un est couché sur le dos immobile
L'autre accroupi à l'avant pagaie nonchalemment
Le soleil joue sur les deux faces de sa pagaie
Ils font lentement le tour du bateau puis retournent à la rive

La Plage de Guaruja

Il est quatorze heures nous sommes enfin à quai
J'ai découvert un paquet d'hommes à l'ombre dans l'ombre ramassée d'une grue
Certificats médicaux passeport douane
Je débarque
Je ne suis pas assis dans l'auto qui m'emporte mais dans la chaleur molle épaisse
    rembourrée comme une carosserie
Mes amis qui m'attendent depuis sept heures du matin sur le quai ensoleillé ont encore
    tout juste la force de me serrer la main
Toute la ville retentit de jeunes klaxons qui se saluent
De jeunes klaxons qui nous raniment
De jeunes klaxons qui nous donnent faim
De jeunes klaxons qui nous mènent déjeuner sur la plage de Guarujà
Dans un restaurant rempli d'appareils à sous tirs électriques oiseaux mécaniques
    appareils automatiques qui vous font les lignes de la main gramophones qui vous
    disent la bonne aventure et où l'on mange de la bonne vieille cuisine brésilienne
    savoureuse épicée nègre indienne

Bananeraie

Nous faisons encore un tour en auto avant de prendre le train
Nous traversons des bananeraies poussiéreuses
Les abattoirs puants
Une banlieue misérable et une brousse florissante
Puis nous longeons une montagne en terre rouge où s'amoncellent des maisons
    cubiques peinturlurées en rouge et en bleu noir des maisons de bois construites sur
    des placers abandonnés
Deux chèvres naines broutent les plantes rares qui poussent au bord de la route deux
    chèvres naines et un petit cochon bleu

Mictorio

Le mictorio c'est les W. C. de la gare
Je regarde toujours cet endroit avec curiosité quand j'arrive dans un nouveau pays
Les lieux de la gare de Santos sont un petit réduit où une immense terrine qui me
    rappelle les grandes jarres qui sont dans les vignes en Provence où une immense
    terrine est enfouie jusqu'au col dans le sol
Un gros boudin de bois noir large et épais est posé en couronne sur le bord et sert
    de siège
Cela doit être bien mal commode et trop bas
C'est exactement le contraire des tinettes de la Bastille qui elles sont trop haut perchées

Les Tinettes de la Bastille

Les tinettes de la Bastille servent encore dans les cachots de la caserne de Reuilly à Paris
Ce sont des pots de grès en forme d'entonnoir renversé d'environ un mètre trente-cinq
    de haut
Elles sont au centre des cachots la partie la plus évasée reposant sur le sol et le petit bout
    la partie la plus étroite en l'air
C'est dans cette espèce d'embouchure de trompette qui est beaucoup trop haut placée
    que le soldat puni de cachot doit réussir à faire ses besoins
Sans rien laisser choir à l'extérieur sinon il rebiffe pour la même durée de tôle
C'est le supplice de Tantale à rebours
Au début de la guerre j'ai connu des poilus qui pour ce motif et de vingt-quatre en
    vingt-quatre heures ont passé des mois en cachot puis ils finissaient par passer au
    tourniquet comme fortes têtes
On racontait que ces tinettes étaient les anciennes tinettes de l'ancienne prison de la
    Bastille

Sâo-Paulo Railway Cº

Le rapide est sous pression
Nous nous installons dans un Pullman pompéien qui ressemble aux confortables
    wagons des chemins de fer égyptiens
Nous sommes autour d'une table de bridge dans de larges fauteuils d'osier
Il y a un bar au bout du wagon où je bois le premier café de Santos
Au départ nous croisons un convoi de wagons blancs qui portent cette inscription
Caloric Cy
Tu parles
J'étouffe

Paysage

La terre est rouge
Le ciel est bleu
La végétation est d'un vert foncé
Ce paysage est cruel dur triste malgré la variété infinie des formes végétatives
Malgré la grâce penchée des palmiers et les bouquets éclatants des grands arbres
    en fleurs fleurs de carême

Dans le Train

Le train va assez vite
Les signaux aiguilles et passages à niveau fonctionnent comme en Angleterre
La nature est d'un vert beaucoup plus foncé que chez nous
Cuivrée
Fermée
La forêt a un visage d'indien
Tandis que le jaune et le blanc dominent dans nos prés
Ici c'est le bleu céleste qui colore les campos fleuris

Paranapiaçaba

Le Paranapiaçaba est la Serra do Mar
C'est ici que le train est hissé par des câbles et franchit la dure montagne en plusieurs
    sections
Toutes les stations sont suspendues dans le vide
Il y a beaucoup de chutes d'eau et il a fallu entreprendre de grands travaux d'art pour
    étayer partout la montagne qui s'effrite
Car la Serra est une montagne pourrie comme les Rognes au-dessus de Bionnasay mais
    les Rognes couvertes de forêts tropicales
Les mauvaises herbes qui poussent sur les talus dans la tranchée entre les voies sont
    toutes des plantes rares qu'on ne voit à Paris que dans les vitrines des grands
    horticulteurs
Dans une gare trois métis indolents étaient en train de les sarcler

Ligne Télégraphique

Vous voyez cette ligne télégraphique au fond de la vallée et dont le tracé rectiligne
    coupe la forêt sur la montagne d'en face
Tous les poteaux en sont de fer
Quand on l'a installée les poteaux étaient en bois
Au bout de trois mois il leur poussait des branches
On les a alors arrachés retournés et replantés la tête en bas les racines en l'air
Au bout de trois mois il leur repoussait de nouvelles branches ils reprenaient racine et
    recommençaient à vivre
Il fallut tout arracher et pour rétablir une nouvelle ligne faire venir à grands frais des
    poteaux de fer de Pittsburg

Trouées

Échappées sur la mer
Chutes d'eau
Arbres chevelus moussus
Lourdes feuilles caoutchoutées luisantes
Un vernis de soleil
Une chaleur bien astiquée
Reluisance
Je n'écoute plus la conversation animée de mes amis qui se partagent les nouvelles que
    j'ai apportées de Paris
Des deux côtés du train toute proche ou alors de l'autre côté de la vallée lointaine
La forêt est là et me regarde et m'inquiète et m'attire comme le masque d'une momie
Je regarde
Pas l'ombre d'un œil

Visage Raviné

Il y a les frondaisons de la forêt les frondaisons
Cette architecture penchée ouvragée comme la façade d'une cathédrale avec des niches
et des enjolivures des masses perpendiculaires et des fûts frêles

Piratininga

Quand on franchit la crête de la Serra et qu'on est sorti des brouillards qui
l'encapuchonnent le pays devient moins inégal
Il finit par n'être plus qu'une vaste plaine ondulée bornée au nord par des montagnes
bleues
La terre est rouge
Cette plaine offre des petits bouquets de bois peu élevés d'une étendue peu considérable
très rapprochés les uns des autres qui souvent se touchent par quelque point et sont
disséminés au milieu d'une pelouse presque rase
Il est difficile de déterminer s'il y a plus de terrain couvert de bois qu'il n'y en a de
pâturages
Cela fait une sorte de marqueterie de deux nuances de vert bien différentes et bien
tranchées
Celle de l'herbe d'une couleur tendre
Celle des bois d'une teinte foncée

Botanique

L'araucaria attire les regards
On admire sa taille gigantesque
Et surtout ses branches
Qui nées à différentes hauteurs
S'élèvent en manière de candélabre
Et s'arrêtent toutes au même point pour former un plateau parfaitement égal
On voit aussi le grand seneçon aux fleurs d'un jaune d'or les myrtées
Les térébinthacées
La composée si commune qu'on nomme Alecrim do campo le romarin des champs
Et le petit arbre à feuilles ternées n° 1204 *bis*
Mais mon plus grand bonheur est de ne pas pouvoir mettre de nom sur des tas de
plantes toutes plus belles les unes que les autres
Et que je ne connais pas
Et que je vois pour la première fois
Et que j'admire

Ignorance

Je n'écoute plus toutes les belles histoires que l'on me raconte sur l'avenir le passé le
    présent du Brésil
Je vois par la portière du train qui maintenant accélère sa marche
La grande fougère ptéris caudata
Qu'il n'y a pas un oiseau
Les grandes fourmilières maçonnées
Que les lys forment ici des buissons impénétrables
Les savanes se composent tantôt d'herbes sèches et de sous-arbrisseaux tantôt au milieu
    des herbes d'arbres épars çà et là presque toujours tortueux et rabougris
Que les ricins atteignent plusieurs mètres de hauteur
Il y a quelques animaux dans les prés des bœufs à longues cornes des chevaux maigres à
    allure de moustang et des taureaux zébus
Qu'il n'y a aucune trace de culture
Puis je ne sais plus rien de tout ce que je vois
Des formes
Des formes de végétation
Des palmiers des cactus on ne sait plus comment appeler ça des manches à balai
    surmontés d'aigrettes roses il paraît que c'est un fruit aphrodisiaque

Sâo-Paulo

Enfin voici des usines une banlieue un gentil petit tramway
Des conduites électriques
Une rue populeuse avec des gens qui vont faire leurs emplettes du soir
Un gazomètre
Enfin on entre en gare
Saint-Paul
Je crois être en gare de Nice
Ou débarquer à Charring-Cross à Londres
Je trouve tous mes amis
Bonjour
C'est moi

Le Hâvre-Saint-Paul, fév. 1924

II. SÂO-PAULO

Debout

La nuit s'avance
Le jour commence à poindre
Une fenêtre s'ouvre
Un homme se penche au dehors en fredonnant
Il est en bras de chemise et regarde de par le monde
Le vent murmure doucement comme une tête bourdonnante

La Ville Se Réveille

Les premiers trams ouvriers passent
Un homme vend des journaux au milieu de la place
Il se démène dans les grandes feuilles de papier qui battent des ailes et exécute une
　　espèce de ballet à lui tout seul tout en s'accompagnant de cris gutturaux…
　　STADO… ERCIO… EIO
Des klaxons lui répondent
Et les premières autos passent à toute vitesse

Klaxons Électriques

Ici on ne connaît pas la Ligue du Silence
Comme dans tous les pays neufs
La joie de vivre et de gagner de l'argent s'exprime par la voix des klaxons et la pétarade
　　des pots d'échappement ouverts

Menu Fretin

Le ciel est d'un bleu cru
Le mur d'en face est d'un blanc cru
Le soleil cru me tape sur la tête
Une négresse installée sur une petite terrasse fait frire de tout petits poissons sur un
　　réchaud découpé dans une vieille boîte à biscuits
Deux négrillons rongent une tige de canne à sucre

Paysage

Le mur ripoliné de la PENSION MILANESE s'encadre dans ma fenêtre
Je vois une tranche de l'avenue Sao-Joao
Trams autos trams
Trams-trams trams trams
Des mulets jaunes attelés par trois tirent de toutes petites charrettes vides
Au-dessus des poivriers de l'avenue se détache l'enseigne géante de la CASA TOKIO
Le soleil verse du vernis

Saint-Paul

J'adore cette ville
Saint-Paul est selon mon cœur
Ici nulle tradition
Aucun préjugé
Ni ancien ni moderne
Seuls comptent cet appétit furieux cette confiance absolue cet optimisme cette audace
　　ce travail ce labeur cette spéculation qui font construire dix maisons par heure de
　　tous styles ridicules grotesques beaux grands petits nord sud égyptien yankee cubiste

Sans autre préoccupation que de suivre les statistiques prévoir l'avenir le confort l'utilité
  la plus value et d'attirer une grosse immigration
Tous les pays
Tous les peuples
J'aime ça
Les deux trois vieilles maisons portugaises qui restent sont des faïences bleues

III

Départ

Pour la dernière fois je reprends le caminho do Mar
Mais je n'en jouis pas à cause d'Oswald qui a le cafard
Et qui fait le sombre ténébreux
La Serra est dans le brouillard
L'auto a des à-coups
Le moteur des ratés

A Quai

Au revoir mes bons amis Au revoir
Rentrez vite à São-Paulo avant la nuit
On parle une dernière fois des mitrailleuses de la révolution
Moi je reste seul à bord de ce grand bateau hollandais plein d'Allemands de Hollandais
  d'Argentins enfantins brillants cosmétiqués et de 2–3 faux Anglais
Les émigrants espagnols rentrent dans leur pays
Ils ont gagné un peu d'argent puisqu'ils peuvent se payer un billet de retour et ils ont
  l'air bien content
Un couple danse au son d'un accordéon
C'est encore une jota

Cabine 2

C'est la mienne
Elle est toute blanche
J'y serai très bien
Tout seul
Car il me faut beaucoup travailler
Pour rattraper les 9 mois au soleil
Les 9 mois au Brésil
Les 9 mois aux Amis
Et je dois travailler pour Paris
C'est pourquoi j'aime déjà ce bateau archibondé où je ne vois personne avec qui faire
  causette

A Table

J'ai donné un bon pourboire au maître-d'hôtel pour avoir dans un coin une petite table
    à moi tout seul
Je ne ferai pas de connaissances
Je regarde les autres et je mange
Voici le premier menu de goût européen
J'avoue que je mange avec plaisir ces plats d'Europe
Potage Pompadour
Culotte de bœuf à la bruxelloise
Perdreau sur canapé
Le goût est le sens le plus atavique le plus réactionnaire le plus national
Analytique
Aux antipodes de l'amour du toucher du toucher de l'amour en pleine évolution et
    croissance universelle
Révolutionnaire
Synthétique

Retard

Il est près de deux heures du matin et nous ne partons toujours pas
On n'arrête pas d'embarquer du café
Les sacs vont vont et vont sur les monte-charge continus et tombent à fond de cale
    comme les porcs gonflés de Chicago
J'en ai marre
Je vais me coucher

Réveil

Je suis nu
J'ai déjà pris mon bain
Je me frictionne à l'eau de Cologne
Un voilier lourdement secoué passe dans mon hublot
Il fait froid ce matin
Il y a de la brume
Je range mes papiers
J'établis un horaire
Mes journées seront bien remplies
Je n'ai pas une minute à perdre
J'écris

La Brise

Pas un bruit pas une secousse
Le «Gelria» tient admirablement la mer
Sur ce paquebot de luxe avec ses orchestres tziganes dans chaque cache-pot on se lève
    tard
La matinée m'appartient
Mes manuscrits sont étalés sur ma couchette
La brise les feuillette d'un doigt distrait
Présences

Rio-de-Janeiro

Une lumière éclatante inonde l'atmosphère
Une lumière si colorée et si fluide que les objets qu'elle touche
Les rochers roses
Le phare blanc qui les surmonte
Les signaux du sémaphore en semblent liquéfiés
Et voici maintenant que je sais le nom des montagnes qui entourent cette baie
    merveilleuse
Le Géant couché
La Gavéa
Le Bico de Papagaio
Le Corcovado
Le Pain de Sucre que les compagnons de Jean de Léry appelaient le Pot de Beurre
Et les aiguilles étranges de la chaîne des Orgues
Bonjour Vous

Dîner en Ville

Mr. Lopart n'était plus à Rio il était parti samedi par le «Lutetia»
J'ai dîné en ville avec le nouveau directeur
Après avoir signé le contrat de 24 F/N type Grand Sport je l'ai mené dans un petit
    caboulot sur le port
Nous avons mangé des crevettes grillées
Des langues de dorade à la mayonnaise
Du tatou
(La viande de tatou a le goût de la viande de renne chère à Satie)
Des fruits du pays mamans bananes oranges de Bahia
Chacun a bu son fiasco de chianti

Le Matin M'Appartient

Le soleil se lève à six heures moins le quart
Le vent a beaucoup fraîchi
Le matin le pont m'appartient jusqu'à 9 heures
Je regarde les matelots qui récurent le spardeck
Les hautes vagues

Un vapeur brésilien que nous rattrapons
Un seul et unique oiseau blanc et noir
Quand apparaissent les premières femmes que le vent secoue et les fillettes qu'il trousse
    en découvrant leur petit derrière hérissé je redescends dans ma cabine
Et me remets au travail

Écrire

Ma machine bat en cadence
Elle sonne au bout de chaque ligne
Les engrenages grasseyent
De temps en temps je me renverse dans mon fauteuil de jonc et je lâche une grosse
    bouffée de fumée
Ma cigarette est toujours allumée
J'entends alors le bruit des vagues
Les gargouillements de l'eau étranglée dans la tuyauterie du lavabo
Je me lève et trempe ma main dans l'eau froide
Ou je me parfume
J'ai voilé le miroir de l'armoire à glace pour ne pas me voir écrire
Le hublot est une rondelle de soleil
Quand je pense
Il résonne comme la peau d'un tambour et parle fort

Mauvaise Foi

Ce sacré maître-d'hôtel à qui j'avais tout de même donné un bon pourboire pour être
    seul vient me trouver avec son air de chat miteux
Il me prie de la part du commandant de venir prendre place à la table d'honneur
Je suis furieux mais ne puis refuser
Au dîner il se trouve que le commandant est un homme très sympathique
Je suis entre un attaché d'ambassade à la Haye et un consul anglais à Stockholm
De l'autre côté il y a une sommité mondiale en bactériologie et son épouse qui est une
    femme douce et gourmande toute blanche de peau avec des yeux ronds et mats
Mes paradoxes antimusicaux et mes théories culinaires secouent la table d'indignation
L'attaché à la Haye trempe son monocle dans le bouillon
Le consul à Stockholm devient vert-congestion comme un pyjama rayé
La sommité bactériologique allonge encore sa tête pointue de furet
Son épouse glousse et se ride du centre vers la périphérie si bien que tout son visage
    finit par ressembler à un nombril de poussah
Le commandant cligne de l'œil avec malice

Smoking

Il n'y a que les miteux qui n'ont pas de smoking à bord
Il n'y a que les gens trop bien élevés qui ont des smokings à bord
Je mets un petit complet en cheviote d'Angleterre et la mer est d'un bleu aussi uni que
    mon complet bleu tropical

La Nuit Monte

J'ai bien observé comment cela se passait
Quand le soleil est couché
C'est la mer qui s'assombrit
Le ciel conserve encore longtemps une grande clarté
La nuit monte de l'eau et encercle lentement tout l'horizon
Puis le ciel s'assombrit à son tour avec lenteur
Il y a un moment où il fait tout noir
Puis le noir de l'eau et le noir du ciel reculent
Il s'établit une transparence éburnéenne avec des reflets dans l'eau et des poches
        obscures au ciel
Puis le Sac à Charbon sous la Croix du Sud
Puis la Voie Lactée

Traversée sans Histoire

Hollande Hollande Hollande
Fumée plein le fumoir
Tziganes plein l'orchestre
Fauteuils plein le salon
Familles familles familles
Trous plein les bas
Et les femmes qui tricotent qui tricotent

Chaleur

De La Plata à Pernambouc il y a six jours en transatlantique rapide
On voit souvent la côte mais pas un seul oiseau
Comme à l'intérieur de l'immense état de Saint-Paul on reste des jours entiers à rouler
        sur les routes dans la poussière
Sans faire lever un seul oiseau
Tant il fait chaud

Cap Frie

J'ai entendu cette nuit une voix d'enfant derrière ma porte
Douce
Modulée
Pure
Ça m'a fait du bien

Incognito Dévoilé

Voici déjà quelques jours que j'intriguais énormément mes compagnons de table
Ils se demandaient ce que je pouvais bien être
Je parlais bactériologie avec la sommité mondiale
Femmes et boîtes de nuit avec le commandant
Théories kantiennes de la paix avec l'attaché à la Haye
Affaires de fret avec le consul anglais
Paris cinéma musique banque vitalisme aviation
Ce soir à table comme je lui faisais un compliment la femme de la sommité mondiale
    dit C'est vrai
Monsieur est poète
Patatras
Elle l'a appris de la femme du jockey qui est en deuxième
Je ne puis pas lui en vouloir car son sourire en forme de nombril gourmand m'amuse
    plus que tout au monde
Je voudrais bien savoir comment elle arrive à si bien plisser un visage grassouillet et rond

Nourrices et Sports

Il y a plusieurs nourrices à bord
Des sèches et des pas sèches
Quand on joue aux palets sur le pont
Chaque fois que la jeune Allemande se penche elle montre deux petits seins blottis au
    fond de son corsage
Tous les hommes du passager des premières aux matelots connaissent ce jeu et tous
    passent par le pont babord pour voir ces deux choses rondes au nid
On doit en parler jusque dans la cambuse
Au bout d'un banc
Dans un coin sombre
Un nourrisson se pend et fait gicler un grand sein de négresse abondant et gommeux
    comme un régime de bananes

Vie Dangereuse

Aujourd'hui je suis peut-être l'homme le plus heureux du monde
Je possède tout ce que je ne désire pas
Et la seule chose à laquelle je tienne dans la vie chaque tour de l'hélice m'en rapproche
Et j'aurai peut-être tout perdu en arrivant

Coquilles

Les fautes d'orthographe et les coquilles font mon bonheur
Il y a des jours où j'en ferais exprès
C'est tricher
J'aime beaucoup les fautes de prononciation les hésitations de la langue et l'accent de
    tous les terroirs

Un Jour Viendra

Un jour viendra
La technique moderne n'y suffit plus
Chaque traversée coûte un million aux électeurs
Avec les avions et les dirigeables cela coûtera dix millions
Les câbles sous-marins ma cabine de luxe les roues les travaux des ports les grandes
    industries mangent de l'argent
Toute cette activité prodigieuse qui fait notre orgueil
Les machines n'y suffisent plus
Faillite
Sur son fumier Job se sert encore de son face-massage électrique
C'est gai

Coucher de Soleil

Nous sommes en vue des côtes
Le coucher de soleil a été extraordinaire
Dans le flamboiement du soir
D'énormes nuages perpendiculaires et d'une hauteur folle
Chimères griffons et une grande victoire ailée sont restés toute la nuit au-dessus de
    l'horizon
Au petit jour tout le troupeau se trouvait réuni jaune et rose au-dessus de Bahia en
    damier

Bahia

Lagune églises palmiers maisons cubiques
Grandes barques avec deux voiles rectangulaires renversées qui ressemblent aux jambes
    immenses d'un pantalon que le vent gonfle
Petites barquettes à aileron de requin qui bondissent entre les lames de fond
Grands nuages perpendiculaires renflés colorés comme des poteries
Jaunes et bleues

Hic Haec Hoc

J'ai acheté trois ouistitis que j'ai baptisés Hic Haec Hoc
Douze colibris
Mille cigares
Et une main de bahiana grande comme un pied
Avec ça j'emporte le souvenir du plus bel éclat de rire

Pernambouco

Victor Hugo l'appelle Fernandbouc aux Montagnes Bleues
Et un vieil auteur que je lis Ferdinandbourg aux mille Eglises
En indien ce nom signifie la Bouche Fendue
Voici ce que l'on voit aujourd'hui quand on arrive du large et que l'on fait une escale
    d'une heure et demie
Des terres basses sablonneuses
Une jetée en béton armé et une toute petite grue
Une deuxième jetée en béton armé et une immense grue
Une troisième jetée en béton armé sur laquelle on édifie des hangars en béton armé
Quelques cargos à quai
Une longue suite de baraques numérotées
Et par derrière quelques coupoles deux trois clochers et un observatoire astronomique
Il y a également les tanks de l'*American Petroleum* Cᵒ et de la *Caloric*
Du soleil de la chaleur et de la tôle ondulée

Adrienne Lecouvreur et Cocteau

J'ai encore acheté deux tout petits ouistitis
Et deux oiseaux avec des plumes comme en papier moiré
Mes petits singes ont des boucles d'oreilles
Mes oiseaux ont les ongles dorés
J'ai baptisé le plus petit singe Adrienne Lecouvreur l'autre Jean
J'ai donné un oiseau à la fille de l'amiral argentin qui est à bord
C'est une jeune fille bête et qui louche des deux yeux
Elle donne un bain de pied à son oiseau pour lui dédorer les pattes
L'autre chante dans ma cabine dans quelques jours il imitera tous les bruits familiers et
    sonnera comme ma machine à écrire
Quand j'écris mes petits singes me regardent
Je les amuse beaucoup
Ils s'imaginent qu'ils me tiennent en cage

Chaleur

Je meurs de chaleur dans ma cabine et je ne puis pas aérer pour ne pas exposer ma
    petite famille de petites bêtes au courant d'air
Tant pis
Je reste dans ma cabine
J'étouffe et j'écris j'écris
J'écris pour leur faire plaisir
Ces petites bêtes sont bien gentilles et moi aussi

Requins

On m'appelle
Il y a des requins dans notre sillage
Deux trois monstres qui bondissent en virant du blanc quand on leur jette des poules
J'achète un mouton que je balance par-dessus bord
Le mouton nage les requins ont peur je suis volé

Entrepont

Je passe la soirée dans l'entrepont et dans le poste de l'équipage
C'est une véritable ménagerie à bord
Bengalis perroquets singes un fourmilier un cachorro do matto
De la marmaille nue
Des femmes qui sentent fort

Un Trait

Un trait qui s'estompe
Adieu
C'est l'Amérique
Il y a au-dessus une couronne de nuages
Dans la nuit qui vient une étoile de plus belle eau
Maintenant on va cingler vers l'est et à partir de demain la piscine sera installée sur le
    pont supérieur

Le Charpentier

Hic Haec Hoc sont chez le charpentier
Je ne garde dans ma cabine que l'oiseau et les singes Adrienne et Cocteau
Chez le charpentier c'est plein de perroquets de singes de chiens de chats
Lui est un bonhomme qui fume sa pipe
Il a ces yeux gris des buveurs de vin blanc
Quand on parle il vous répond en donnant de grands coups de rabot qui font sauter des
    buchies
En vrille
Je le surnomme Robinson Crusoé
Alors il daigne sourire

Je l'Avais Bien Dit

Je l'avais dit
Quand on achète des singes
Il faut prendre ceux qui sont bien vivants et qui vous font presque peur
Et ne jamais choisir un singe doux endormi qui se blottit dans vos bras
Car ce sont des singes drogués qui le lendemain sont féroces
C'est ce qui vient d'arriver à une jeune fille qui a été mordue au nez

Christophe Colomb

Ce que je perds de vue aujourd'hui en me dirigeant vers l'est c'est ce que Christophe
    Colomb découvrait en se dirigeant vers l'ouest
C'est dans ces parages qu'il a vu un premier oiseau blanc et noir qui l'a fait tomber à
    genoux et rendre grâces à Dieu
Avec tant d'émotion
Et improviser cette prière baudelairienne qui se trouve dans son journal de bord
Et où il demande pardon d'avoir menti tous les jours à ses compagnons en leur
    indiquant un faux point
Pour qu'ils ne puissent retrouver sa route

Rire

Je ris
Je ris
Tu ris
Nous rions
Plus rien ne compte
Sauf ce rire que nous aimons
Il faut savoir être bête et content

Le Commandant Est un Chic Type

Le commandant est tout de même un chic type
Hier il a fait monter la piscine pour moi seul
Aujourd'hui sans rien dire à personne et tout simplement pour me faire plaisir
Il fait un crochet
Et longe Fernando do Noronha de si près que je pourrais presque cueillir un bouquet

Fernando de Noronha

De loin on dirait une cathédrale engloutie
De près
C'est une île aux couleurs si intenses que le vert de l'herbe est tout doré

Grotte

Il y a une grotte qui perce l'île de part en part

Pic

Il y a un pic dont personne n'a pu me dire le nom
Il ressemble au Cervin et c'est le dernier pilier de l'Atlantide
Quelle émotion quand je crois découvrir à la lunette les traces d'une terrasse atlante

Plage

Dans une baie
Derrière un promontoire
Une plage de sable jaune et des palmiers de nacre

Bagne

Un mur blanc
Haut comme celui d'un cimetière
Il porte l'inscription suivante en caractères gigantesques que l'on peut très bien
    dèchiffrer à l'œil nu
Logement des prises

Civilisation

Il y a quelques traces de cultures
Quelques maisons
Une station de T. S. F. deux pylônes et deux tours Eiffel en construction
Un vieux port portugais
Un calvaire
A la lunette je distingue sur le mur du bagne un homme nu qui agite un chiffon blanc
Les nuits sont les plus belles sans lune avec des étoiles immenses et la chaleur ne va que
    grandissante
Comme l'agitation des hélices rend l'eau nocturne de plus en plus phosphorescente
    dans notre sillage

Passagers

Ils sont tous là à faire de la chaise longue
Ou à jouer aux cartes
Ou à prendre le thé
Ou à s'ennuyer
Il y a tout de même un petit groupe de sportifs qui jouent aux galets
Ou au deck-tennis
Et un autre petit groupe qui vient nager dans la piscine
La nuit quand tout le monde est couché les fauteuils vides alignés sur le pont
    ressemblent à une collection de squelettes dans un musée
Vieilles femmes desséchées
Caméléons pellicules ongles

L'Oiseau Bleu

Mon oiseau bleu a le ventre tout bleu
Sa tête est d'un vert mordoré
Il a une tache noire sous la gorge
Ses ailes sont bleues avec des touffes de petites plumes jaune doré
Au bout de la queue il y a des traces de vermillon
Son dos est zébré de noir et de vert
Il a le bec noir les pattes incarnat et deux petits yeux de jais
Il adore faire trempette se nourrit de bananes et pousse un cri qui ressemble au
    sifflement d'un tout petit jet de vapeur
On le nomme le septicolore

Pourquoi

L'oiseau siffle
Les singes le regardent
Maîtrise
Je travaille en souriant
Tout ce qui m'arrive m'est absolument égal
Et tout ce que je fais m'est absolument indifférent
Je suis des yeux quelqu'un qui n'est pas là
J'ècris en tournant le dos à la marche du navire
Soleil dans le brouillard
Avance
Retard
Oui

Oiseaux

Les rochers guaneux sont remplis d'oiseaux

Jangada

Trois hommes nus au large
Montés sur une jangada ils chassent au cachalot
Trois poutres blanches une voile triangulaire un balancier

Sillage

La mer continue à être d'un bleu de mer
Le temps continue à être le plus beau temps que j'ai jamais connu en mer
Cette traversée continue à être la plus calme et la plus dépourvue d'incidents que l'on
  puisse imaginer

Bal

Un couple américain danse des danses apaches
Les jeunes Argentines boudent l'orchestre et méprisent cordialement les jeunes gens
  du bord
Les Portugais éclatent en applaudissements dès qu'on joue un air portugais
Les Français font bande à part rient fort et se moquent de tout le monde
Seules les petites bonnes ont envie de danser dans leurs belles robes
J'invite la nourrice nègre au grand scandale des uns et pour l'amusement des autres
Le couple américain redanse des danses apaches

Podomètre

Quand on fait les cent pas sur le pont…

Pourquoi J'Écris?

Parce que…

1924

Sud-Américaines

I

La route monte en lacets
L'auto s'élève brusque et puissante
Nous grimpons dans un tintamarre d'avion qui va plafonner
Chaque tournant la jette contre mon épaule et quand nous virons dans le vide elle
  se cramponne inconsciente à mon bras et se penche au-dessus du précipice

Au sommet de la serra nous nous arrêtons court devant la faille géante
Une lune monstrueuse et toute proche monte derrière nous
«Lua, lua!» murmure-t-elle
Au nom de la lune, mon ami, comment Dieu autorise-t-il ces gigantesques travaux qui
    nous permirent de passer?
Ce n'est pas la lune, chérie, mais le soleil qui en précipitant les brouillards fit cette
    énorme déchirure
Regarde l'eau qui coule au fond parmi les débris des montagnes et qui s'engouffre dans
    les tuyaux de l'usine
Cette station envoie de l'électricité jusqu'à Rio

II

Libertins et libertines
Maintenant nous pouvons avouer
Nous sommes quelques-uns de par le monde
Santé intégrale
Nous avons aussi les plus belles femmes du monde
Simplicité
Intelligence
Amour
Sports
Nous leur avons aussi appris la liberté
Les enfants grandissent avec les chiens les chevaux les oiseaux au milieu des belles
    servantes toutes rondes et mobiles comme des tournesols

III

Il n'y a plus de jalousie de crainte ou de timidité
Nos amies sont fortes et saines
Elles sont belles et simples et grandes
Et elles savent toutes s'habiller
Ce ne sont pas des femmes intelligentes mais elles sont très perspicaces
Elles n'ont pas peur d'aimer
Elles ne craignent pas de prendre
Elles savent tout aussi bien donner
Chacune d'elles a dû lutter avec sa famille leur position sociale le monde ou autre chose
Maintenant
Elles ont simplifié leur vie et sont pleines d'enfantillages
Plus de meubles plus de bibelots elles aiment les animaux les grandes automobiles et
    leur sourire
Elles voyagent
Elles détestent la musique mais emportent toutes un phono

IV

Il y en a trois que j'aime particulièrement
La première

Une vieille dame sensible belle et bonne
Adorablement bavarde et d'une souveraine élégance
Mondaine mais d'une gourmandise telle qu'elle s'est libérée de la mondanité
La deuxième est la sauvageonne de l'Hôtel Meurice
Tout le jour elle peigne ses longs cheveux et grignote son rouge de chez Guerlain
Bananiers nourrice nègre colibris
Son pays est si loin qu'on voyage six semaines sur un fleuve recouvert de fleurs de
    mousses de champignons gros comme des œufs d'autruche
Elle est si belle le soir dans le hall de l'hôtel que tous les hommes en sont fous
Son sourire le plus aigu est pour moi car je sais rire comme les abeilles sauvages
    de son pays
La dernière est trop riche pour être heureuse
Mais elle a déjà fait de grands progrès
Ce n'est pas du premier coup que l'on trouve son équilibre et la simplicité de la vie au
    milieu de toutes les complications de la richesse
Il y faut de l'entêtement
Elle le sait bien elle qui monte si divinement à cheval et qui fait corps avec son grand
    étalon argentin
Que ta volonté soit comme ta cravache
Mais ne t'en sers pas
Trop
Souvent

V

Il y en a encore une autre qui est encore comme une toute petite fille
Malgré son horrible mari ce divorce affreux et la détention au cloître
Elle est farouche comme le jour et la nuit
Elle est plus belle qu'un œuf
Plus belle qu'un rond
Mais elle est toujours trop nue sa beauté déborde elle ne sait pas encore s'habiller
Elle mange aussi beaucoup trop et son ventre s'arrondit comme si elle était enceinte de
    deux petits mois
C'est qu'elle a un tel appétit et une telle envie de vivre
Nous allons lui apprendre tout ça et lui apprendre à s'habiller
Et lui donner les bonnes adresses

VI

Une
Il y en a encore une
Une que j'aime plus que tout au monde
Je me donne à elle tout entier comme une pepsine car elle a besoin d'un fortifiant
Car elle est trop douce
Car elle est encore un peu craintive
Car le bonheur est une chose bien lourde à porter
Car la beauté a besoin d'un petit quart d'heure d'exercice tous les matins

VII

Nous ne voulons pas être tristes
C'est trop facile
C'est trop bête
C'est trop commode
On en a trop souvent l'occasion
C'est pas malin
Tout le monde est triste
Nous ne voulons plus être tristes

1924

Poèmes Divers

Shrapnells

I

Dans le brouillard la fusillade crépite et la voix du canon vient jusqu'à nous
Le bison d'Amérique n'est pas plus terrible
Ni plus beau
Affût
Pareil au cygne du Caméroun

II

Je t'ai rogné les ailes, ô mon front explosible
Et tu ne veux pas du képi
Sur la route nationale 400 mille pieds battent des étincelles aux cliquetis des gamelles
Je pense
Je passe
Cynique et bête
Puant bélier

III

Tous mes hommes sont couchés sous les acacias que les obus saccagent
Oh Ciel bleu de la Marne
Femme
Avec le sourire d'un aéroplane…
On nous oublie

Octobre 1914

Hommage à Guillaume Apollinaire

Le pain lève
La France
Paris
Toute une génération
Je m'adresse aux poètes qui étaient présents
Amis
Apollinaire n'est pas mort
Vous avez suivi un corbillard vide
Apollinaire est un mage
C'est lui qui souriait dans la soie des drapeaux aux fenêtres
Il s'amusait à vous jeter des fleurs et des couronnes
Tandis que vous passiez derrière son corbillard
Puis il a acheté une petite cocarde tricolore
Je l'ai vu le soir même manifester sur les boulevards
Il était à cheval sur le moteur d'un camion américain et brandissait un énorme drapeau
     international déployé comme un avion
VIVE LA FRANCE!

Les temps passent
Les années s'écoulent comme des nuages
Les soldats sont rentrés chez eux
A la maison
Dans leur pays
Et voilà que se lève une nouvelle génération
Le rêve des MAMELLES se réalise!
Des petits français, moitié anglais, moitié nègre, moitié russe, un peu belge, italien,
     annamite, tchèque
L'un à l'accent canadien, l'autre les yeux hindous
Dents face os jointures galbe démarche sourire
Ils ont tous quelque chose d'étranger et sont pourtant bien de chez nous
Au milieu d'eux, Apollinaire, comme cette statue du Nil, le père des eaux, étendu avec
     des gosses qui lui coulent de partout
Entre les pieds, sous les aisselles, dans la barbe
Ils ressemblent à leur père et se départent de lui
Et ils parlent tous la langue d'Apollinaire

Paris, novembre 1918

Dictés par Téléphone

DANS LA FORÊT DE BROCÉLIANDE (OPÉRA FÉERIE)

Bien au contraire de Caruso
Côté cour, côté jardin
Quand Cycca, le ténor de la route, chante
Seules les poules ne l'entendent pas

KLAXON

Jazz vient de tanguer
Et de jaser tango
Qu'importe l'étymologie
Si ce petit Klaxon m'amuse

SORTIE DE PARIS

Bébé Cadum vous souhaite bon voyage
Merci, Michelin, pour quand je rentrerai
Comme les fétiches nègres dans la brousse
Les pompes à essence sont nues

PROVERBE A L'AMÉRICAINE

Le temps c'est de l'argent,
Oui, mais Bugatti le double en vitesse

Actualité

Platon n'accorde pas le droit de cité au poète

Les amis, les proches
Tu n'as plus de coutumes et pas encore d'habitudes
Il faut échapper à la tyrannie des journaux
Littérature
Vie pauvre
Orgueil déplacé
La femme, la danse que Nietzsche a voulu nous apprendre à danser
La femme
Mais l'ironie?

Va-et-vient continuel
Vagabondage spécial
Tous les hommes, tous les pays
C'est ainsi que tu n'es plus à charge
Que tu ne te fais plus sentir
Etc.

Au Cœur du Monde
(Fragments)

Ce ciel de Paris est plus pur qu'un ciel d'hiver lucide de froid.
Jamais je ne vis de nuits plus sidérales et plus touffues que ce printemps
Où les arbres des boulevards sont comme les ombres du ciel,
Frondaisons dans les rivières mêlées aux oreilles d'éléphant,
Feuilles de platanes, lourds marronniers.

Un nénuphar sur la Seine, c'est la lune au fil de l'eau.
La Voie Lactée dans le ciel se pâme sur Paris et l'étreint
Folle et nue et renversée, sa bouche suce Notre-Dame.
La Grande Ourse et la Petite Ourse grognent autour de Saint-Merry.
Ma main coupée brille au ciel dans la constellation d'Orion.

Dans cette lumière froide et crue, tremblotante, plus qu'irréelle,
Paris est comme l'image refroidie d'une plante
Qui réapparaît dans sa cendre. Triste simulacre.
Tirées au cordeau et sans âge, les maisons et les rues ne sont
Que pierre et fer en tas dans un désert invraisemblable.

Babylone et la Thébaïde ne sont pas plus mortes, cette nuit, que la ville morte de Paris
Bleue et verte, encre et goudron, ses arêtes blanchies aux étoiles.
Pas un bruit. Pas un passant. C'est le lourd silence de guerre.
Mon œil va des pissotières à l'œil violet des réverbères.
C'est le seul espace éclairé où traîner mon inquiétude.

C'est ainsi que tous les soirs je traverse tout Paris à pied
Des Batignolles au Quartier Latin comme je traverserais les Andes
Sous les feux de nouvelles étoiles, plus grandes et plus consternantes,
La Croix du Sud plus prodigieuse à chaque pas que l'on fait vers elle émergeant
    de l'ancien monde
Sur son nouveau continent.

Je suis l'homme qui n'a plus de passé.—Seul mon moignon me fait mal.—
J'ai loué une chambre d'hôtel pour être bien seul avec moi-même.
J'ai un panier d'osier tout neuf qui s'emplit de mes manuscrits.
Je n'ai ni livres ni tableau, aucun bibelot esthétique.

Un journal traîne sur ma table.
Je travaille dans ma chambre nue, derrière une glace dépolie,
Pieds nus sur du carrelage rouge, et jouant avec des ballons et une petite trompette
    d'enfant:
Je travaille à la FIN DU MONDE.

Hôtel Notre-Dame

Je suis revenu au Quartier
Comme au temps de ma jeunesse
Je crois que c'est peine perdue
Car rien en moi ne revit plus
De mes rêves de mes désespoirs
De ce que j'ai fait à dix-huit ans

On démolit des pâtés de maisons
On a changé le nom des rues
Saint-Séverin est mis à nu
La place Maubert est plus grande
Et la rue Saint-Jacques s'élargit
Je trouve cela beaucoup plus beau
Neuf et plus antique à la fois

C'est ainsi que m'étant fait sauter
La barbe et les cheveux tout court
Je porte un visage d'aujourd'hui
Et le crâne de mon grand-père

C'est pourquoi je ne regrette rien
Et j'appelle les démolisseurs
Foutez mon enfance par terre
Ma famille et mes habitudes
Mettez une gare à la place
Ou laissez un terrain vague
Qui dégage mon origine

Je ne suis pas le fils de mon père
Et je n'aime que mon bisaïeul
Je me suis fait un nom nouveau
Visible comme une affiche bleue
Et rouge montée sur un échafaudage
Derrière quoi on édifie
Des nouveautés des lendemains

Soudain les sirènes mugissent et je cours à ma fenêtre.
Déjà le canon tonne du côté d'Aubervilliers.
Le ciel s'étoile d'avions boches, d'obus, de croix, de fusées,
De cris, de sifflets, de mélisme qui fusent et gémissent sous les ponts.

La Seine est plus noire que gouffre avec les lourds chalands qui sont
Longs comme les cercueils des grands rois mérovingiens
Chamarrés d'étoiles qui se noient—au fond de l'eau—au fond de l'eau.
Je souffle ma lampe derrière moi et j'allume un gros cigare.

Les gens qui se sauvent dans la rue, tonitruants, mal réveillés,
Vont se réfugier dans les caves de la Préfectance qui sentent la poudre et le salpêtre.
L'auto violette du préfet croise l'auto rouge des pompiers,
Féeriques et souples, fauves et câlines, tigresses comme des étoiles filantes.

Les sirènes miaulent et se taisent. Le chahut bat son plein. Là-haut. C'est fou.
Abois. Craquements et lourd silence. Puis chute aiguë et sourde véhémence des
   torpilles.
Dégringolade de millions de tonnes. Eclairs. Feu. Fumée. Flamme.
Accordéon des 75. Quintes. Cris. Chute. Stridences. Toux. Et tassement des
   effondrements.

Le ciel est tout mouvementé de clignements d'yeux imperceptibles
Prunelles, feux multicolores, que coupent, que divisent, que raniment les hélices
   mélodieuses.
Un projecteur éclaire soudain l'affiche du bébé Cadum
Puis saute au ciel et y fait un trou laiteux comme un biberon.

Je prends mon chapeau et descends à mon tour dans les rues noires.
Voici les vieilles maisons ventrues qui s'accotent comme des vieillards.
Les cheminées et les girouettes indiquent toutes le ciel du doigt.
Je remonte la rue Saint-Jacques, les épaules enfoncées dans mes poches.

Voici la Sorbonne et sa tour, l'église, le lycée Louis-le-Grand.
Un peu plus haut je demande du feu à un boulanger au travail.
J'allume un nouveau cigare et nous nous regardons en souriant.
Il a un beau tatouage, un nom, une rose et un cœur poignardé.

Ce nom je le connais bien: c'est celui de ma mère.
Je sors dans la rue en courant. Me voici devant la maison.
Cœur poignardé—premier point de chute—
Et plus beau que ton torse nu, beau boulanger—
La maison où je suis né.

Le Ventre de Ma Mère

C'est mon premier domicile
Il était tout arrondi
Bien souvent je m'imagine
Ce que je pouvais bien être…

Les pieds sur ton cœur maman
Les genoux tout contre ton foie
Les mains crispés au canal
Qui aboutissait à ton ventre

Le dos tordu en spirale
Les oreilles pleines les yeux vides
Tout recroquevillé tendu
La tête presque hors de ton corps

Mon crâne à ton orifice
Je jouis de ta santé
De la chaleur de ton sang
Des étreintes de papa

Bien souvent un feu hybride
Electrisait mes ténèbres
Un choc au crâne me détendait
Et je ruais sur ton cœur

Le grand muscle de ton vagin
Se resserrait alors durement
Je me laissais douloureusement faire
Et tu m'inondais de ton sang

Mon front est encore bosselé
De ces bourrades de mon père
Pourquoi faut-il se laisser faire
Ainsi à moitié étranglé?

Si j'avais pu ouvrir la bouche
Je t'aurais mordu
Si j'avais pu déjà parler
J'aurais dit:
Merde, je ne veux pas vivre

Je suis debout sur le trottoir d'en face et contemple longuement la maison.
C'est la maison où fut écrit le *Roman de la Rose*.
216 de la rue Saint-Jacques, *Hôtel des Etrangers*.
Au 218 est l'enseigne d'une sage-femme de 1ʳᵉ classe.

Comme elle était au complet elle envoya ma mère coucher et accoucher à l'hôtel
    d'à côté.
Cinq jours après je prenais le paquebot à Brindisi. Ma mère allant rejoindre mon père
    en Egypte.
(Le paquebot, *packet-boat*, le paquet, le courrier, la malle; on dit encore la malle des
    Indes et l'on appelle toujours long-courrier le trois-mâts qui fait croisière par
    le cap Horn.)

Suis-je pélagien comme ma nounou égyptienne ou suisse comme mon père
Ou italien, français, écossais, flamand comme mon grand-père ou je ne sais plus quel
    grand aïeul constructeur d'orgues en Rhénanie et en Bourgogne, ou cet autre
Le meilleur biographe de Rubens?
Et il y en a encore un qui chantait au *Chat-Noir*, m'a dit Erik Satie.
Pourtant je suis le premier de mon nom puisque c'est moi qui l'ai inventé de toutes
    pièces.

J'ai du sang de Lavater dans les veines et du sang d'Euler,
Ce fameux mathématicien appelé à la cour de Russie par Catherine II et qui, devenu
    aveugle à 86 ans, dicta à son petit-fils Hans, âgé de 12 ans,
Un traité d'algèbre qui se lit comme un roman
Afin de se prouver que s'il avait perdu la vue, il n'avait pas perdu sa lucidité
Mentale ni sa logique.

Je suis sur le trottoir d'en face et je regarde l'étroite et haute maison d'en face
Qui se mire au fond de moi-même comme dans du sang. Les cheminées fument.
Il fait noir. Jamais je ne vis de nuit plus sidérale. Les bombes éclatent. Les éclats
    pleuvent.
La chaussée éventrée met à jour ce cimetière étrusque établi sur le cimetière des
    mammouths mis à jour
Dans ce chantier où s'édifie l'*Institut Océanographique* du prince de Monaco
Contre la palissade duquel je recule et je chancelle et me colle
Affiche neuve sur les vieilles affiches lacérées.

O rue Saint-Jacques! vieille fente de ce Paris qui a la forme d'un vagin et dont j'aurais
    voulu tourner la vie au cinéma, montrer à l'écran la formation, le groupement, le
    rayonnement autour de son noyau,
Notre-Dame,
Vieille fente en profondeur, long cheminement
De la porte des Flandres à Montrouge,
O rue Saint-Jacques! Oui, je chancelle, mais je ne suis pas frappé à mort, ni même
    touché.

Au Coeur du Monde   353

Si je chancelle, c'est que cette maison m'épouvante et j'entre
—Deuxième point de chute—dans cet *Hôtel des Etrangers*, où souvent déjà j'ai loué
    une chambre à la journée
Ou pour la nuit, maman,
Avec une femme de couleur, avec une fille peinte, du d'Harcourt ou du Boul'Mich'

Et où je suis resté un mois avec cette jeune fille américaine qui devait rentrer dans sa
    famille à New York
Et qui laissait partir tous les bateaux
Car elle était nue dans ma chambre et dansait devant le feu qui brûlait
Dans ma cheminée et que nous nous amusions à faire l'amour chaque fois que la
    fleuriste du coin nous apportait une corbeille de violettes de Parme
Et que nous lisions ensemble, en allant jusqu'au bout, la *Physique de l'Amour* ou le
    Latin mystique de Remy de Gourmont.

Mais cette nuit, maman, j'entre seul.

Hôtel des Étrangers

    Quel est Amour le nom de mon amour?
    On entre On trouve un lavabo une épingle
    A cheveux oubliée au coin
    Ou sur le marbre
    De la cheminée ou tombée
    Dans une rainure du parquet
    Derrière la commode
Mais son nom Amour quel est le nom de mon amour
    Dans la glace?
. . . .

Paris, 1917

Translator's Notes on the Poems

Easter in New York

Written during the author's stay in New York, December 1911–May 1912. The dedication is to Agnès Hall, wife of BC's brother Georges and daughter of painter Richard Hall (1862–1943). The epigraph is from the hymn "Pange lingua," which is still in the Roman breviary and is sung on Good Friday during the adoration of the Cross. Remy de Gourmont translates the hymn in his *Le Latin mystique*, calling it a "masterpiece of theological poetry." It was written either by Claudien Mamert (fifth century A.D.), the archbishop of Vienna, or by Saint Fortunatus (530–609), bishop of Poitiers. BC admired Gourmont's book so much that he copied the entire volume (more than 350 pages) by hand, in the Imperial Library in Saint Petersburg in 1907. In the epigraph, he seems to have miscopied *durement* as *rudement*.

Your feast day: Good Friday.

Carrière: Eugène Carrière (1849–1906), French artist whose work tends to be dark, quiet, and serious, as in his 1899 etching, "The Mother of Christ."

Around the ninth hour: Around three P.M., as described in Luke 23:44.

I'm sitting at the ocean's edge: Miriam Cendrars speculates that perhaps BC took the subway out to a beach.

Burrié-Vladislasz: Apparently in eastern Europe or Russia.

Dic nobis, Maria, quid vidisti in via?: Latin for "Tell us, Mary, what hast thou seen on the road?" From the Catholic liturgy for Easter Sunday.

The Prose of the Trans-Siberian and of Little Jeanne of France

This poem recounts a train trip that BC claims to have taken across Russia soon after his arrival in 1904, during the Russian-Japanese War. *The Trans-Siberian* was published in 1913 in an accordion format with beautiful pochoir designs by Sonia Delaunay (1885–1979) and a variety of typefaces and indentations to indicate stanza breaks. Fully unfolded, each copy was about 6' 7'' tall. The first edition of 150 copies, BC pointed out, was to have been as tall as the Eiffel Tower. One journalist pointed out that it would be a useful book to take out to the country: "If you're caught in a sudden downpour, you can take shelter under it: it's a real portable villa." *The Trans-Siberian* was the first French book illustrated with abstract art; it was the first "simultaneous book"; and it might well qualify as the first book *as art object*. To get an idea of what it looks like in color, see Arthur A. Cohen's *Sonia Delaunay* (New York: Harry N. Abrams, 1975) or S. A. Buckberrough's *Sonia Delaunay: A Retrospective* (Buffalo, N.Y.: Albright-Knox Gallery, 1980).

The Temple at Ephesus: The Artemision, the grandest version of several temples dedicated to the goddess Artemis, at Ephesus, an ancient Ionian city on the west coast of Asia Minor. The temple is said to have been burned to the ground by an arsonist named Herostratus in 356 B.C., on the evening when Alexander the Great was born. The site of the Artemision was first excavated in 1863–74; further discoveries were made when work resumed in 1904, when BC was in Russia.

Novgorod: Novgorod (now Gorky) was one of the most important medieval Russian cities, the capital of the principality of Novgorod. According to BC, his first published literary work was called *The Legend of Novgorod* (1909). It is supposed to have appeared in an edition of fourteen copies in Russian translation, but none survive, and the manuscript has never been found. There are some interesting tales and legends associated with Novgorod, but none that I know of called "The Legend of Novgorod."

I foresaw the coming . . . of the Russian Revolution: The young BC was in Saint Petersburg on Red Sunday, the beginning of the Revolution of 1905.

Amur: River in eastern Asia that forms the boundary between Manchuria and Russia.

Malmo: This seaport was, at the turn of the century, second only to Stockholm in Swedish industry.

Traveling jewel merchant: A Varsovian merchant named Rogovine who took the seventeen-year-old BC under his wing in 1904. They traveled thousands of miles across Russia and China, dealing in antiques, jewels, spices, cuckoo clocks, and rugs.

Harbin: Town in Manchuria that became an important military town during the Russian-Japanese War because it served as a junction on the Trans-Manchurian railway (the part of the Trans-Siberian that crossed Manchuria) with the line leading to Port Arthur.

Golconda: A fortress and ruined city in India that lent its name to the diamonds found in the dominions of the Kutb Shahi dynasty (founded in 1512), which ruled a large and powerful kingdom, with Golconda as its capital and treasury.

Khunkhuz: In his book *Siberia* (1943), Emil Lengyel says, "The . . . Khunkhuz brigands . . . [of Manchuria] took a perverse pleasure in destroying the [railroad] line for no apparent reason whatever."

Boxers: Members of an intensely patriotic organization, the Righteous Harmony Fists (popularized by journalists as "Boxers") retaliated against foreigners and Christians in China in 1900.

"Railroad nerves": In a 1930 letter to John Dos Passos, BC explained this phrase as a technical term used by American psychiatrists to describe "a softening of the spinal marrow due to the trepidations of modern life or some such nonsense." He hazarded "railroad brain" as a translation.

Taciturns: Apparently Siberian hills or mountains.

Patagonia: An area in South America lying partly in Chile, partly in Argentina, it was discovered in 1520 by Magellan and named Tierra del Patagones because of the large footprints of the natives, whose average height was around six feet two inches. Hence, "Patagonia, which befits my immense sadness."

I'm on the road with little Jeanne of France: All we know of Jeanne is in this poem.

Tomsk Chelyabinsk Kansk etc.: Russian towns, most of which are on the Trans-Siberian line.

Cockaigne: The Land of Cockaigne, an imaginary country, a medieval utopia where life was a continual round of luxurious idleness. In literature, Cockaigne is sometimes used as a euphemism for London or Paris—"the big city."

Rousseau: The French painter Henri Rousseau (1844–1910) allowed his artist and poet friends to believe that he had been to Mexico. Guillaume Apollinaire (see note below), whose brother worked in a bank in Mexico, was an enthusiastic perpetuator of this legend.

Land of the thousand lakes: Finland. The Finnish national anthem describes Finland as "you land of a thousand lakes."

Ufa: Russian town.

Grodno: Russian town.

Bruges-the-Dead: Bruges is the capital of West Flanders, Belgium. The belfry of the market hall dates from the end of the thirteenth century. The chimes are famous.

Syracuse: Ancient Sicilian town, the birthplace of Archimedes.

Archimedes: Greek mathematician and inventor (ca. 287–212 B.C.), famous for inventing various mechanical devices, some of which were used as weapons. His most important discoveries were in physics and mathematics. He was killed by a Roman soldier while drawing mathematical figures in the sand, although orders had been given that he be spared.

Chagall: Marc Chagall (1887–1985), Russian-born painter who was virtually discovered by BC.

Guillaume Apollinaire: French poet (1880–1918) and friend of BC. Like Cendrars, he was a foreign national who became a naturalized French citizen and changed his name. See also BC's poems "Hammock" and "Homage to Guillaume Apollinaire."

Kuropotkin: Probably Aleksey Nikolayevich Kuropotkin (1848–1925), commander of the Russian army in the Russian-Japanese War of 1904–5, although BC could also have had in the back of his mind Pyotr Kropotkin, the anarchist, who explored Siberia in the nineteenth century. Both men wrote memoirs.

Irkutsk: A town on the Trans-Siberian line, on Lake Baikal.

Lake Baikal: An enormous Siberian lake (over 400 miles long), surrounded by mountains and filled with salt water and salt-water marine life—2,000 miles from the nearest salt water. Because of various difficulties, the construction of the railroad line was interrupted on one side of Lake Baikal and continued on the other, so that this stretch remained the final one, at last completed in 1905.

Krasnoyarsk: A town on the Trans-Siberian line.

Khilok: A town on the Trans-Siberian line.

Port Arthur: An ice-free port on the southern tip of the Liaotung Peninsula in China, Port Arthur was thus the hope of an expanding, imperialist Russia at the turn of the century.

Chita: A town on the Trans-Siberian line.

Maeterlinck: Maurice Maeterlinck (1862–1949), Belgian-born French poet and dramatist.

Tsitsihar: A town on the Trans-Manchurian line.

Yellow the proud color: A big series of novels from the French publisher Albin Michel had yellow covers.

Lapin Agile: A rustic cabaret in Montmartre frequented before World War I. It was so named because it displayed a large painting of a rabbit, apparently dancing, by an artist named A. Gill.

The great Gibbet: Perhaps BC's nickname for the Eiffel Tower; in "Tower" he says, "I'd like to . . . hang from the Eiffel Tower." It could also be a reference to the Paris of François Villon.

The Wheel: The Ferris wheel erected, like the Eiffel Tower, for the Universal Exposition of 1889. The Universal Exposition of 1900 had a Trans-Siberian Railway pavilion that simulated a train trip across Russia.

Panama, or the Adventures of My Seven Uncles

Written in 1913–14 and published in 1918 by Editions de la Sirène with a cover (a slightly modified version of the timetables for the Union Pacific railroad) designed by BC and executed by Raoul Dufy. The edition was even folded to resemble its model: the back and front covers became, in effect, the back cover when the book was unfolded to be read. Stanza breaks were indicated by bits of American railway maps.

The name *Paname* was also slang for "Paris." BC didn't have seven uncles, but his wife Féla had seven brothers.

The Panama crash: Originally the Panama Canal was a French undertaking. When the enterprise failed, the investors lost a lot of money.

Ahasuerus: The legendary "wandering Jew." Eugène Sue's novel *Le Juif errant* (1844–45) was enormously popular.

Dourak: Polish word for "dummy." BC's first wife Féla was Polish. Miriam Cendrars recalls that *dourak* was a word she and her two brothers used around the house a lot.

Kabyle: A type of Berber in Algeria and Tunisia.

Musset: Alfred de Musset (1810–1857), French poet and dramatist.

General Sutter: Johann August Sutter (Suter, in French), a legendary Swiss adventurer ruined by the discovery of gold on his land in California. BC's most popular novel, *Gold*, tells what he called the "marvelous" story.

Sejera: A small village seven miles outside of Nazareth, founded in 1902. Also known as Ilaniya or Ilanaya.

On board the Volturno *for 35 francs*: Apparently true. The French franc was worth about twenty cents at the time.

The baptism of the line: Refers to the custom of "baptizing" people on board as the ship crossed the equator or one of the tropics. The baptism consisted of dressing up in costumes, having more than a few drinks, and getting drenched. Perhaps that's what the "Splash / Buckets of water" a few lines later refers to. BC mentions such baptisms later in *Travel Notes*. In the Blaise Cendrars collection at the Swiss National Library, there is even a baptismal "certificate" BC saved from one of his trips.

Gaoupa: I have not yet been able to find out what this word means. The next line ("The dirtiest Hungarian word") may refer to it.

Kishinev: The capital of Moldavia.

Solothurnians: Natives of Solothurn (or, in French, Soleure) in Switzerland, not far from where BC was born.

The Uranium Steamship Co.: One of whose steamers was the *Volturno*.

The god Tangaloa: Apparently a Polynesian deity.

Urlu: It is possible that BC originally meant *Urdu*. It is also possible that someone pointed out the mistake to him. According to Miriam Cendrars, he rejected such criticisms. Besides, his taste for fabulation sometimes led him to prefer invention over "reality." He let *Urlu* stand in edition after edition.

I feel like killing someone with a sap or a waffle iron: The French is *au boudin ou à la gaufre*, literally "with a sausage or a waffle." *Boudin* was slang for "black-jack" and the expression *prendre un gaufre* means "to take a blow." I've tried to retain the suggestion of slang, as well as the oddness and humor of the phrasing, as well as the food imagery (sap, syrup, waffles . . .).

General Robertson: Possibly Sir William Robert Robertson, first baronet (1860–1933), who was a member of the intelligence staff of the British forces during the Boer War (1899–1902).

Tugela: River in southern Africa and scene of important military operations in the Boer War during the siege of Ladysmith (1899–1900).

Remy de Gourmont: French writer (1858–1915) much admired by BC.

Cartridge thread or twine: The original is *filagore ou seizaine*. In a 1930 letter to John Dos Passos, BC confessed that he had been seduced by the sound of the technical term *filagore*.

Hananiah Mishael Azariah: Also known as Shadrach, Meshach, and Abed-nego, the three companions of Daniel who were thrown into the blazing furnace of King Nebuchadnezzar because they refused to worship his gods. See the first three chapters of the Book of Daniel in the Bible.

Froggy went a-courtin': The French *brebis qui broute* means "the grazing goat," no doubt suggested by the *saute-mouton* (literally, "leap-sheep") in the previous line. It's hard to say whether the "goat" line continues the game imagery of the "sheep" line or whether it goes off in another direction. Within the context of the line that follows ("Springboard woman"), the "goat" line has a faint suggestion of sexuality. There is probably no connection with the Café Brebis celebrated in Pierre MacOrlan's *La Clique du café brebis*.

"Siméon, Siméon": Simeon was the son of Jacob in the Bible. Miriam Cendrars recalls that around the First World War it was also a popular song that BC sang with Robert and Sonia Delaunay. Perhaps he's referring to the three of them as the "three hot-blooded young people" a few lines before.

Quai-d'Orsay–Saint-Nazaire: The Gare d'Orsay train station in Paris served Saint-Nazaire, an important port for the Americas.

You go under the Eiffel Tower . . . to come down on the other side of the world: An early draft of this poem suggests that BC is referring to the San Francisco Panama-Pacific Exposition of 1915.

Acaraguan Bananan: Apparently the name of a company.

Those islands of the blessed: A reference to what in ancient times were called the Fortunate Isles, now the Canary Islands, the westernmost of which, Hierro (formerly Ferro) was believed by ancient geographers to be the western limit of the world, and therefore the spot from which they measured longitude. Cendrars has quite a few references to longitude, latitude, meridians, the equator, the tropical lines, etc. in his poetry.

Tupa: Possibly the municipality in the state of São Paulo.

Lives of the Saints, etc.: Book titles. *Cymbalum mundi* is a polemical religious and philosophical tract in four dialogues by Bonaventure Despériers (1498–1544). *The Crocodile of Saint-Martin* is an allegorical poem by Louis-Claude de Saint-Martin (1743–1803), sometimes known as the Unknown Philosopher, in which he embraces the mystical doctrines of Jakob Böhme.

Strindberg: August Strindberg (1849–1912), the Swedish playwright and novelist.

Gavarni: The pen name of Sulpice Guillaume Chevalier (1801–1866), French caricaturist who was also interested in aerial navigation. See E. and J. Goncourt's *Gavarni, l'homme et l'oeuvre* (1873).

The propeller of gems: This phrase also appears in "Titles," the sixteenth poem in *Nineteen Elastic Poems.*

Maggi: The brand name of a Swiss beef extract.

Byrrh: The brand name of an aperitif.

A shudder of wreckage: The *frissoulis* in the original *frissoulis de bris* is an invented word.

Press Argus: A clipping service. In fact it was BC's first wife Féla who collected newspaper mentions of BC by using the services of Press Argus.

Aspinwall: The old name for Colón.

The Trunk: In British Stock Exchange language, "Trunk" originally was short for Grand Trunk Railway of Canada. There have been several Canadian trunk lines. The term is often used loosely.

Toyo Kisen Kaisha: The last one may be Kaishu, the Japanese name for the North Korean town of Haeju.

900 million: "400 million" in an earlier version. No one seems to have figured out what BC meant here.

The Rotonde: A Montparnasse bar frequented by writers and artists.

Nineteen Elastic Poems

First edition published by Au Sans Pareil in 1919 with a frontispiece portrait of the author by Modigliani. An individual date of composition follows each poem. See Jean-Pierre Goldenstein's *Dix-neuf poèmes élastiques de Blaise Cendrars* (Paris: Méridiens Klincksieck, 1986) for a brilliant study of these poems, from which some of the following notes are derived.

1. NEWSPAPER

My paintings: Cendrars did paint at various times, including during his recuperation from a broken leg the same month he wrote this poem.

I'm the other one: BC is quoting Gérard de Nerval's comment on seeing his portrait by Nadar, but one can't help thinking also of Rimbaud's "*Je est un autre*" ("I is another"). On 5 May 1912, BC did a self-portrait pencil drawing, under which he wrote, "*Je suis l'autre.*" Therefore, in this poem BC is, in a sense, quoting both Nerval and himself. An appropriate quotation for this dualistic operation.

2. TOWER

Castellammare: Castellammare di Stabia, a port near Naples, not far from the location of ancient Stabia, which was destroyed by an eruption of Mount Vesuvius in A.D. 79. There is no evidence that BC was in Italy in 1910.

The cloud of grasshoppers, one of the ten plagues of Egypt: See Exodus 7–12, in the Bible.

The heralded Trumpet: In the Bible, the trumpet of resurrection at the end of the world. Or possibly the trumpet sounded by the seven angels of the Apocalypse, unleashing total disaster.

Pierre Brisset's frog: Jean-Pierre Brisset, the so-called Prince of Thinkers, claimed that man had descended from frogs.

I didn't vow you to the Python: A reference to the black python in chapter 10 of Flaubert's *Salammbô.*

Rood of David or Wood of the Cross: References to the cross on which Christ was crucified.

Lignum Crucis: Latin for "Wood of the Cross."

Giant fireworks of the Universal Exposition: The Eiffel Tower, built for the Universal Exposition of 1889, originally was painted with newly invented pigments that produced an iridescence (see the first line of the poem "Crackling").

Bonnot's head rolls beneath the guillotine: Jean Bonnot (1876–1912), the legendary French gangster, was not guillotined. He was shot dead in a gun battle with the police.

The Simultaneous Delaunay: Robert Delaunay (1885–1941), French painter whose work at one point involved ideas of simultaneity. Delaunay did many paintings of the Eiffel Tower. BC met Robert Delaunay and his wife Sonia at the end of 1912 or beginning of 1913, and they became fast friends. Sonia designed the original edition of BC's *Trans-Siberian.*

World tour tower: An attempt to convey some of BC's pun: *tour du monde* usually means "world tour" but could also mean "world tower," especially in this poem. I added a little wordplay in the last line by translating *tour en mouvement* ("tower in motion") as "moving tower."

3. CONTRASTS

BC's title is the same as that of some of the paintings of his new friend, Robert Delaunay.

At the Chamber: The French Chamber of Deputies.

The numbers game: The French *poule au gibier* was a betting game in bars. The name comes from a play on the English word *pool*, as in "betting pool."

A gangster goes by in a car: The famous Bonnot Gang was one of the first to use cars for getaways.

M. Cochon: Ernest Georges Cochon, who made the news in 1913 for his protests on behalf of the homeless.

The Samaritaine sign: The electric sign of the Samaritaine department store, near the Seine.

Saint-Séverin: A church in Paris, the subject of paintings (1907 and 1909) by Robert Delaunay.

Montrouge Gare de l'Est Métro Nord-Sud Seine omnibus: Montrouge, a suburb immediately south of Paris, and the Gare de l'Est, a train station, were linked at that time by a trolley line. Nord-Sud was the name of the (then) new subway line that linked Montparnasse and Montmartre. In those days, there was boat-bus service in Paris along the Seine, similar to the *vaporetti* in Venice today.

L'Intransigeant and *Paris-Sports:* A newspaper and a daily sports journal.

Cimabue: Giovanni Cimabue (originally Bencivieni di Pepo, ca. 1251–1302), Florentine painter. Perhaps BC is thinking of the gold-leaf backgrounds in Cimabue's paintings of the Madonna and child.

4. I. PORTRAIT and II. STUDIO

This poem in two parts gives us a sense of what it was like to go see Marc Chagall in his studio. When BC first met him in 1911, Chagall was virtually unknown. Perhaps the fact that BC had lived in Russia and spoke Russian enabled the two to become friends quickly.

The Beehive: La Ruche (in French) was an artists' colony in what had been the Wine Pavilion of the Universal Exposition. Chagall moved into La Ruche near the end of 1911.

Léger: Fernand Léger (1881–1955), French artist and friend of BC, had a studio at La Ruche, beginning in 1908. The nineteenth poem in this series is about him and his work.

Tobeen: Félix Elie Tobeen (1880–?) was an early cubist who became an academic painter after the First World War.

Pétrus Borel: Known as the Lycanthrope, Joseph-Pierre Borel d'Hauterive (1809–1859) was a French author of fiction.

Lautréamont: Isidore Ducasse (1846–1870), the Equadorian-born French writer who published the extraordinary *Chants de Maldoror* under the name of Comte de Lautréamont. BC published the first twentieth-century edition of the *Chants* in 1920, at La Sirène editions.

My wife: When this poem was written, BC's common-law wife, whom he married the following year, was Féla Poznanska.

Morose delectation: In Catholic moral theology, the term *delectatio morosa* (French *délectation morose*) refers to taking pleasure in a sinful thought, but without really desiring the object of that thought. The subtle distinctions between this and related sins are discussed in *Moral Theology*, by the Rev. Heribert Jone, O.F.M. CAP., J.D.C., translated by the Rev. Urban Adelman, O.F.M. CAP., J.D.C., and published by The Newman Press (Westminster, Md: 1952), pp. 52–55 and 158–159. The subtext is mainly sexual, associated sometimes with masturbation, a subject that interested BC.

Zina: One of Chagall's sisters.

In the graduations of light: BC's phrase *les échelles de la lumière* suggests *l'échelle des couleurs* (a color chart). Other meanings of *échelle* are hovering about: ladder, succession or series, musical scale, arithmetical or geometric progression, and the scale of a map.

5. MY DANCE

Plato: In *The Republic*, Plato banned poets from the city because they got people too stirred up.

Procuring in the street: The French term *vagabondage spécial* is a legal term for pimping.

6. SHE HAS A BODY ON HER DRESS

This poem is about the amazing "simultaneous" dresses designed and worn by Sonia Delaunay, the first of which she created in 1913.

Bal Bullier: A dance hall in the place de l'Observatoire in Paris, especially popular among students. Sonia Delaunay did four paintings called "The Bal Bullier."

7. HAMMOCK

Onoto-face: Onoto was a brand of fountain pen. Apparently at that time Onoto had some advertising near the Gare Saint-Lazare that included an image that looked like Apollinaire in profile.

Gare Saint-Lazare: Paris train station.

Oxo-Liebig: Liebig was a beef extract, Oxo a brand of bouillon.

Julie, or I Lost My Rose: A reference to Apollinaire's erotic poem "Julie, or I Lent My Rose."

In the shade of a painting: An early draft of this poem suggests that the painting in question was Henri Rousseau's "The Snake Charmer."

Your portrait: Henri Rousseau (1844–1910) did two portraits of Apollinaire called "The Muse Inspiring the Poet" (sometimes called "The Poet and His Muse").

Among the stars: This line might have been inspired by Apollinaire's poem "Inscription for the Tomb of the Painter Henri Rousseau, Douanier," which had appeared in the April 1913 issue of *Les Soirées de Paris.* In that poem, the poet tells Rousseau in heaven that he would be brought "brushes colors canvas / So that your holy leisures in the real light / Can be devoted to painting as you did my portrait / The face of the stars."

The sweet williams oeillets du poète: The *oeillet de poète* (literally "poet's eyelet") is French for the sweet william. BC is playing on words here: Guillaume is French for William. These flowers appear in the foreground of Rousseau's second portrait of Apollinaire.

8. MARDI GRAS

Canudo: Ricciotto Canudo (1879–1923), Italian-born French writer and editor of *Montjoie!* magazine, which published three of the *Nineteen Elastic Poems.*

Your improvisation: Canudo had written a book about Beethoven's Ninth Symphony.

Areopagites: Members of the supreme tribunal in ancient Athens.

Spiritual pyramid: Canudo had referred to Beethoven's Ninth Symphony as "the spiritual Pyramid of the West."

"Imperialism": *Montjoie!* described itself as "the organ of French artistic imperialism." Canudo was, I should add, trying to redefine the word *imperialism.*

Wistiti: A type of small monkey.

Montjoie!: The name of Canudo's magazine came from the traditional French battle cry found in the French epic poem *The Song of Roland.*

Roland's Oliphant: Roland, the hero of *The Song of Roland.* Oliphant (derived from *elephant*) was the name of his ivory horn.

9. CRACKLING

The Tower: The Eiffel Tower.

Paris-Midi: A daily newspaper.

Intransigeant: A Parisian newspaper.

Poems for postcards: BC was irked by Apollinaire's publishing these in the newspaper.

Futurism: BC is referring to the Italian avant-garde art movement.

Simultaneity: The avant-garde art—mostly that of Robert and Sonia Delaunay—that was something like cubism with bright colors. Apollinaire called it orphism. A similar movement was called synchronism. BC is expressing his distrust of the idea of any "movement."

Bodin: Jean Bodin (1530–1596), author of *La Démonomanie des sourciers* (1580).

My friend R . . . : Ludwig Rubiner (1881–1920), German expressionist poet.

10. NEWS FLASH

This poem—perhaps the first found poem—is a lightly revised version of an article that appeared in the newspaper *Paris-Midi* on 21 January 1914. In the article, Mr. Thomas is killed during the escape. BC brings him back to life.

11. BOMBAY EXPRESS

Mascagni: Pietro Mascagni (1863–1945), Italian composer of *Cavalliera Rusticana* and other works.

12. F.I.A.T.

No one is yet sure what this title refers to—perhaps to the FIAT automobile company, which had been founded in 1899. According to Rino Cortiana, the setting of this poem, the hospital where BC's wife had just given birth to their first child, was near a Renault automobile factory. There is also the suggestion of the Latin word *fiat* ("so be it").

Pneumatiques: In certain big cities in France, special delivery letters sent from post office to post office in little canisters propelled by suction through underground tubes.

Sainte-Clothilde: A church in Paris's seventh arrondissement.

Blériot: Louis Blériot (1872–1936), the first person to fly across the English Channel (1909). Robert Delaunay painted an "Homage to Blériot" (1913–1914), about which he wrote the following notes: "Creation of a constructive disk. Solar fireworks. Depth and life of the sun. Constructive mobility of the solar spectrum; dawn, fire, evolution of airplanes. . . . Everything is roundness, sun, earth, horizons, intense plenitude of life."

13. AT THE 5 CORNERS

A café at the carrefour de Buci (where five streets intersect) in Paris. BC frequented the 5 Corners, especially with Fernand Léger.

I'm ripe: The French *Je suis mûr* could also mean "I'm drunk." In fact, BC later commented that when he wrote this poem, he *was* drunk.

Golden tongue: An oblique reference to Saint John Chrysostom (ca. 347–407), also known as Saint John *bouche d'or,* the patriarch of Constantinople, famed for his preaching. The early Christian church of the Chrysostom rite is not far from the 5 Corners.

14. STILL LIFES

Roger de La Fresnaye: French painter (1885–1925). La Fresnaye exhibited his "Still Life" in the Salon des Indépendents about the time this poem was written.

The artillerymen: In 1912 Roger de La Fresnaye had shown his first big Cubist work, "The Artillery."

The geometry: There are many geometric shapes, as well as military images, in La Fresnaye's work.

15. FANTÔMAS

Fantômas is the main character in a series of very popular crime novels by Marcel Allain (1885–1969) and Pierre Souvestre (1874–1914). One of BC's friends, Emil Szittya, quoted BC as saying, "*Fantômas* is the *Iliad* of our time."

Simultaneism: An avant-garde artistic mini-movement of the time. Robert and Sonia Delaunay were its chief proponents.

Father Moche: One of Fantômas's many false identities.

Alma Mater Humanity Holy Cow: According to Jean-Pierre Goldenstein, the French word *vache,* when used in the expression *la grande vache,* was turn-of-the-century anarchist slang for "humanity." Since there is no English equivalent, I decided to have some anarchic fun with the translation.

Monsieur Barzum: Henri-Martin Barzun (1881–?), poet with whom BC had a bitter literary quarrel.

I was in jail: In 1912, BC was detained in jail (for one day) for shoplifting a book by Apollinaire he couldn't afford to buy.

I studied the trademarks: BC had been a university student in Bern, the location of the International Bureau for the Protection of Industrial Property, which includes trademarks as well as patents.

16. TITLES

Shapes Sweats Tresses: A line from Rimbaud's poem "Barbare."

Accidents in Fairyland: Another reference to a line of Rimbaud's, this one from *Illuminations.*

17. MEE TOO BUGGI

BC derived most of this poem from A. J. B. Defauconpret's 1817 French translation of John Mariner's *An Account of the Natives of the Tonga Islands in the South Pacific Ocean,* edited by John Martin. The title is the name of a native dance. It doesn't mean "I too boogie."

Jay Bochner did a radical translation of this poem by going back to Mariner's book and finding the original wordings. If BC's poem is a found poem, Bochner's translation is a found translation. For more information, see Bochner's article "The Voyage Out and the Voyage Back in a Poem by Blaise Cendrars" in *Explorations* magazine, vol. 1, December 1973, published by Illinois State University.

Fango-fango: A nasal flute used in the South Seas.

Bolotoo: An island.

Papalangi: The Tonga name for Europe.

Mee low folla: Not, as some have guessed, pidgin English; rather, the name of a native dance described by Captain Cook.

18. THE HEAD

Christopher Columbus's egg: Apparently the story of Christopher Columbus's egg used to be better known than it is now. Washington Irving, in his *Life and Voyages of Christopher Columbus* (New York: Putnam, 1868), retells the 1572 version of the Italian historian Benzoni: "Pedro Gonzalez de Mendoza, the grand cardinal of Spain, and first subject of the realm . . . invited Columbus to a banquet, where he assigned him the most honorable place at table, and had him served with the ceremonials which in those punctilious times were observed towards sovereigns. At this repast it is said to have occurred the well-known anecdote of the egg. A shallow courtier present, impatient of the honors paid to Columbus, and meanly jealous of him as a foreigner, abruptly asked him whether he thought that, in case he had not discovered the Indies, there were not other men in Spain who would have been capable of the enterprise? To this Columbus made no immediate reply, but, taking an egg, invited the company to make it stand on one end. Everyone attempted it, but in vain; whereupon he struck it upon the table so as to break the end, and left it standing on the broken part; illustrating in this simple manner, that when he had once shown the way to the New World, nothing was easier than to follow it." See also the contemporary retelling in Ingri and Edgar Parin d'Aulaire's *Columbus* (Garden City, N.Y.: Doubleday, 1955).

Archipenko: Aleksandr Archipenko (1887–1964), Ukrainian-born sculptor who arrived in Paris in 1908.

19. CONSTRUCTION

Some of the images in this poem may have influenced *The Creation of the World*, a ballet created by BC (scenario), Fernand Léger (decor and costumes), Jean Borlin (choreography), and Darius Milhaud (music) for the Ballets Suédois in 1923.

Léger: Fernand Léger (1881–1955), French painter and good friend of BC.

A 75 mm breech: The breech of a cannon, one of the objects that influenced Léger's painting at one point. (Léger was a soldier at the front during the First World War.) One of Léger's portraits of BC shows this influence.

At the end of *Nineteen Elastic Poems* BC included a parting shot:

A LITTLE NOTE ON LITERARY HISTORY
(1912–1914)

Born on the occasion of an encounter, a friendship, a painting, a polemic, or something I read, the few preceding poems belong to the highly disparaged genre of occasional poetry. With the exception of two or three of them, they were published by foreign magazines. The *Mercure de France, Vers et Prose, Les Soirées de Paris,* and *Poème et Drame,* that is, the older writers, the established poets, and the so-called avant-garde rejected my work. Because at that time, it was not good to be truly young among the "young."

This note is more a reflection of the frustration BC felt early in his career than it is an accurate statement of the facts. In fact, five of the poems were published originally in *Les Soirées de Paris.* The Paris literary magazine *Montjoie!* published another three. Three others were published by young members of the avant-garde: *Cabaret Voltaire, Avanscoperta,* and *Littérature.* (To BC's credit, we should note that the "Little Note" is preceded by an accurate list detailing the magazine publication of all the poems—many in 1914.) In the "Little Note," BC was settling some old scores and making it clear that he was not to be pigeonholed in any group or movement.

Only twice did BC add notes to his books of poetry, and in both cases he refers to genre. In *Nineteen Elastic Poems* he rehabilitates the occasional poem, and in *Kodak* he creates what is perhaps a new genre, the documentary poem.

The War in the Luxembourg

That is, the Luxembourg Garden in Paris. The first edition of this poem was published by D. Niestlé (Paris, 1916), with six drawings by Moïse Kisling, who had been with BC at the front.

Navarin Farm: BC's right arm was blown off in this attack 28 September 1915.

The Paris meridian: At that time the French used a different meridian than that of Greenwich.

Bois de Boulogne . . . Meudon: Large wooded parks.

Place de l'Etoile: Literally, Star Square. Hence BC's image of it rising into the sky.

Unnatural Sonnets

"OpOetic" was first published in the program notes of a poetry and music presentation, Paris, 1917. It was reprinted, with the two others in this group, in *L'Oeuf dur* no. 14 (Paris, 1923).

OPOETIC

Jean COctO: Jean Cocteau (1889–1963), French writer, artist, and filmmaker. BC, as director of the publishing house Editions de la Sirène, consulted with and published Cocteau.

What crimes . . . . : A paraphrase of Mme. Roland's last words before her death (1793) on the guillotine: "O liberty! O liberty! What crimes are committed in thy name!"

Aretino: Pietro Aretino (1492–1556), Italian author of licentious works.

Ozenfant: A pun on the French word *enfant* (child) and Amédée Ozenfant (1886–1966), French painter and theoretician who edited *L'Elan* magazine (1915–1916), which published typographically daring poems.

ACADÉMIE MÉDRANO

That is, the Cirque Médrano, located at the corner of the rue des Martyrs and the boulevard de Rochechouart in Paris. On Sundays and holidays a circus was held there, with equestrian performances, acrobatics, pantomimes, etc.

Conrad Moricand: Swiss-born French writer and astrologer (ca. 1885–ca. 1951); later a friend of Henry Miller.

On one handwritten manuscript, the title is broken into "The Music Kiss Me."

Erik Satie: French composer (1866–1925) and friend of BC.

Venizélos: Eleuthérios Venizélos (1864–1936), Greek statesman. President of the Council (1910–1915, 1917–1920, and 1928).

Raymond Duncan: Brother of Isadora Duncan, he wore ancient-style Greek sandals and robes in the streets of Paris right up to his death in 1966.

Charlie Chaplin: BC claimed that in London he had once shared a room with the then unknown Chaplin. He later realized that he had confused him with a long-lost friend named Perlberg.

Quod erat demonstrandum: In Euclidean geometry, the expression (Q.E.D.) comes at the end of a proof and means, "Which was to be shown."

Black African Poems

These poems were first published in magazines in 1922: "Dark Continent" in *L'Oeuf dur* no. 9, Paris; "The Great Fetishes" in *Le Disque vert* no. 1, Brussels.

DARK CONTINENT

Strabo: Greek author (ca. 60 B.C.–A.D. 25) of *Geography,* a description of the world as the ancients knew it. A new edition of A. Tardieu's French translation was brought out in Paris in 1909. I have been unable to find the observations BC ascribes to Strabo.

Mojos: Amulets.

The marvelous island of Saint Borandion: Or Saint Brendan; a legendary island named after Brendan (or Brandon or Brandan) (ca. 484–578), Irish saint and hero of an equally legendary Atlantic voyage celebrated in medieval sagas. The best surviving manuscript of it is in Old French, reprinted in *The Anglo-Norman Voyage of St. Brendan by Benedeit,* edited by E. G. R. Waters (Oxford University Press, 1928). Saint Brendan's Island was the object of voyages of discovery as late as 1759, when it was decided that previous sightings had been mirages.

Madeira: Portuguese islands north of the Canaries; also the name of one of these islands.

The sacatra, the griff, etc.: BC is satirizing the anthropologists' system of racial classification. The quadroon and quarteron were one-quarter black and three-quarters white; the mulatto, half-breed, and half-caste were half black and half white; the mameluco was half Brazilian Indian and half white; the griff was three-quarters black and one-quarter white; the sacatra and marabou were seven-eighths black and one-eighth white. Thus, BC's list approaches gibberish.

THE GREAT FETISHES

There seems to be no evidence that BC was in London in February of 1916.

Kodak (Documentary)

Most of the poems in *Kodak* consist of lightly revised passages from *The Mysterious Doctor Cornelius*, by Gustave Le Rouge, the voluminous author of pulp fiction and other works. BC, who was a great admirer of Le Rouge, wrote this book to prove to Le Rouge that the latter was indeed a poet. The original title of this collection was changed to *Documentaries*, as BC explained in the preface to a subsequent edition:

DOCUMENT

Just as this volume was going to press, I received a letter from Editions Stock that included the following excerpt:

"Paris, March 25, 1943 . . . When Blaise Cendrars's *Kodak* appeared, we received a notarized letter from the American firm of Kodak Co., pointing out that we had used, without authorization, the name of its company as the title of one of our publications. To our objection that this name was that of an object in everyday use, and that we were in effect giving them free publicity, they replied that according to legal counsel they own the name "Kodak" and that the unlawful and wrongful use of this word, far from serving as publicity, was on the contrary detrimental to it, because it distracted customers from the precise uses of the products sold by their company.

"We had no choice but to accede, but the Kodak Co. was kind enough not to require the removal of the book from bookstores. They simply asked us to promise to change the title should the book be reprinted. We are now doing so as an express condition of our assignment of rights. You can, of course, refer to the title *Kodak* in a bibliography, as requested above, but the general title of the pieces published by you in your collection must be changed."

When I received this letter I seriously considered debaptizing my book and calling it, for example, *Pathé Baby*, but I feared that the powerful Kodak Co. Ltd., with capital of no telling how many millions of dollars, would then accuse me of disloyal competition. Poor poets, let's keep working. What does a title matter. Poetry isn't in a title but in a fact, and since in fact these poems, which I conceived of as verbal photographs, form a documentary, I will henceforth title them *Documentaries*. Their former subtitle. It might be a new genre.

B. C.

AMPHITRYON

In Greek mythology, Zeus disguised himself as Amphitryon and paid a conjugal visit to the latter's wife. In Molière's *Amphitryon*, Amphitryon's servant, who can't tell which is the real Amphitryon, decides that the real one is the one who invites him to dinner. (He was wrong.)

YOUNG MAN

Beau Brummell: An excessively well-dressed man, a dandy; named after George Bryan Brummell (1778–1840).

TRESTLE WORK

Saint Andrew's crosses: A Saint Andrew's cross is in the shape of an X.

CUCUMINGO

It's possible that the title is a misspelling of Cucamonga.
   The cottontail: The French text has always had a nice misprint ("cottontrail").
   The jackass: This one isn't an error on BC's part. Our modern term "jackrabbit" is a shortened form of the older "jackass rabbit."

VANCOUVER

The Canadian Northern the Grand Trunk: According to Jim Christy, a Cendrarsian living in Vancouver, the "Canadian" was probably the Canadian Northern line. For "The Grand Trunk," see the note for the "Trunk" in *Panama*.

VOMITO NEGRO

Spanish for the "black vomit" associated with yellow fever.

OYSTER BAY

Smoke smoker smoke smoke spirals away: This line can be translated differently, depending on whether you read *l'hélice* as "spiral" or "propeller" (in which case the line would be "Smoke smoker smoke smoke goes the propeller"). Since the setting is on a boat, the logical choice is propeller. I like both versions, but I've chosen spiral.

THE BAHR EL ZERAF

A waterway in the Nile Delta.

MENUS

In *Panama* BC says, "Your menus / Are the new poetry."
Ravensara: A fruit whose nut smells like cloves.

Travel Notes

These poems were originally published in three separate groups. Part I ("The *Formosa*") was issued by Au Sans Pareil (Paris, 1924), with cover and illustrations by Tarsila. Part II ("São Paulo") was brought out by the Percier Gallery (Paris, 1926). Part III appeared in two issues of *Montparnasse* magazine, 1927 and 1928.

The title (*Feuilles de route*) may have been inspired by Whitman's *Leaves of Grass*, which appeared in French translation in 1909 as *Feuilles d'herbe*. Whitman's "Song of the Open Road" is also suggestive in this context. It is also possible that BC was echoing a selection of André Gide's journals published in *Vers et Prose* magazine in 1911 under the title *Feuilles de route 1895–1896*. The French *feuilles de route* also means "packing slips," "bills of lading," or simply "logbook." In any case, by 1928 travel poetry in French was practically a genre; one thinks of Henri J. M. Levet's *Postcards*, Valery Larbaud's *The Poems of A. O. Barnabooth*, and Philippe Soupault's *Westwego*.

In January of 1924 BC sailed from Le Havre on board the *Formosa*.

In the dedication: Paulo Prado (Paulo da Silva Prado, ca. 1867–1943) was a Brazilian millionaire, a patron and friend of BC. Prado's coffee plantations covered an area the size of Switzerland.

WAKING UP

The dock where I arrived from New York in 1911: It was actually in 1912.

YOU ARE MORE BEAUTIFUL THAN THE SKY AND THE SEA

The hand the leg the   the eye: The discreet blank space is intentional.

LETTER

My Remington: BC had just bought or rented this portable typewriter, described in "Baggage" as "the latest model."

LA PALLICE

La Pallice and the Ile de Ré: La Pallice is a port of La Rochelle, on the west coast of France. Ile de Ré is an island just off La Pallice.

Real true-ism: The French expression *une vérité de la Palice* (Jacques de Chabannes de la Palice, 1470–1525) means "a truism." BC is playing on the name of the town and the name of the man.

BILBAO

A Spanish port.

LA CORUÑA

A Spanish port, where Picasso (see previous poem) was brought up and learned to paint.

VILLA GARCÍA

A Spanish port. The *Formosa* is hugging the coast of Spain, the same route taken by sailors of antiquity.

PÔRTO DE LEIXÕES

The Portuguese harbor of Porto (sometimes called Oporto).

EN ROUTE TO DAKAR

Dakar is the port city and capital of Senegal.

WITHIN SIGHT OF THE ISLAND OF FUERTEVENTURA

Fuerteventura is one of the Canary Islands.

ON BOARD THE *FORMOSA*

Jota: A dance, also mentioned in "At the Pier."
Baku: The capital of Azerbaijan, an oil-producing region of the USSR.
Manille: A card game.

Santander: A Spanish seaport.

Mogador: A Moroccan port, now called Essaouira.

OFF RÍO DE ORO

Río de Oro is a bay of Spanish Sahara.

IN SIGHT OF CAPE BLANC

Cape Blanc is on the southernmost tip of Spanish Sahara.

GORÉE

Gorée is an island and town across from Dakar. Formerly a slave-trading center.

Salon d'automne: The *Salon d'automne* was an important annual exhibition of avant-garde art, begun in 1903.

THE MUMUS

Mumu: A long, straight dress, sometimes called a shift.

The Pincio: One of the hills of Rome, with a nice park.

BIJOU-CONCERT

The name of a club in Dakar. The Bijou-Club ticket BC bought is now in the Swiss National Library in Bern.

THE VULTURES

Saint-Ouen: A Paris suburb, known for its poverty.

WHITE SUIT

Caporal Ordinaires: A brand of cheap French cigarettes.

BAGGAGE

Grasset: Bernard Grasset was the French publisher of BC's novel *Moravagine* in 1926.

Au Sans Pareil: Au Sans Pareil brought out BC's *Le Plan de l'Aiguille* in 1929.

Raymone: Raymone Duchâteau (1898–1986), French actress BC fell in love with in 1917 and eventually married in 1949.

Anthology: The first volume of BC's *Anthologie nègre* had been published by

Editions de la Sirène in 1921. It was published in English translation under the title *African Saga* in 1927.

Babouche: A type of Arab slipper.

CROSSING THE LINE

Baptism of the line: See the note under "Panama."

SAN FERNANDO DE NORONHA

An island off the northeastern coast of Brazil.

Santos: A Brazilian seaport.

I send an ocean letter: This ocean letter is now in the Swiss National Library, Bern.

AMARALINA

Small coastal town in Brazil, near Salvador (formerly São Salvador or Bahia).

THE BLOWERS

Bahia: A state in eastern Brazil.

THE PITCH POST

This whole poem is based on a pun: *pot au noir* (pitch pot, or doldrums) and *poteau noir* (black pole), as Monique Chefdor explains in the notes to her version of this poem, found in *Complete Postcards from the Americas* (Berkeley and Los Angeles: University of California Press, 1976), which includes her translations of *Documentaires* and *Feuilles de route*.

LANDS

Pernambuco: BC is referring to the port now called Recife, in northeastern Brazil. Pernambuco is still the name of the state, of which Recife is the capital.

IN PORT

Chargeurs Réunis: The *Formosa* was one of the ships of the Chargeurs Réunis line.

THE GANGWAY

The last line may have been inspired by a bawdy popular song that began: "Monte là dessus et tu verras Montmartre / Monte là dessus et tu verras . . ."

BANQUET

Pinga: Portuguese slang for white rum.

PARIS

The people named in this poem are friends of BC: Jean Cocteau, Erik Satie, Fernand Léger, Eugenia Errazuriz, Marcel Lévesque, Mariette Prado, Francis Picabia, Germaine Everling, and Abel Gance. Sanders might have been the name of a café.

ISLANDS

There is a wonderful recording of BC reading this poem in his rather high-pitched, nasal voice.

GUARUJÁ BEACH

A suburb of Santos and one of Brazil's main seaside resorts.

MICTORIO

The title is Portuguese for "toilet."

THE BASTILLE TANKS

Tantalus: In Greek mythology, Tantalus was condemned to stand up to his chin in a vat of water, with fruit suspended overhead. Every time he tried to drink or eat, the water and fruit receded just out of reach. Hence our word *tantalizing.*

PARANAPIAÇABA

A mountain range southwest of São Paulo. BC definitely took the scenic route, a big loop from Santos to São Paulo.
    Serra do Mar: Portuguese for "coastal mountain range."
    Les Rognes above Bionnasay: In the south of France, near Marseilles.

PIRATININGA

Small town on a railway line, not far from Bauru, in the state of São Paulo.

SÃO PAULO

Charing Cross: A train station.

THE CITY WAKES UP

STADO . . . ERCIO . . . EIO: The cry of news vendors selling three major newspapers of that time, *O Estado de São Paulo, Jornal do Comércio,* and *Correio Paulistano.*

ELECTRIC HORNS

The League of Silence: Apparently a civic-minded group that banded together to reduce urban noise.

LEAVING

Caminho do Mar: Portuguese for "the sea road."

Oswald: Oswaldo de Andrade, one of the young Brazilian modernist writers who admired BC and who helped organize his trip to Brazil.

AT THE PIER

This big Dutch ship: The *Gelria* (of the Lloyd Royal Hollandais line), which BC took on 19 August 1924. The agreeable captain was named Kolkman.

Jota: A dance, also mentioned in "On Board the *Formosa.*"

NIGHT RISES

The Coal Sack: In the note to her translation of this poem, Monique Chefdor quotes BC's explanation of the Coal Sack. Near the Southern Cross, it's a black patch of the night sky in the Southern Hemisphere, believed by some to be the entrance to hell, or the exit from the world, or the doorway to fairyland, etc.

CAPE FRIA

Possibly the Cape Fria in northern Namibia.

HIC HAEC HOC

A Bahian's hand: It was an ebony carving.

ADRIENNE LECOUVREUR AND COCTEAU

Adrienne Lecouvreur: French actress (1692–1730), the most popular of her day.

STEERAGE

Cachorro do mato: Portuguese for "wild dog." The French has *mato* with two *t*'s.

According to Jay Bochner, this is a paradise tanager (*Tangara Chilensis*).

JANGADA

A *jangada* is a fishing raft or float especially common along the coast of Brazil.

DANCE

Apache dances: Not American Indian dances, but rather those of Parisian tough guys of the time. Apache dance is used in many films set in louche Paris: the steely-eyed man in a dark suit (or sometimes a red-and-white striped sailor's shirt and beret) hurls a moll around the floor.

South American Women

This series of poems was first published in *Feuilles Libres* no. 44 (Paris, 1926).
    "*Lua, lua!*": Portuguese for "moon, moon."

Various Poems

SHRAPNELS

This poem, the only one that BC wrote at the front, was first published in *Valori Plastici* (Rome, 1919). BC did take part in some heavy fighting during the war.

HOMAGE TO GUILLAUME APOLLINAIRE

First published in *SIC* (Paris, 1919), the special issue devoted to Apollinaire, who had died in November of 1918.
    BREASTS: A reference to Apollinaire's play *The Breasts of Tiresias.*

DICTATED OVER THE TELEPHONE

In the Forest of Broceliande (Fairy Opera)
Broceliande: A large forest (today called the Forest of Paimpont) in Brittany where the wizard Merlin was said to live.
    Caruso: Enrico Caruso (1873–1921), the great tenor, whom BC visited in New York in early 1912.
Klaxon
A slightly different version of this poem first appeared in *Verde* no. 3, a Brazilian magazine, under the title "*Aux Jeunes gens de Catacazes,*" dated Rio, 9 Novem-

ber 1927. The word *Klaxon* was originally the brand name of a horn, the type that went ooga-ooga.

Leaving Paris

Baby Cadum: French advertising symbol depicting a cute, chubby baby.

   Michelin: The tire company.

American-Style Proverb

Bugatti: A make of very fast Italian car, whose designer, Ettore Bugatti, when once reproached for bad brakes, replied, "I make my cars to go, not stop."

CURRENT EVENTS

Compare this poem to "My Dance" in *Nineteen Elastic Poems.*

To the Heart of the World

The first section and "Hôtel Notre-Dame" were first published in *Littérature* no. 16 (Paris, 1919); "My Mother's Belly" in *Montparnasse* no. 1 (Paris, 1922). *To the Heart of the World* is mentioned in "Baggage" (*Travel Notes*).

"THIS PARIS SKY IS PURER THAN A WINTER SKY . . ."

Saint-Merry: A Paris church.

   Thebaid: A desolate region around Thebes, in ancient Egypt. Early Christian ascetics took to this region; hence, the suggestion of deep solitude.

   THE END OF THE WORLD: An unfinished text, not to be confused with BC's book *La Fin du monde filmée par l'Ange Nôtre Dame.*

HÔTEL NOTRE-DAME

Saint-Séverin . . . The place Maubert . . . rue Saint-Jacques: All in the Latin Quarter in Paris.

"SUDDENLY THE SIRENS WAIL AND I RUN TO MY WINDOW . . ."

Aubervilliers: Suburb on the northeastern edge of Paris.

   75s: Seventy-five-millimeter cannons. Also mentioned in "Construction" in *Nineteen Elastic Poems.*

"I STAND ON THE SIDEWALK ACROSS THE STREET . . ."

Romance of the Rose: The French medieval epic poem by Guillaume de Lorris (born ca. 1235) and Jean de Meung (ca. 1240–ca. 1305).

At 218 [rue Saint-Jacques] . . . : Frédéric Louis Sauser was born at 27 rue de la Paix, La Chaux-de-Fonds, Switzerland.

The Chat Noir: A literary cabaret in Montmartre, where Erik Satie played the piano for a few months in 1891.

Lavater: Johann Caspar Lavater (1741–1801), Swiss poet, mystic, Protestant theologian, and the inventor of physiognomy.

Euler: Leonhard Euler (1707–1783), Swiss mathematician who also wrote on astronomy, physics, chemistry, and metaphysics.

The d'Harcourt or the Boul' Mich': My guess is that these were bars. Boul' Mich' is short for the boulevard Saint-Michel, which is a minute or two away from the Hôtel des Etrangers. Formerly at 42–44 boulevard Saint-Michel was the Collège d'Harcourt.

Select Bibliography

By Jay Bochner and Ron Padgett

I. Available French editions of the poetry, in order of preference

Du Monde entier au coeur du monde: Poèmes de Blaise Cendrars. Paris: Denoël, 1957; reissued in paperback, 1987. Text established during the lifetime of the author. The most available authoritative text.

Oeuvres complètes, vol. 1. Paris: Denoël, 1963. Essentially the same text as above, along with other works, in the standard edition of Cendrars's works in eight vols.

Du Monde entier au coeur du monde: Poésies complètes: 1912–1924. Two vols. Paris: NRF, 1967. Preface by Paul Morand. Convenient pocket edition, but with a good number of misprints.

II. Criticism

A. FULL-LENGTH STUDIES THAT INCLUDE DISCUSSIONS OF THE POETRY

Bochner, Jay. *Blaise Cendrars, Discovery and Re-creation.* Toronto: University of Toronto Press, 1978. A comprehensive study of Cendrars's style of mythmaking.

Cendrars, Miriam. *Blaise Cendrars.* Paris: Balland, 1984. A fond and detailed biography, in French, with selections from private documents, including the invaluable diaries of Cendrars's first wife.

Chefdor, Monique. *Blaise Cendrars.* Boston: Twayne, 1980. A far-reaching study of Cendrars as a transnational avant-gardist.

Goldenstein, Jean-Pierre. *Les Dix-neuf poèmes élastiques.* Paris: Klincksieck, 1986. The critical edition; exhaustively researched historical and textual details for these difficult poems.

B. RECENT COLLOQUIA

Bernard, Jacqueline, ed. *Le Texte cendrarsien.* Grenoble: Centre de Création Littéraire, 1988. About one-third of the papers delivered at this international conference are on the poetry. Culmination of the recent effort to concentrate on the adventures of Cendrars the writer instead of Cendrars the man.

Chefdor, Monique, Claude Leroy, and Frédérick-Jacques Temple, eds. *Blaise Cendrars*. Special issue of *Sud* (Marseilles, 1988) devoted to the colloquium Modernités de Blaise Cendrars, held at Cerisy-la-Salle (Normandy) in July of 1987. Many papers on the poetry and on the general issues of modernity, modernism, and the avant-garde.

III. English translations

Complete Postcards from the Americas. Translated by Monique Chefdor. Berkeley, Los Angeles, London: University of California Press, 1976. Includes *Documentaires*, *Feuilles de route*, and *Sud-Américaines*, with a good introduction and notes by the translator, who is also one of the leading Cendrars scholars.

Panama or the Adventures of My Seven Uncles. Translated by John Dos Passos. New York and London: Harper & Brothers, 1931. Includes *The Trans-Siberian*, *Panama*, and selections from *Kodak* and *Feuilles de route*. Illustrated by the translator.

Selected Poems. Translated by Peter Hoida. Harmondsworth, England: Penguin, 1979. Introduction by Mary Ann Caws. Not available in the U.S.

Selected Writings. Edited with an introduction by Walter Albert, and translated by Walter Albert, John Dos Passos, and Scott Bates. New York: New Directions, 1966.

IV. Further sources

See Bochner, above, pp. 273–294; consult the bibliography updated biannually in *Feuille de routes*, the bulletin of the Blaise Cendrars International Society, from 1990 onward edited by Jacqueline Bernard, 30 Galerie de l'arlequin, App. 2201, 38100 Grenoble, France; and see the bibliography updated annually in *Continent Cendrars*, published by the Centre d'Etudes Blaise Cendrars at the University of Bern, 5 Hallerstrasse, CH-3012, Switzerland.

For information on membership in the Blaise Cendrars International Society, write to Georgiana Colvile, Dept. of Romance Languages, University of Colorado, Boulder, Colo. 80309.

Index of English Titles

Index of French Titles

Designer:	David Bullen
Compositor:	G & S Typesetters, Inc.
Text:	11/14 Electra
Display:	Electra
Printer:	Bookcrafters, Inc.
Binder:	Bookcrafters, Inc.